D.D. Jonathan Swift

# The Prose Works Of Jonathan Swift,D.D.

Vol III.

D.D. Jonathan Swift

**The Prose Works Of Jonathan Swift,D.D.**
*Vol III.*

ISBN/EAN: 9783741103568

Manufactured in Europe, USA, Canada, Australia, Japa

Cover: Foto ©Andreas Hilbeck / pixelio.de

Manufactured and distributed by brebook publishing software (www.brebook.com)

D.D. Jonathan Swift

**The Prose Works Of Jonathan Swift,D.D.**

*Jonathan Swift.*
*from a picture by Francis Bindon*
*in the possession of Sir J.R.Falkiner*

# THE PROSE WORKS
## OF
# JONATHAN SWIFT, D.D.

### EDITED BY
### TEMPLE SCOTT

WITH A BIOGRAPHICAL INTRODUCTION BY
THE RT. HON. W. E. H. LECKY, M.P.

### VOL. III

LONDON
GEORGE BELL AND SONS
1898

CHISWICK PRESS:—CHARLES WHITTINGHAM AND CO.
TOOKS COURT, CHANCERY LANE, LONDON.

# SWIFT'S
# WRITINGS ON RELIGION AND THE CHURCH

## VOL. I

EDITED BY
TEMPLE SCOTT

LONDON
GEORGE BELL AND SONS
1898

# PREFACE.

THE inquiry into the religious thought of the eighteenth century forms one of the most interesting subjects for speculation in the history of the intellectual development of western nations. It is true, that in that history Swift takes no special or distinguished part; but he forms a figure of peculiar interest in a special circle of his own. Swift had no natural bent for the ministry of a church; his instincts, his temperament, his intellect, were of that order which fitted him for leadership and administration. He was a born magistrate and commander of men. It is, therefore, one of the finest compliments we can pay Swift to say, that no more faithful, no more devoted, no stauncher servant has that Church possessed; for we must remember the proud and haughty temper which attempted to content itself with the humdrum duties of a parish life. Swift entered the service of that Church at a time when its need for such a man was great; and in spite of its disdain of his worth, in spite of its failure to recognize and acknowledge his transcendent qualities, he never forgot his oath, and never shook in his allegiance. To any one, however, who reads carefully his sermons, his "Thoughts on Religion," and his "Letter to a Young Clergyman," there comes a question—whether, for his innermost conscience, Swift found a satisfying conviction in the doctrines of Christianity. "I am not answerable to God," he says, "for the doubts that arise in my own breast, since they are the consequence of that reason which he hath planted in me, if I take care to conceal those doubts from others, if I use my best endeavours to subdue them, and if they have no influence on the conduct of my life." We search in vain, in any of his writings, for any definite expression of doubt or want of faith in these doctrines. When he touches on them, as he does in the sermon "On the Trinity," he seems to avoid of set purpose, rational inquiry, and contents himself with insisting on the necessity for a belief in those mysteries concerning God about which we cannot hope to know anything. "I do not find," he says, in his "Letter to a Young Clergyman," "that you are anywhere directed in the canons or articles to attempt explaining the mysteries of the Christian religion; and, indeed, since Providence intended there should be mysteries, I don't see how it can be agreeable to piety, orthodoxy, or good sense to go about such a work. For to me there seems a manifest dilemma in the case; if you explain them, they are mysteries no longer; if you fail, you have laboured to no purpose."

It must at once be admitted that Swift had not the metaphysical bent; philosophy—in our modern sense of the word—was to him only a species of word spinning. That only was valuable which had a practical bearing on life— and Christianity had that. He found in Christianity, as he knew it—in the Church of England, that is to say—an excellent organization, which recognized the frailties of human nature, aimed at making healthier men's souls, and gave mankind a reasonable guidance in the selection of the best motives to action. He himself, as a preacher, made it his principal business, "first to tell the people what is their duty, and then to convince them that it is so." He had a profound faith in existing institutions, which to him were founded on the fundamental traits of humanity. The Church of England he considered to be such an institution; and it was, moreover, regulated and settled by order of the State.

To follow its teachings would lead men to become good citizens, honest dealers, truthful and cleanly companions, upright friends. What more could be demanded of any religion?

The Romish Church led away from the Constitution as by law established. Dissent set up private authority, which could no more be permitted in religious than it was in political matters; it meant dissension, revolution, and the upheaval of tried and trusted associations. Therefore, the Church of Rome and the teachings of Dissent were alike dangerous; and against both, whenever they attempted the possession of political power, he waged a fierce and uncompromising war. "Where sects are tolerated in a State," he says, in his "Sentiments of a Church of England Man," "it is fit they should enjoy a full liberty of conscience, and every other privilege of free-born subjects, to which no power is annexed. And to preserve their obedience upon all emergencies, a government cannot give them too much ease, nor trust them with too little power."

Swift had no passionate love for ideals—indeed, he may have thought ideals to be figments of an overheated and, therefore, aberrated imagination. The practically real was the best ideal; and by the real he would understand that power which most capably and most regulatively nursed, guided, and assisted the best instincts of the average man. The average man was but a sorry creature, and required adventitious aids for his development. Gifted as he was with a large sympathy, Swift yet was seemingly incapable of appreciating those thought-forms which help us to visualize mentally our religious aspirations and emotions. A mere emotion was but subject-matter for his satire. He suspected any zeal which protested too much for truth, and considered it "odds on" it being "either petulancy, ambition, or pride."

Whatever may have been his private speculations as to the truth of the doctrines of Christianity they never interfered with his sense of his responsibilities as a clergyman. "I look upon myself," he says, "in the capacity of a clergyman, to be one appointed by Providence for defending a post assigned me, and for gaining over as many enemies as I can. Although I think my cause is just, yet one great motive is my submitting to the pleasure of Providence, and to the laws of my country." If anyone had asked him, what was the pleasure of Providence, he would probably have answered, that it was plainly shown in the Scriptures, and required not the aid of the expositions of divines who were "too curious, or too narrow, in reducing orthodoxy within the compass of subtleties, niceties, and distinctions." Truth was no abstraction—that was truth which found its expression in the best action; and this explains Swift's acceptance of any organization which made for such expression. He found one ready in the Church of England; and whatever his doubts were, those only moved him which were aroused by action from those who attempted to interfere with the working of that organization. And this also helps to explain his political attitude at the time when it was thought he had deserted his friends. The Church was always his first consideration. He was not a Churchman because he was a politician, but a politician because he was a Churchman. These, however, are matters which are more fully entered into by Swift himself in the tracts herewith reprinted, and in the notes prefixed to them by the editor.

It was originally intended that Swift's writings on Religion and the Church should occupy a single volume of this edition of his works. They are, however, so numerous that it has been found more convenient to divide them into two volumes—the first including all the tracts, except those relating to the Sacramental Test; the second containing the Test pamphlets and the twelve sermons, with the Remarks on Dr. Gibbs's paraphrase of the Psalms, in an appendix. It is hoped that this division, while it entails upon the student the necessity for a double reference, will yet preserve the continuity of form enabling him to view Swift's religious standpoint and work with as much advantage as he would have obtained by the original plan.

    The editor again takes the opportunity to thank Colonel F. Grant for the service he has rendered him in placing at his disposal his fine collection of Swift's tracts. The portrait which forms the frontispiece to this volume is one of those painted by Francis Bindon, and was formerly in the possession of Judge Berwick. For permission to photograph and reproduce it here, thanks are due to Sir Frederick R. Falkiner, Recorder of Dublin.

TEMPLE SCOTT.

# CONTENTS.

|  | PAGE |
|---|---|
| ARGUMENT AGAINST ABOLISHING CHRISTIANITY . . . | 1 |
| PROJECT FOR THE ADVANCEMENT OF RELIGION . . . | 21 |
| SENTIMENTS OF A CHURCH OF ENGLAND MAN . . . | 49 |
| REMARKS UPON "THE RIGHTS OF THE CHRISTIAN CHURCH" | 77 |
| PREFACE TO THE BISHOP OF SARUM'S "INTRODUCTION" . | 125 |
| ABSTRACT OF COLLINS'S "DISCOURSE OF FREETHINKING" | 163 |
| SOME THOUGHTS ON FREETHINKING . . . . . | 193 |
| LETTER TO A YOUNG CLERGYMAN . . . . . | 195 |
| ARGUMENTS AGAINST ENLARGING THE POWER OF BISHOPS IN LETTING LEASES . . . . . . . . | 219 |
| REASONS OFFERED TO THE ARCHBISHOP OF DUBLIN . . | 239 |
| ON THE BILL FOR THE CLERGY'S RESIDING ON THEIR LIVINGS . . . . . . . . . . | 249 |
| CONSIDERATIONS UPON TWO BILLS RELATING TO THE CLERGY OF IRELAND . . . . . . . | 257 |
| REASONS AGAINST THE MODUS . . . . . . | 273 |
| ESSAY ON THE FATES OF CLERGYMEN . . . . | 289 |
| CONCERNING THAT UNIVERSAL HATRED WHICH PREVAILS AGAINST THE CLERGY . . . . . . . | 299 |
| THOUGHTS ON RELIGION . . . . . . . | 305 |
| FURTHER THOUGHTS ON RELIGION . . . . . | 310 |
| PRAYERS FOR MRS. JOHNSON . . . . . . | 311 |
| AN EVENING PRAYER . . . . . . . . | 315 |
| OBSERVATIONS ON HEYLIN'S "HISTORY OF PRESBYTERIANS" . . . . . . . . . . | 319 |

ERRATUM.

P. 73, *note.* *For* " Peter the Great " *read* " Pedro of Castile."

# AN ARGUMENT

TO PROVE THAT THE

## ABOLISHING OF CHRISTIANITY IN ENGLAND

MAY, AS THINGS NOW STAND, BE ATTENDED WITH SOME INCONVENIENCES, AND PERHAPS NOT PRODUCE THOSE MANY GOOD EFFECTS PROPOSED THEREBY.

WRITTEN IN THE YEAR 1708.

## NOTE.

IN November, 1707, Swift left Dublin in the train of the then Lord Lieutenant, Lord Pembroke. His travelling companion was Sir Andrew Fountaine, who, on landing in England, set out with Lord Pembroke for Wilton, while Swift went on to Leicester to visit his mother. He stayed with her until some time in December, but, by the middle of the same month, he was in London. During this absence from Ireland Swift corresponded somewhat freely with Archbishop King of Dublin, and with Archdeacon Walls—the letters to the former were first printed in Forster's "Life of Swift." For these Forster was indebted to the Rev. Mr. Reeves (vicar of Lusk, co. Dublin), who discovered them in the record-room of the see of Armagh (see "Life," p. 205 *et seq.* and note). One of Swift's intentions, while in the metropolis, was to push forward the claim of the Irish clergy for the remission of the First Fruits and Tenths, a grant which had already been conceded to the English clergy; and his letters to King often include requests for the necessary papers by means of which he could lay the matter before either Godolphin or Somers. Walls had written to Swift of the vacancy of the see of Waterford, and, from the reply to the archdeacon, we learn that even at so early a date Swift suffered a grievous disappointment; for in January, 1708, the bishopric, of which Swift had hopes, was presented to Dr. Thomas Milles. In his letter to Walls Swift confesses that he "once had a glimpse that things would have gone otherwise. . . . But let us talk no further on this subject. I am stomach-sick of it already. . . . Pray send me an account of some smaller vacancy in the Government's gift." It was to Somers, and through him to Lord Halifax, that Swift looked for recognition, either for services rendered, or because of their appreciation of his abilities. But, however much he may have been disappointed at their inaction, it may not be argued, as it has been, that Swift's so-called change in his political opinions was the outcome either of spleen or chagrin against the Whigs for their ingratitude towards him. It is, indeed, questionable whether Swift ever changed his political opinions, speaking of these as party opinions. From the day of his entrance, it may be said, into the orders of the Church, his first thought was for it; and on all political questions which touched Church matters Swift was neither Whig nor Tory, but churchman. It was because of the attitude of the Whigs towards the Church that Swift left them; and in his writings he does not spare the Tories even when he finds them taking up similar attitudes. On purely political questions Swift was too independent a thinker to be influenced by mere party views. That he wrote for the Tories must be put down to Harley's personal influence, and to his foresight which saw in

Swift a man who must be treated as an equal with the highest in the land. Swift's intercourse with the leading men of his day only served to accentuate his consciousness of his superiority; and a party which would permit him the free play of his powers would be the party to which Swift would give his adhesion. Godolphin, Somers, and Walpole either did not recognize the genius of the man, or their own "points of view" did not permit them to give him the free play they felt he would obtain. Be that as it may, Harley gained not only a splendid party fighter, but a friend on whose affection he could ever rely.

In these tracts on Religion and the Church, which he wrote in the year 1708, Swift is not a party man, speaking for party purposes. He believed, and sincerely believed, that for such beings as were the men and women of this kingdom, the Church was, if not the highest and noblest instrument for good, yet the worthiest and ablest they had. Swift never lost himself in theories. He was, however, not blind to the dangers which an established religion might engender; but whatever its dangers, these would be inevitable to the most perfect system so long as human nature was as base as it was. The "Argument" is written in a vein of satirical banter; but the Swiftian cynicism permeates every line. It is the first of four tracts which form Swift's most important expression of his thoughts on Religion and the Church. Scott well describes it as "one of the most felicitous efforts in our language, to engage wit and humour on the side of religion," and Forster speaks of it as "having also that indefinable subtlety of style which conveys not the writer's knowledge of the subject only, but his power and superiority over it."

I have not been able to find a copy of the original edition of the "Argument" upon which to base the present text—for that I have gone to the first edition of the "Miscellanies," published in 1711; but I have collated this with those given by the "Miscellanies" (1728), Faulkner, Hawkesworth, Scott, Morley, and Craik.

[T. S.]

# AN ARGUMENT AGAINST ABOLISH-
## ING CHRISTIANITY.

I AM very sensible what a weakness and presumption it is, to reason against the general humour and disposition of the world. I remember it was with great justice, and a due regard to the freedom both of the public and the press, forbidden upon several penalties to write,[1] or discourse, or lay wagers against the Union, even before it was confirmed by parliament, because that was looked upon as a design, to oppose the current of the people, which, besides the folly of it, is a manifest breach of the fundamental law that makes this majority of opinion the voice of God. In like manner, and for the very same reasons, it may perhaps be neither safe nor prudent to argue against the abolishing of Christianity, at a juncture when all parties appear[2] so unanimously determined upon the point, as we cannot but allow from their actions, their discourses, and their writings. However, I know not how, whether from the affectation of singularity, or the perverseness of human nature, but so it unhappily falls out, that I cannot be entirely of this opinion. Nay, though I were sure an order were issued for my immediate prosecution by the Attorney-General, I should still confess that in the present posture of our affairs at home or abroad, I do not

---

[1] This refers to the Jacobitism of the time, particularly among those who were opposed to the Union. A reference to Lord Mahon's "Reign of Queen Anne" will show how strong was the opposition in Scotland, and how severe were the measures taken to put down that opposition. [T. S.]

[2] Craik and Hawkesworth print the word "seem," but the "Miscellanies," Faulkner, and Scott give it as in the text. [T. S.]

yet see the absolute necessity of extirpating the Christian religion from among us.

This perhaps may appear too great a paradox even for our wise and paradoxical age to endure; therefore I shall handle it with all tenderness, and with the utmost deference to that great and profound majority which is of another sentiment.

And yet the curious may please to observe, how much the genius of a nation is liable to alter in half an age. I have heard it affirmed for certain by some very old people, that the contrary opinion was even in their memories as much in vogue as the other is now; and, that a project for the abolishing of Christianity would then have appeared as singular, and been thought as absurd, as it would be at this time to write or discourse in its defence.

Therefore I freely own that all appearances are against me. The system of the Gospel, after the fate of other systems is generally antiquated and exploded; and the mass or body of the common people, among whom it seems to have had its latest credit, are now grown as much ashamed of it as their betters; opinions, like fashions, always descending from those of quality to the middle sort, and thence to the vulgar, where at length they are dropped and vanish.

But here I would not be mistaken, and must therefore be so bold as to borrow a distinction from the writers on the other side, when they make a difference between nominal and real Trinitarians. I hope no reader imagines me so weak to stand up in the defence of real Christianity, such as used in primitive times (if we may believe the authors of those ages) to have an influence upon men's belief and actions: To offer at the restoring of that would indeed be a wild project; it would be to dig up foundations; to destroy at one blow all the wit, and half the learning of the kingdom; to break the entire frame and constitution of things; to ruin trade, extinguish arts and sciences with the professors of them; in short, to turn our courts, exchanges, and shops into deserts; and would be full as absurd as the proposal of Horace,[1] where he advises the Romans all in a body to leave

---

[1] This proposal is embodied in the 16th Epode, where, in an appeal "to the Roman people," Horace advises them to fly the evils of tyranny

their city, and seek a new seat in some remote part of the world, by way of cure for the corruption of their manners.

Therefore I think this caution was in itself altogether unnecessary, (which I have inserted only to prevent all possibility of cavilling) since every candid reader will easily understand my discourse to be intended only in defence of nominal Christianity; the other having been for some time wholly laid aside by general consent, as utterly inconsistent with our present schemes of wealth and power.

But why we should therefore cast off the name and title of Christians, although the general opinion and resolution be so violent for it, I confess I cannot (with submission) apprehend the consequence necessary.[1] However, since the undertakers propose such wonderful advantages to the nation by this project, and advance many plausible objections against the system of Christianity, I shall briefly consider the strength of both, fairly allow them their greatest weight, and offer such answers as I think most reasonable. After which I will beg leave to shew what inconveniences may possibly happen by such an innovation, in the present posture of our affairs.

*First*, One great advantage proposed by the abolishing of Christianity is, that it would very much enlarge and establish liberty of conscience, that great bulwark of our nation, and of the Protestant Religion, which is still too much limited by priestcraft, notwithstanding all the good intentions of the legislature, as we have lately found by a severe instance. For it is confidently reported, that two young gentlemen of real hopes, bright wit, and profound judgment, who upon a thorough examination of causes and effects, and by the mere force of natural abilities, without the least tincture of learning, having made a discovery, that there was no God, and generously communicating their thoughts for the good of the public, were some time ago, by an unparalleled severity,

and civil war by sailing away to "the happy land, those islands of the blest:"

"Nos manet Oceanus circumvagus! arva, beata
Petamus arva, divites et insulas!" [T. S.]

[1] I give the reading of the "Miscellanies" (1711), Faulkner and Hawkesworth. Scott and Craik print it: "I confess I cannot (with submission) apprehend, nor is the consequence necessary." [T. S.]

and upon I know not what obsolete law, broke for blasphemy.[1] And as it hath been wisely observed, if persecution once begins, no man alive knows how far it may reach, or where it will end.

In answer to all which, with deference to wiser judgments, I think this rather shews the necessity of a nominal religion among us. Great wits love to be free with the highest objects; and if they cannot be allowed a God to revile or renounce, they will speak evil of dignities, abuse the government, and reflect upon the ministry; which I am sure few will deny to be of much more pernicious consequence, according to the saying of Tiberius, *Deorum offensa diis curæ.*[2] As to the particular fact related, I think it is not fair to argue from one instance, perhaps another cannot be produced; yet (to the comfort of all those who may be apprehensive of persecution) blasphemy we know is freely spoken a million of times in every coffeehouse and tavern, or wherever else good company meet. It must be allowed indeed, that to break an English free-born officer only for blasphemy, was, to speak the gentlest of such an action, a very high strain of absolute power. Little can be said in excuse for the general; perhaps he was afraid it might give offence to the allies, among whom, for aught we know, it may be the custom of the country to believe a God. But if he argued, as some have done, upon a mistaken principle, that an officer who is guilty of speaking blasphemy, may some time or other proceed so far as to raise a mutiny, the consequence is by no means to be admitted; for, surely the commander of an English army is likely to be but ill obeyed, whose soldiers fear and reverence him as little as they do a Deity.

It is further objected against the Gospel System, that it obliges men to the belief of things too difficult for freethinkers, and such who have shaken off the prejudices that usually cling to a confined education. To which I answer, that men should be cautious how they raise objections which reflect upon the wisdom of the nation. Is not every body freely allowed to believe whatever he pleases, and to publish his belief to the world whenever he thinks fit, especially if it

---

[1] No record of this " breaking " has been discovered. [T. S.]
[2] Tacitus, "Annals," bk. i., c. lxxiii. [T. S.]

serves to strengthen the party which is in the right? Would any indifferent foreigner, who should read the trumpery lately written by Asgil, Tindal, Toland, Coward,[1] and forty

[1] John Asgill (1659-1738), became a member of Lincoln's Inn, and went over to Ireland in 1697, where he practised as a barrister, amassed a large fortune, and was elected to the Irish parliament. For writing "An Argument, proving that Man may be translated from hence without passing through Death," he was, in 1700, expelled the House, and the book ordered to be burnt. On returning to England he was elected to parliament for Bramber, but suffered a second expulsion in 1712, also on account of this book. He was imprisoned for debt, and remained under the rules of the Fleet and King's Bench for thirty years, during which time he wrote and published various political tracts. His "Argument" attempted to "interpret the relations between God and man by the technical rules of English law," and Coleridge thought no little of its power and style.

Matthew Tindal (1657-1733) was born at Beer Ferrers, in Devonshire. He studied at Oxford, and obtained a fellowship in All Souls. He was made LL.D. in 1685, and, although he professed himself a Roman Catholic in James II.'s reign, he managed to keep his fellowship after that monarch's flight by becoming Protestant again. His most important work was "The Rights of the Christian Church Asserted," which the House of Commons in 1710 adjudged fit for burning by the hangman. In 1730 he published anonymously, the first part of "Christianity as Old as Creation," a work which attacked strongly the authority of the Scriptures; a second volume was never published.

John Toland (1669-1722), born near Londonderry, and educated in a Catholic school. He professed himself a Protestant, and was sent to Glasgow and Edinburgh. In the latter university he graduated in his master's degree. While studying at Leyden he became a sceptic, and in 1695 published his "Christianity not Mysterious," a work which aroused a wide controversy. In his "Life of Milton" (1698) he denied that King Charles was the author of "Eikon Basiliké," and also attacked the Gospels. This also brought upon him rejoinders from Dr. Blackall and Dr. Samuel Clarke. He died at Putney, in easy circumstances, due to the presents made him while visiting German courts. He wrote other works, chief among which may be mentioned, "Socinianism truly Stated" (1705), "Nazarenas" (1718), and "Tetradymus." His "Posthumous Works" were issued in two volumes in 1726, with a life by Des Maizeaux. Craik calls him "a man of utterly worthless character," and refers to his being "mixed up in some discreditable episodes as a political spy."

William Coward (1656?—1724?) was born at Winchester. He studied medicine and became a fellow of Wadham College, Oxford. His "Second Thoughts concerning Human Souls," published in 1702, occasioned fierce disputes, on account of its materialism. The House of Commons ordered the work to be burnt by the hangman.

Asgill, Toland, Tindal, Collins, and Coward are classed as the Deistical writers of the eighteenth century. In his "History of English Thought

more, imagine the Gospel to be our rule of faith, and confirmed by parliaments? Does any man either believe, or say he believes, or desire to have it thought that he says he believes one syllable of the matter? And is any man worse received upon that score, or does he find his want of nominal faith a disadvantage to him in the pursuit of any civil or military employment? What if there be an old dormant statute or two against him, are they not now obsolete, to a degree, that Empsom and Dudley[1] themselves if they were now alive, would find it impossible to put them in execution?

It is likewise urged, that there are, by computation, in this kingdom, above ten thousand parsons, whose revenues added to those of my lords the bishops, would suffice to maintain at least two hundred young gentlemen of wit and pleasure, and freethinking, enemies to priestcraft, narrow principles, pedantry, and prejudices; who might be an ornament to the Court and Town: And then, again, so great a number of able [bodied] divines might be a recruit to our fleet and armies. This indeed appears to be a consideration of some weight: But then, on the other side, several things deserve to be considered likewise: As, first, whether it may not be thought necessary that in certain tracts of country, like what we call parishes, there shall be one man at least of abilities to read and write. Then it seems a wrong computation, that the revenues of the Church throughout this island would be large enough to maintain two hundred young gentlemen, or even half that number, after the present refined way of living; that is, to allow each of them such a rent, as in the modern form of speech, would make them easy. But still there is in this project a greater mischief behind; and we ought to beware of the woman's folly, who killed the hen that every morning laid her a golden egg. For, pray what would become of the race of men in the next age, if we had nothing to trust to beside the scrofulous, consumptive productions, furnished by our men of wit and

in the Eighteenth Century" Mr. Leslie Stephen gives an admirable exposition of their views, and their special interpretation of Locke's theories. [T. S.]

[1] Of Henry VII. notoriety, who aided the king, by illegal exactions, to amass his large fortune. They were executed by Henry VIII. [T. S.]

pleasure, when, having squandered away their vigour, health and estates, they are forced by some disagreeable marriage to piece up their broken fortunes, and entail rottenness and politeness on their posterity? Now, here are ten thousand persons reduced by the wise regulations of Henry the Eighth,[1] to the necessity of a low diet, and moderate exercise, who are the only great restorers of our breed, without which the nation would in an age or two become one great hospital.

Another advantage proposed by the abolishing of Christianity, is the clear gain of one day in seven, which is now entirely lost, and consequently the kingdom one seventh less considerable in trade, business, and pleasure; besides the loss to the public of so many stately structures now in the hands of the Clergy, which might be converted into playhouses, exchanges, market-houses, common dormitories, and other public edifices.

I hope I shall be forgiven a hard word, if I call this a perfect *cavil*. I readily own there has been an old custom time out of mind, for people to assemble in the churches every Sunday, and that shops are still frequently shut, in order as it is conceived, to preserve the memory of that ancient practice, but how this can prove a hindrance to business or pleasure, is hard to imagine. What if the men of pleasure are forced one day in the week, to game at home instead of the chocolate-houses?[2] Are not the taverns and coffeehouses open? Can there be a more convenient season for taking a dose of physic? Are fewer claps got upon Sundays than other days? Is not that the chief day for traders to sum up the accounts of the week, and for lawyers to prepare their briefs? But I would fain know how it can be pretended that the churches are misapplied? Where are more appointments and rendezvouzes of gallantry? Where more care to appear in the foremost box with greater advantage of dress? Where more meetings for business? Where more bargains driven of all sorts? And where so many conveniences or enticements to sleep?

There is one advantage greater than any of the foregoing,

---

[1] His seizures of the revenues of the Church. [T. S.]

[2] The chocolate-houses seem to have been largely used for gambling purposes. They were not so numerous as the coffee-houses. [T. S.]

proposed by the abolishing of Christianity: that it will utterly extinguish parties among us, by removing those factious distinctions of High and Low Church, of Whig and Tory, Presbyterian and Church of England, which are now so many mutual clogs upon public proceedings, and are apt to prefer the gratifying themselves, or depressing their adversaries, before the most important interest of the state.

I confess, if it were certain that so great an advantage would redound to the nation by this expedient, I would submit and be silent: But will any man say, that if the words *whoring, drinking, cheating, lying, stealing,* were by act of parliament ejected out of the English tongue and dictionaries, we should all awake next morning chaste and temperate, honest and just, and lovers of truth? Is this a fair consequence? Or, if the physicians would forbid us to pronounce the words *pox, gout, rheumatism* and *stone,* would that expedient serve like so many talismans to destroy the diseases themselves? Are party and faction rooted in men's hearts no deeper than phrases borrowed from religion, or founded upon no firmer principles? And is our language so poor that we cannot find other terms to express them? Are *envy, pride, avarice* and *ambition* such ill nomenclators, that they cannot furnish appellations for their owners? Will not *heydukes* and *mamalukes, mandarins* and *patshaws,* or any other words formed at pleasure, serve to distinguish those who are in the ministry from others who would be in it if they could? What, for instance, is easier than to vary the form of speech, and instead of the word church, make it a question in politics, whether the Monument be in danger? Because religion was nearest at hand to furnish a few convenient phrases, is our invention so barren, we can find no other? Suppose, for argument sake, that the Tories favoured Margarita, the Whigs Mrs Tofts,[1] and the

---

[1] Margarita was a famous Italian singer of the day. Her name was Francesca Margherita de l'Epine, and she was known as "the Italian woman." In his "Journal to Stella" for August 6th, 1711, Swift writes: "We have a music meeting in our town [Windsor] to-night. I went to the rehearsal of it, and there was Margarita and her sister, and another drab, and a parcel of fiddlers; I was weary, and would not go to the meeting, which I am sorry for, because I heard it was a great assembly." (See present edition, vol. ii. p. 219).

Mrs. Catherine Tofts was an Englishwoman, who also sang in Italian

Trimmers[1] Valentini,[2] would not *Margaritians, Toftians,* and *Valentinians* be very tolerable marks of distinction? The *Prasini* and *Veniti*,[3] two most virulent factions in Italy, began (if I remember right) by a distinction of colours in ribbons, which we might do with as good a grace[4] about the dignity of the blue and the green, and would serve as properly to divide the Court, the Parliament, and the Kingdom between them, as any terms of art whatsoever, borrowed from religion. And therefore I think, there is little force in this objection against Christianity, or prospect of so great an advantage as is proposed in the abolishing of it.

'Tis again objected, as a very absurd ridiculous custom, that a set of men should be suffered, much less employed and hired, to bawl one day in seven against the lawfulness of those methods most in use toward the pursuit of greatness, riches and pleasure, which are the constant practice of all men alive on the other six. But this objection is, I think, a little unworthy so refined an age as ours. Let us argue this matter calmly: I appeal to the breast of any polite freethinker, whether in the pursuit of gratifying a predominant passion, he hath not always felt a wonderful incitement, by reflecting it was a thing forbidden; and therefore we see, in order to cultivate this taste, the wisdom of the nation hath taken special care, that the ladies should be furnished with prohibited silks, and the men with prohibited wine. And

---

opera. She had a fine figure and a beautiful voice. Steele in the "Tatler," No. 20, refers to her when in her state of insanity. Her mind, evidently, could not stand the strain of her great popularity, and she became mad in 1709. In the "Tatler" she is called Camilla; and Cibber also speaks of the "silver tone of her voice." [T. S.]

[1] By the Trimmers Swift referred to the nickname given to the party in the time of Charles II., which consisted of those who wished to compromise between the advocates of the Crown and the supporters of the Protestant succession as against the Duke of York. [T. S.]

[2] Another Italian singer of the time, who was the rival of Margarita and Mrs. Tofts. [T. S.]

[3] This refers to the Roman chariot races. They gave rise to the factions called *Albati, Russati, Prasini,* and *Veniti.* The Prasini (green) and Veniti (blue) were the principal, and their rivalry landed the empire, under Justinian, in a civil war. [T. S.]

[4] Scott has "and we might contend with as good a grace," &c. Craik follows Scott. The reading in the text is that of the "Miscellanies" (1711), Faulkner, and Hawkesworth. [T. S.]

indeed it were to be wished, that some other prohibitions were promoted, in order to improve the pleasures of the town; which, for want of such expedients begin already, as I am told, to flag and grow languid, giving way daily to cruel inroads from the spleen.

'Tis likewise proposed as a great advantage to the public, that if we once discard the system of the Gospel, all religion will of course be banished for ever; and consequently, along with it, those grievous prejudices of education, which under the names of *virtue, conscience, honour, justice,* and the like, are so apt to disturb the peace of human minds, and the notions whereof are so hard to be eradicated by right reason or freethinking, sometimes during the whole course of our lives.

Here first, I observe how difficult it is to get rid of a phrase, which the world is once grown fond of, though the occasion that first produced it, be entirely taken away. For several years past, if a man had but an ill-favoured nose, the deep-thinkers of the age would some way or other contrive to impute the cause to the prejudice of his education. From this fountain were said to be derived all our foolish notions of justice, piety, love of our country, all our opinions of God, or a future state, Heaven, Hell, and the like: And there might formerly perhaps have been some pretence for this charge. But so effectual care has been taken to remove those prejudices, by an entire change in the methods of education, that (with honour I mention it to our polite innovators) the young gentlemen who are now on the scene, seem to have not the least tincture of those infusions, or string of those weeds; and, by consequence, the reason for abolishing nominal Christianity upon that pretext, is wholly ceased.

For the rest, it may perhaps admit a controversy, whether the banishing of all notions of religion whatsoever, would be convenient for the vulgar. Not that I am in the least of opinion with those who hold religion to have been the invention of politicians, to keep the lower part of the world in awe by the fear of invisible powers; unless mankind were then very different to what it is now: For I look upon the mass or body of our people here in England, to be as freethinkers, that is to say, as staunch unbelievers, as any of the highest rank. But I conceive some scattered notions about a superior power to be of singular use for the common people, as furnishing excellent materials to keep children quiet when they grow peevish, and providing topics of amusement in a tedious winter-night.

Lastly, 'tis proposed as a singular advantage, that the abolishing of Christianity will very much contribute to the uniting of Protestants, by enlarging the terms of communion so as to take in all sorts of dissenters, who are now shut out of the pale upon account of a few ceremonies which all sides confess to be things indifferent: That this alone will effectually answer the great ends of a scheme for comprehension, by opening a large noble gate, at which all bodies may enter; whereas the chaffering with dissenters, and dodging about this or t'other ceremony, is but like opening a few wickets, and leaving them at jar, by which no more than one can get in at a time, and that, not without stooping, and sideling, and squeezing his body.[1]

To all this I answer; that there is one darling inclination of mankind, which usually affects to be a retainer to religion, though she be neither its parent, its godmother, or its friend; I mean the spirit of opposition, that lived long before Christianity, and can easily subsist without it. Let us, for instance, examine wherein the opposition of sectaries among us consists, we shall find Christianity to have no share in it at all. Does the Gospel any where prescribe a starched, squeezed countenance, a stiff, formal gait, a singularity of manners and habit, or any affected modes of speech different from the reasonable part of mankind? Yet, if Christianity did not lend its name to stand in the gap, and to employ or divert these humours, they must of necessity be spent in contraventions to the laws of the land, and disturbance of the public peace. There is a portion of enthusiasm assigned to every nation, which, if it hath not proper objects to work on, will burst out, and set all into a flame. If the quiet of a state can be bought by only flinging men a few ceremonies to devour, it

---

[1] "In this passage," says Scott, "the author's High Church principles, and jealousy of the Dissenters, plainly shew themselves; and it is, perhaps, in special reference to what is here said, that he ranks it among the pamphlets he wrote in opposition to the party then in power." [T. S.]

is a purchase no wise man would refuse. Let the mastiffs amuse themselves about a sheep's skin stuffed with hay, provided it will keep them from worrying the flock. The institution of convents abroad, seems in one point a strain of great wisdom, there being few irregularities in human passions, which may not have recourse to vent themselves in some of those orders, which are so many retreats for the speculative, the melancholy, the proud, the silent, the politic and the morose, to spend themselves, and evaporate the noxious particles; for each of whom we in this island are forced to provide a several sect of religion, to keep them quiet: And whenever Christianity shall be abolished, the legislature must find some other expedient to employ and entertain them. For what imports it how large a gate you open, if there will be always left a number who place a pride and a merit in not coming in?[1]

Having thus considered the most important objections against Christianity, and the chief advantages proposed by the abolishing thereof; I shall now with equal deference and submission to wiser judgments as before, proceed to mention a few inconveniences that may happen, if the Gospel should be repealed; which perhaps the projectors may not have sufficiently considered.

And first, I am very sensible how much the gentlemen of wit and pleasure are apt to murmur, and be choqued[2] at the sight of so many draggled-tail parsons, that happen to fall in their way, and offend their eyes; but at the same time, these wise reformers do not consider what an advantage and felicity it is, for great wits to be always provided with objects of scorn and contempt, in order to exercise and improve their talents, and divert their spleen from falling on each other or on themselves; especially when all this may be done without the least imaginable danger to their persons.

And to urge another argument of a parallel nature: If Christianity were once abolished, how could the freethinkers, the strong reasoners, and the men of profound learning, be able to find another subject so calculated in all points

---

[1] So the "Miscellanies" (1711) and Hawkesworth. Faulkner, Scott, and Craik print, "in refusing to enter." [T. S.]
[2] Shocked. Swift's habit when using a word of French origin was to keep the French spelling. [T. S.]

whereon to display their abilities? What wonderful productions of wit should we be deprived of, from those whose genius by continual practice hath been wholly turned upon raillery and invectives against religion, and would therefore never be able to shine or distinguish themselves upon any other subject! We are daily complaining of the great decline of wit among us, and would we take away the greatest, perhaps the only topic we have left? Who would ever have suspected Asgil for a wit, or Toland for a philosopher, if the inexhaustible stock of Christianity had not been at hand to provide them with materials? What other subject, through all art or nature, could have produced Tindal for a profound author, or furnished him with readers? It is the wise choice of the subject that alone adorns and distinguishes the writer. For, had a hundred such pens as these been employed on the side of religion, they would have immediately sunk into silence and oblivion.

Nor do I think it wholly groundless, or my fears altogether imaginary, that the abolishing of Christianity may perhaps bring the Church into danger, or at least put the senate to the trouble of another securing vote. I desire I may not be mistaken; I am far from presuming to affirm or think that the Church is in danger at present, or as things now stand; but we know not how soon it may be so when the Christian religion is repealed. As plausible as this project seems, there may a dangerous design lurk under it:[1] Nothing can be more notorious, than that the Atheists, Deists, Socinians, Anti-trinitarians, and other subdivisions of freethinkers, are persons of little zeal for the present ecclesiastical establishment: Their declared opinion is for repealing the Sacramental Test; they are very indifferent with regard to ceremonies; nor do they hold the *jus divinum* of Episcopacy. Therefore this may be intended as one politic step toward altering the constitution of the Church established, and setting up Presbytery in the stead, which I leave to be further considered by those at the helm.

In the last place, I think nothing can be more plain, than that by this expedient, we shall run into the evil we chiefly

---

[1] Craik follows Scott in altering this sentence to "there may be a dangerous design lurking under it"; but all other editors, except Morley and Roscoe, give it as printed in the text. [T. S.]

pretend to avoid; and that the abolishment of the Christian religion will be the readiest course we can take to introduce popery. And I am the more inclined to this opinion, because we know it has been the constant practice of the Jesuits to send over emissaries, with instructions to personate themselves members of the several prevailing sects among us. So it is recorded, that they have at sundry times appeared in the guise of Presbyterians, Anabaptists, Independents and Quakers, according as any of these were most in credit; so, since the fashion hath been taken up of exploding religion, the popish missionaries have not been wanting to mix with the freethinkers; among whom, Toland the great oracle of the Antichristians is an Irish priest, the son of an Irish priest; and the most learned and ingenious author of a book called "The Rights of the Christian Church,"[1] was in a proper juncture reconciled to the Romish faith, whose true son, as appears by a hundred passages in his treatise, he still continues. Perhaps I could add some others to the number; but the fact is beyond dispute, and the reasoning they proceed by is right: For, supposing Christianity to be extinguished, the people will never be at ease till they find out some other method of worship; which will as infallibly produce superstition, as this will end in popery.

And therefore, if notwithstanding all I have said, it still be thought necessary to have a bill brought in for repealing Christianity, I would humbly offer an amendment; that instead of the word, Christianity, may be put religion in general; which I conceive will much better answer all the good ends proposed by the projectors of it. For, as long as we leave in being a God and his providence, with all the necessary consequences which curious and inquisitive men will be apt to draw from such premises, we do not strike at the root of the evil, though we should ever so effectually annihilate the present scheme of the Gospel: For, of what use is freedom of thought, if it will not produce freedom of action, which is the sole end, how remote soever in

[1] Dr. Matthew Tindal (see previous note, p. 9). The book was afterwards specially criticised by Swift in his "Remarks upon a Book entitled 'The Rights of the Christian Church.'" See also note to the present reprint of these "Remarks." [T. S.]

appearance, of all objections against Christianity? And therefore, the freethinkers consider it as a sort of edifice, wherein all the parts have such a mutual dependence on each other, that if you happen to pull out one single nail, the whole fabric must fall to the ground. This was happily expressed by him who had heard of a text brought for proof of the Trinity, which in an ancient manuscript was differently read; he thereupon immediately took the hint, and by a sudden deduction of a long *sorites*, most logically concluded; "Why, if it be as you say, I may safely whore and drink on, and defy the parson." From which, and many the like instances easy to be produced, I think nothing can be more manifest, than that the quarrel is not against any particular points of hard digestion in the Christian system, but against religion in general; which, by laying restraints on human nature, is supposed the great enemy to the freedom of thought and action.

Upon the whole, if it shall still be thought for the benefit of Church and State, that Christianity be abolished; I conceive however, it may be more convenient to defer the execution to a time of peace, and not venture in this conjuncture to disoblige our allies, who, as it falls out, are all Christians, and many of them, by the prejudices of their education, so bigoted, as to place a sort of pride in the appellation. If upon being rejected by them, we are to trust an alliance with the Turk, we shall find ourselves much deceived: For, as he is too remote, and generally engaged in war with the Persian emperor, so his people would be more scandalized at our infidelity, than our Christian neighbours. For they [the Turks] are not only strict observers of religious worship, but what is worse, believe a God; which is more than required of us even while we preserve the name of Christians.

To conclude: Whatever some may think of the great advantages to trade by this favourite scheme, I do very much apprehend, that in six months time after the act is passed for the extirpation of the Gospel, the Bank, and East-India Stock, may fall at least one *per cent.* And since that is fifty times more than ever the wisdom of our age thought fit to venture for the preservation of Christianity, there is no reason we should be at so great a loss, merely for the sake of destroying it.

# A PROJECT

### FOR THE

## ADVANCEMENT OF RELIGION,

### AND THE

## REFORMATION OF MANNERS.

## BY A PERSON OF QUALITY.

# NOTE.

In placing this tract second in chronological order I am following Forster and Craik. All the collected editions of Swift's works, including the "Miscellanies" of 1711, begin with "The Sentiments of a Church of England Man," continue with the "Argument," and then the "Project." But the short intervals which separated the publication of all three tracts and the "Letter on the Sacramental Test," make a strict chronological order of less value than the order of development of the subject-matter with which they deal, granting even that the "Project" appeared after "The Sentiments." There seems, however, nothing improbable in the suggestion made by Forster, that Swift planned the writing of both the "Argument" and the "Project" while on a visit to the Earl of Berkeley, at Cranford, in 1708; and his dedication of the latter to Lady Berkeley lends this suggestion added weight. That the original edition of the "Project" is dated 1709 is nothing to the point, since it is well-known that the booksellers often antedated their publications, as publishers do now, when the issue occurred towards the end of a year. Moreover, the letter of the Earl of Berkeley to Swift, which Scott misdates 1706-1707, but which should be 1708, makes special reference to this very tract, showing that it was certainly published in 1708. "I earnestly entreat you," writes the earl, "if you have not done it already, that you would not fail of having your bookseller enable the Archbishop of York [Dr. Sterne] to give a book to the queen; for, with Mr. Nelson, I am entirely of opinion, that Her Majesty's reading of that book on the Progress for the Increase of Morality and Piety, may be of very great use to that end." I have never seen a copy of the first edition of "The Sentiments," and I cannot fix the exact date of its publication; but it was certainly not written before the "Project." The "Project," therefore, must be considered in the light of a preliminary essay to the fuller and more digested statement of "The Sentiments of a Church of England man"; and I have, on this account, placed it as the second tract written by Swift in the year 1708.

Whatever may be thought of the particular methods which Swift suggested for realizing his reformatory scheme, and they were, no doubt, artificial and wooden enough; the tract itself remains an excellent survey of the evils and gross habits of the time. The methods may be Utopian (Swift himself thought they were open to discussion), but the spirit of sincerity and piety is unmistakable. It is worth remembering, however, that several of the proposals, such as those for closing the public-houses at twelve o'clock at night; the penalizing of publicans who supplied drink to drunken customers; the building of churches, have since been adopted.

I cannot agree with Mr. Churton Collins ("Jonathan Swift," pp. 59-61) in suspecting Swift of a special policy of self-interest in writing the "Project." Swift was too honest a man to use the religious sentiment for the purpose of counteracting any bad impression his previous writings had made on those who had the power to advance him. However much he might delight in the possession of high worldly station, he would never so prostitute himself to obtain it. Nor did he care to let the world into the secret of his heart. Indeed, all his life Swift seemed to hide, almost jealously, the genuine piety of his nature. Whatever suspicion of policy has surrounded the tract must be ascribed to the well-intentioned letter of the Earl of Berkeley above quoted; and the Earl would not have written thus had he felt Swift's motive to be any other than a purely impersonal one.

Steele, in his review of the "Project" in the fifth "Tatler" (April 20th, 1709), makes some interesting observations, and seems to take special note of the "Person of Honour," in the character of which Swift wrote it. Writing from Will's Coffee-House, Steele says: "This week being sacred to holy things, and no public diversions allowed, there has been taken notice of even here, a little Treatise, called 'A Project for the Advancement of Religion: dedicated to the Countess of Berkeley.' The title was so uncommon, and promised so peculiar a way of thinking, that every man here has read it, and as many as have done so have approved it. It is written with the spirit of one who has seen the world enough to undervalue it with good breeding. The author must certainly be a man of wisdom, as well as piety, and have spent as much time in the exercise of both. The real causes of the decay of the interests of religion are set forth in a clear and lively manner, without unseasonable passions; and the whole air of the book, as to the language, the sentiments, and the reasonableness, show it was written by one whose virtue sits easy about him, and to whom vice is thoroughly contemptible. It was said by one of this company, alluding to that knowledge of the world the author seems to have, the man writes much like a gentleman, and goes to Heaven with a very good mien."

In his "Apology" Steele refers to this "Tatler" note, and remarks: "The gentleman I here intended was Dr. Swift, this kind of man I thought him at that time. We have not met of late, but I hope he deserves this character still."

The present text is based upon the first edition; but this edition was so wretchedly printed that I have carefully collated it with those given in the "Miscellanies" (1711), Faulkner (1735), and Hawkesworth (1762).

[T. S.]

# A PROJECT

## FOR THE

## Advancement of Religion,

### AND THE

## Reformation of Manners.

By a Perſon of QUALITY.

*O quiſquis volet impias*
  *Cædes, & rabiem tollere civicam:*
*Si quæret pater urbium*
  *Subſcribi ſtatuis, indomitam audeat*
*Refrænare licentiam.*

Hor.

## LONDON:

Printed and Sold by *H. Hills*, in *Black-fryars*, near the Water-ſide. For the Benefit of the Poor. 1709.

# A PROJECT FOR THE ADVANCEMENT OF RELIGION AND THE REFORMATION OF MANNERS.

### TO THE COUNTESS OF BERKELEY.[1]

MADAM,

MY intention in prefixing your Ladyship's name, is not after the common form, to desire your protection of the following papers; which I take to be a very unreasonable request; since, by being inscribed to your Ladyship, though without your knowledge, and from a concealed hand, you cannot recommend them without some suspicion of partiality. My real design is, I confess, the very same I have often detested in most dedications; that of publishing your praises to the world. Not upon the subject of your noble birth, for I know others as noble; or of the greatness of your fortune, for I know others far greater; or of that beautiful race (the images of their parents) which call you mother: for even this may perhaps have been equalled in some other age or country. Besides, none of these advantages do derive any accomplishments to the owners, but serve at best only to adorn what they really possess. What I intend, is your piety, truth, good sense, and good nature, affability, and charity; wherein I wish your Ladyship had many equals, or any superiors; and I wish I could say I knew them too, for then your Ladyship might have had a chance to escape this address. In the meantime, I think it highly necessary, for the interest of virtue and religion, that the whole kingdom should be informed in some parts of

---

[1] This is the same Countess of Berkeley whom Swift hoaxed with his "Meditation on a Broomstick." She was the daughter of Viscount Campden and sister to the Earl of Gainsborough. [T. S.]

your character: For instance, that the easiest and politest conversation, joined with the truest piety, may be observed in your Ladyship, in as great perfection, as they were ever seen apart in any other persons. That by your prudence and management under several disadvantages, you have preserved the lustre of that most noble family into which you are grafted, and which the unmeasurable profusion of ancestors for many generations had too much eclipsed. Then, how happily you perform every office of life to which Providence has called you: In the education of those two incomparable daughters, whose conduct is so universally admired; in every duty of a prudent, complying, affectionate wife; in that care which descends to the meanest of your domestics; and, lastly, in that endless bounty to the poor, and discretion where to distribute it. I insist on my opinion, that it is of importance for the public to know this and a great deal more of your Ladyship; yet whoever goes about to inform them, shall instead of finding credit, perhaps be censured for a flatterer. To avoid so usual a reproach, I declare this to be no dedication, but properly an introduction to a proposal for the advancement of religion and morals, by tracing, however imperfectly, some few lineaments in the character of a Lady, who hath spent all her life in the practice and promotion of both.

Among all the schemes offered to the public in this projecting age, I have observed with some displeasure, that there have never been any for the improvement of religion and morals; which beside the piety of the design from the consequence of such a reformation in a future life, would be the best natural means for advancing the public felicity of the state, as well as the present happiness of every individual. For, as much as faith and morality are declined among us, I am altogether confident, they might in a short time, and with no very great trouble, be raised to as high a perfection as numbers are capable of receiving. Indeed, the method is so easy and obvious, and some present opportunities so good, that, in order to have this project reduced to practice, there seems to want nothing more than to put those in mind, who by their honour, duty, and interest, are chiefly concerned.

But because it is idle to propose remedies before we are assured of the disease, or to be in pain,[1] till we are convinced of the danger; I shall first shew in general, that the nation is extremely corrupted in religion and morals; and then I will offer a short scheme for the reformation of both.

As to the first; I know it is reckoned but a form of speech, when divines complain of the wickedness of the age: However, I believe, upon a fair comparison with other times and countries, it would be found an undoubted truth.

For, first; to deliver nothing but plain matter of fact without exaggeration or satire; I suppose it will be granted, that hardly one in a hundred among our people of quality or gentry, appears to act by any principle of religion; that great numbers of them do entirely discard it, and are ready to own their disbelief of all revelation in ordinary discourse. Nor is the case much better among the vulgar, especially in great towns where the profaneness and ignorance of handicraftsmen, small traders, servants, and the like, are to a degree very hard to be imagined greater. Then, it is observed abroad, that no race of mortals hath so little sense of religion, as the English soldiers; to confirm which, I have been often told by great officers in the army, that in the whole compass of their acquaintance, they could not recollect three of their profession, who seemed to regard or believe one syllable of the Gospel: And the same, at least, may be affirmed of the fleet. The consequences of all which upon the actions of men are equally manifest. They never go about, as in former time, to hide or palliate their vices, but expose them freely to view, like any other common occurrences of life, without the least reproach from the world, or themselves. For instance; any man will tell you he intends to be drunk this evening, or was so last night, with as little ceremony or scruple, as he would tell you the time of the day. He will let you know he is going to a whore, or that he has got a clap, with as much indifferency, as he would a piece of public news. He will swear, curse, or blaspheme, without the least passion or provocation. And, though all regard for reputation is not quite laid aside in the other sex,

---

[1] Scott follows Faulkner in using the word "fear." The reading in the text is that of the first edition, the "Miscellanies" (1711), and of Hawkesworth. [T. S.]

'tis, however, at so low an ebb, that very few among them seem to think virtue and conduct of absolute necessity for preserving it. If this be not so, how comes it to pass, that women of tainted reputations find the same countenance and reception in all public places, with those of the nicest virtue, who pay, and receive visits from them without any manner of scruple? which proceeding, as it is not very old among us, so I take it to be of most pernicious consequence: It looks like a sort of compounding between virtue and vice, as if a woman were allowed to be vicious, provided she be not a profligate; as if there were a certain point, where gallantry ends, and infamy begins, or that a hundred criminal amours were not as pardonable as half a score.

Besides those corruptions already mentioned, it would be endless to enumerate such as arise from the excess of play or gaming: The cheats, the quarrels, the oaths and blasphemies among the men; among the women, the neglect of household affairs, the unlimited freedoms, the indecent passion; and lastly, the known inlet to all lewdness, when after an ill run, the person must answer the defects of the purse; the rule on such occasions holding true in play as it does in law; *quod non habet in crumena, luat in corpore.*

But all these are trifles in comparison, if we step into other scenes, and consider the fraud and cozenage of trading men and shopkeepers; that insatiable gulf of injustice and oppression, the law. The open traffic for all civil and military employments, (I wish it rested there) without the least regard to merit or qualifications; the corrupt management of men in office; the many detestable abuses in choosing those who represent the people, with the management of interest and factions among the representatives. To which I must be bold to add, the ignorance of some of the lower clergy; the mean servile temper of others; the pert pragmatical demeanour of several young stagers in divinity, upon their first producing themselves into the world; with many other circumstances, needless, or rather invidious, to mention; which falling in with the corruptions already related, have, however unjustly, almost rendered the whole order contemptible.

This is a short view of the general depravities among us, without entering into particulars, which would be an endless labour. Now, as universal and deep-rooted as these appear to be, I am utterly deceived, if an effectual remedy might not be applied to most of them; neither am I at present upon a wild speculative project, but such a one as may be easily put in execution.

For, while the prerogative of giving all employments continues in the Crown, either immediately, or by subordination; it is in the power of the Prince to make piety and virtue become the fashion of the age, if, at the same time, he would make them necessary qualifications for favour and preferment.

It is clear, from present experience, that the bare example of the best prince will not have any mighty influence, where the age is very corrupt. For, when was there ever a better prince on the throne than the present Queen? I do not talk of her talent for government, her love of the people, or any other qualities that are purely regal; but her piety, charity, temperance, conjugal love, and whatever other virtues do best adorn a private life; wherein, without question or flattery, she hath no superior: yet, neither will it be satire or peevish invective to affirm, that infidelity and vice are not much diminished since her coming to the crown, nor will, in all probability, till some more effectual remedies be provided.

Thus human nature seems to lie under this disadvantage, that the example alone of a vicious prince, will, in time, corrupt an age; but that of a good one, will not be sufficient to reform it, without further endeavours. Princes must therefore supply this defect by a vigorous exercise of that authority, which the law has left them, by making it every man's interest and honour, to cultivate religion and virtue; by rendering vice a disgrace, and the certain ruin to preferment or pretensions: All which they should first attempt in their own courts and families. For instance; might not the Queen's domestics of the middle and lower sort, be obliged, upon penalty of suspension, or loss of their employments, to a constant weekly attendance, at least, on the service of the church; to a decent behaviour in it; to receive the Sacrament four times in the year; to avoid swearing and irreligious profane discourses; and, to the appearance, at least, of temperance and chastity? Might not the care of all this be committed to the strict inspection of proper persons? Might not those of higher rank, and nearer access to her Majesty's person, receive her own commands to the same purpose, and be countenanced, or disfavoured, according as they obey? Might not the Queen lay her injunctions on the Bishops, and other great men of undoubted piety, to make diligent enquiry, to give her notice, if any person about her should happen to be of libertine principles or morals? Might not all those who enter upon any office in her Majesty's family, be obliged to take an oath parallel with that against simony, which is administered to the clergy? 'Tis not to be doubted, but that if these, or the like proceedings, were duly observed, morality and religion would soon become fashionable court virtues; and be taken up as the only methods to get or keep employments there, which alone would have mighty influence upon many of the nobility and principal gentry.

But, if the like methods were pursued as far as possible, with regard to those who are in the great employments of state, it is hard to conceive how general a reformation they might in time produce among us. For, if piety and virtue were once reckoned qualifications necessary to preferment; every man thus endowed, when put into great stations, would readily imitate the Queen's example, in the distribution of all offices in his disposal; especially if any apparent transgression, through favour or partiality, would be imputed to him for a misdemeanour, by which he must certainly forfeit his favour and station: And there being such great numbers in employment, scattered through every town and county in this kingdom; if all these were exemplary in the conduct of their lives, things would soon take a new face, and religion receive a mighty encouragement: Nor would the public weal be less advanced; since, of nine offices in ten that are ill executed, the defect is not in capacity or understanding, but in common honesty. I know no employment, for which piety disqualifies any man; and if it did, I doubt the objection would not be very seasonably offered at present; because, it is perhaps too just a reflection, that in the disposal of places, the question whether a person be *fit* for what he is recommended to, is generally the last that is thought on, or regarded.

I have often imagined, that something parallel to the office of censors anciently in Rome, would be of mighty use among us, and could be easily limited from running into any exorbitances. The Romans understood liberty at least as well as we, were as jealous of it, and upon every occasion as bold assertors. Yet I do not remember to have read any great complaint of the abuses in that office among them; but many admirable effects of it are left upon record. There are several pernicious vices frequent and notorious among us, that escape or elude the punishment of any law we have yet invented, or have had no law at all against them; such as atheism, drunkenness, fraud, avarice, and several others; which, by this institution, wisely regulated, might be much reformed. Suppose, for instance, that itinerary commissioners were appointed to inspect everywhere throughout the kingdom, into the conduct (at least) of men in office, with respect to their morals and religion, as well as their abilities; to receive the complaints and informations that should be offered against them, and make their report here upon oath, to the court, or the ministry, who should reward or punish accordingly. I avoid entering into the particulars of this, or any other scheme, which, coming from a private hand, might be liable to many defects, but would soon be digested by the wisdom of the nation; and surely, six thousand pounds a year would not be ill laid out among as many commissioners duly qualified, who, in three divisions, should be personally obliged to take their yearly circuits for that purpose.

But this is beside my present design, which was only to show what degree of reformation is in the power of the Queen, without the interposition of the legislature, and which her Majesty is, without question, obliged in conscience to endeavour by her authority, as much as she does by her practice.

It will be easily granted, that the example of this great town hath a mighty influence over the whole kingdom; and it is as manifest, that the town is equally influenced by the court, and the ministry, and those who, by their employments, or their hopes, depend upon them. Now, if under so excellent a princess as the present Queen, we would suppose a family strictly regulated, as I have above proposed; a ministry, where every single person was of distinguished piety; if we should suppose all great offices of state and law filled after the same manner, and with such as were equally diligent in choosing persons, who, in their several subordinations, would be obliged to follow the examples of their superiors, under the penalty of loss of favour and place; will not everybody grant, that the empire of vice and irreligion would be soon destroyed in this great metropolis, and receive a terrible blow through the whole island, which hath so great an intercourse with it, and so much affects to follow its fashions?

For, if religion were once understood to be the necessary step to favour and preferment; can it be imagined that any man would openly offend against it, who had the least regard for his reputation or his fortune? There is no quality so contrary to any nature, which men cannot affect, and put on upon occasions, in order to serve an interest, or gratify a prevailing passion. The proudest man will personate humility, the morosest learn to flatter, the laziest will be sedulous and active, where he is in pursuit of what he has much at heart. How ready, therefore, would most men be to step into the paths of virtue and piety, if they infallibly led to favour and fortune!

If swearing and profaneness, scandalous and avowed lewdness, excessive gaming and intemperance, were a little discountenanced in the army, I cannot readily see what ill consequences could be apprehended; if gentlemen of that profession were at least obliged to some external decorum in their conduct; or even if a profligate life and character were not a means of advancement, and the appearance of piety a most infallible hindrance, it is impossible the corruptions there should be so universal and exorbitant. I have been assured by several great officers, that no troops abroad are so ill disciplined as the English; which cannot well be otherwise, while the common soldiers have perpetually before their eyes the vicious example of their leaders; and it is hardly possible for those to commit any crime, whereof these are not infinitely more guilty, and with less temptation.

It is commonly charged upon the gentlemen of the army, that the beastly vice of drinking to excess, hath been lately, from their example, restored among us; which for some years before was almost dropped in England. But, whoever the introducers were, they have succeeded to a miracle; many of the young nobility and gentry are already become great proficients, and are under no manner of concern to hide their talent, but are got beyond all sense of shame or fear of reproach.

This might soon be remedied, if the Queen would think fit to declare, that no young person of quality whatsoever, who was notoriously addicted to that, or any other vice, should be capable of her favour, or even admitted into her presence, with positive command to her ministers, and others in great office, to treat them in the same manner; after which, all men, who had any regard for their reputation, or any prospect of preferment, would avoid their commerce. This would quickly make that vice so scandalous, that those who could not subdue, would at least endeavour to disguise it.

By the like methods, a stop might be put to that ruinous practice of deep gaming; and the reason why it prevails so much is, because a treatment, directly opposite in every point, is made use of to promote it; by which means, the laws enacted against this abuse are wholly eluded.

It cannot be denied, that the want of strict discipline in the universities, hath been of pernicious consequence to the youth of this nation, who are there almost left entirely to their own management, especially those among them of better quality and fortune; who, because they are not under a necessity of making learning their maintenance, are easily allowed to pass their time, and take their degrees, with little or no improvement; than which there cannot well be a greater absurdity. For, if no advancement of knowledge can be had from those places, the time there spent is at best utterly lost, because every ornamental part of education is better taught elsewhere: And as for keeping youths out of harm's way, I doubt, where so many of them are got together, at full liberty of doing what they please, it will not answer the end. But, whatever abuses, corruptions, or deviations from statutes, have crept into the universities through neglect, or length of time; they might in a great degree be reformed, by strict injunctions from court (upon each particular) to the visitors and heads of houses; besides the peculiar authority the queen may have in several colleges, whereof her predecessors were the founders. And among other regulations, it would be very convenient to prevent the excess of drink, with that scurvy custom among the lads, and parent of the former vice, the taking of tobacco, where it is not absolutely necessary in point of health.

From the universities, the young nobility, and others of great fortunes, are sent for early up to town, for fear of contracting any airs of pedantry, by a college education. Many of the younger gentry retire to the Inns of Court, where they are wholly left to their own discretion. And the consequence of this remissness in education appears, by observing that nine in ten of those, who rise in the church or the court, the law, or the army, are younger brothers, or new men, whose narrow fortunes have forced them upon industry and application.

As for the Inns of Court, unless we suppose them to be much degenerated, they must needs be the worst instituted seminaries in any Christian country; but whether they may be corrected without interposition of the legislature, I have not skill enough to determine. However, it is certain, that all wise nations have agreed in the necessity of a strict education, which consisted, among other things, in the observance of moral duties, especially justice, temperance, and chastity, as well as the knowledge of arts, and bodily exercises: But all these among us are laughed out of doors.

Without the least intention to offend the clergy, I cannot but think, that through a mistaken notion and practice, they prevent themselves from doing much service, which otherwise might lie in their power, to religion and virtue: I mean, by affecting so much to converse with each other, and caring so little to mingle with the laity. They have their particular clubs, and particular coffee-houses, where they generally appear in clusters: A single divine dares hardly show his person among numbers of fine gentlemen; or if he happens to fall into such company, he is silent and suspicious, in continual apprehension that some pert man of pleasure should break an unmannerly jest, and render him ridiculous. Now, I take this behaviour of the clergy to be just as reasonable, as if the physicians should agree to spend their time in visiting one another, or their several apothecaries, and leave their patients to shift for themselves. In my humble opinion, the clergy's business lies entirely among the laity; neither is there, perhaps, a more effectual way to forward the salvation of men's souls, than for spiritual persons to make themselves as agreeble as they can, in the conversations of the world; for which a learned education gives them great advantage, if they would please to improve and apply it. It so happens that the men of pleasure, who never go to church, nor use themselves to read books of devotion, form their ideas of the clergy from a few poor strollers they often observe in the streets, or sneaking out of some person of quality's house, where they are hired by the lady at ten shillings a month; while those of better figure and parts, do seldom appear to correct these notions. And let some reasoners think what they please, 'tis certain that men must be brought to esteem and love the clergy, before they can be persuaded to be in love with religion. No man values the best medicine, if administered by a physician, whose person he hates or despises. If the clergy were as forward to appear in all companies, as other gentlemen, and would a little study the arts of conversation to make themselves agreeable, they might be welcome at every party where there was the least regard for politeness or good sense; and consequently prevent a thousand vicious or profane discourses, as well as actions; neither would men of understanding complain, that a clergyman was a constraint upon the company, because they could not speak blasphemy, or obscene jests before him. While the people are so jealous of the clergy's ambition, as to abhor all thoughts of the return of ecclesiastic discipline among them, I do not see any other method left for men of that function to take, in order to reform the world, than by using all honest arts to make themselves acceptable to the laity. This, no doubt, is part of that wisdom of the serpent, which the Author of Christianity directs, and is the very method used by St. Paul, who *became all things to all men, to the Jews a Jew, and a Greek to the Greeks.*

How to remedy these inconveniences, may be a matter of some difficulty; since the clergy seem to be of an opinion, that this humour of sequestering themselves is a part of their duty; nay, as I remember, they have been told so by some of their bishops in their pastoral letters, particularly by one[1] among them of great merit and distinction, who yet, in his own practice, hath all his lifetime taken a course directly contrary. But I am deceived, if an awkward shame and fear of ill usage from the laity, have not a greater share in this mistaken conduct, than their own inclinations: However, if the outward profession of religion and virtue, were once in practice and countenance at court, as well as among all men in office, or who have any hopes or dependence for preferment, a good treatment of the clergy would be the necessary consequence of such a reformation; and they would soon be wise enough to see their own duty and interest in qualifying themselves for lay-conversation, when once they were out of fear of being chocqued by ribaldry or profaneness.

There is one further circumstance upon this occasion, which I know not whether it will be very orthodox to mention: The clergy are the only set of men among us, who constantly wear a distinct habit from others; the consequence of which (not in reason but in fact) is this, that as long as any scandalous persons appear in that dress, it will continue in some degree a general mark of contempt. Whoever happens to see a scoundrel in a gown, reeling home at midnight, (a sight neither frequent nor miraculous), is apt to entertain an ill idea of the whole order, and at the same time to be extremely comforted in his own vices. Some remedy might be put to this, if those straggling gentlemen, who come up to town to seek their fortunes, were fairly dismissed to the West Indies, where there is work enough, and where some better provision should be made for them, than I doubt there is at present. Or, what if no person were allowed to wear the habit, who had not some preferment in the church, or at least some temporal fortune sufficient to keep him out of contempt? Though, in my opinion, it were infinitely better, if all the clergy (except the bishops) were permitted to appear like other men of the graver sort, unless at those seasons when they are doing the business of their function.

[1] Bishop Burnet of Salisbury. See Swift's "Remarks on the Bishop of Sarum's Introduction." [T. S.]

There is one abuse in this town, which wonderfully contributes to the promotion of vice; that such men are often put into the commission of the peace, whose interest it is, that virtue should be utterly banished from among us; who maintain, or at least enrich themselves, by encouraging the grossest immoralities; to whom all the bawds of the ward pay contribution, for shelter and protection from the laws. Thus these worthy magistrates, instead of lessening enormities, are the occasion of just twice as much debauchery as there would be without them. For those infamous women are forced upon doubling their work and industry, to answer double charges, of paying the justice, and supporting themselves. Like thieves who escape the gallows, and are let out to steal, in order to discharge the gaoler's fees.

It is not to be questioned, but the Queen and ministry might easily redress this abominable grievance; by enlarging the number of justices of the peace; by endeavouring to choose men of virtuous principles; by admitting none who have not considerable fortunes; perhaps, by receiving into the number some of the most eminent clergy: Then, by forcing all of them, upon severe penalties, to act when there is occasion, and not permitting any who are offered to refuse the commission; but in these two last cases, which are very material, I doubt there will be need of the legislature.

The reformation of the stage is entirely in the power of the Queen; and in the consequences it hath upon the minds of the younger people, does very well deserve the strictest care. Besides the indecent and profane passages; besides the perpetual turning into ridicule the very function of the priesthood, with other irregularities, in most modern comedies, which have by others been objected to them; it is worth observing the distributive justice of the authors, which is constantly applied to the punishment of virtue, and the reward of vice; directly opposite to the rules of their best critics, as well as to the practice of dramatic poets, in all other ages and countries. For example, a country squire, who is represented with no other vice but that of being a clown, and having the provincial accent upon his tongue, which is neither a fault, nor in his power to remedy, must be condemned to marry a cast wench, or a cracked chambermaid. On the other side, a rakehell of the town, whose character is set off with no other accomplishment, but excessive prodigality, profaneness, intemperance, and lust, is rewarded with a lady of great fortune to repair his own, which his vices had almost ruined. And as in a tragedy, the hero is represented to have obtained many victories in order to raise his character in the minds of the spectators; so the hero of a comedy is represented to have been victorious in all his intrigues, for the same reason. I do not remember, that our English poets ever suffered a criminal amour to succeed upon the stage, till the reign of King Charles the Second. Ever since that time, the alderman is made a cuckold, the deluded virgin is debauched, and adultery and fornication are supposed to be committed behind the scenes, as part of the action. These and many more corruptions of the theatre, peculiar to our age and nation, need continue no longer, than while the court is content to connive at or neglect them. Surely a pension would not be ill employed on some men of wit, learning, and virtue, who might have power to strike out every offensive or unbecoming passage, from plays already written, as well as those that may be offered to the stage for the future. By which, and other wise regulations, the theatre might become a very innocent and useful diversion, instead of being a scandal and reproach to our religion and country.

The proposals I have hitherto made for the advancement of religion and morality, are such as come within reach of the administration; such as a pious active prince, with a steady resolution, might soon bring to effect. Neither am I aware of any objections to be raised against what I have advanced; unless it should be thought, that making religion a necessary step to interest and favour might increase hypocrisy among us; and I readily believe it would. But if one in twenty should be brought over to true piety by this, or the like methods, and the other nineteen be only hypocrites, the advantage would still be great. Besides, hypocrisy is much more eligible than open infidelity and vice; it wears the livery of religion; it acknowledges her authority, and is cautious of giving scandal. Nay, a long continued disguise is too great a constraint upon human nature, especially an English disposition; men would leave off their vices out of mere weariness, rather than undergo the toil and hazard, and perhaps expense, of practising them perpetually in private. And I believe it is often with religion, as it is with love; which, by much dissembling, at last grows real.

All other projects to this great end have proved hitherto ineffectual. Laws against immorality have not been executed; and proclamations occasionally issued out to enforce them are wholly unregarded as things of form. Religious societies, though begun with excellent intention, and by persons of true piety,[1] have dwindled into factious clubs, and grown a trade to enrich little knavish informers of the meanest rank, such as common constables, and broken shopkeepers.

And that some effectual attempt should be made toward such a reformation, is perhaps more necessary than people commonly apprehend; because the ruin of a state is generally preceded by a universal degeneracy of manners, and contempt of religion; which is entirely our case at present.

"Dis te minorem quod geris imperas."—Hor.[2]

Neither is this a matter to be deferred till a more convenient time of peace and leisure: Because a reformation in men's faith and morals is the best natural, as well as religious means, to bring the war to a good conclusion. For, if men in trust performed their duty for conscience sake, affairs would not suffer through fraud, falsehood, and neglect, as they now perpetually do. And if they believed a God, and his Providence, and acted accordingly, they might reasonably hope for his divine assistance, in so just a cause as ours.

Nor could the majesty of the English Crown appear, upon any occasion, in a greater lustre, either to foreigners or subjects, than by an administration, which, producing such great effects, would discover so much power. And power being the natural appetite of princes, a limited monarch cannot so well gratify it in anything, as a strict execution of the laws.

Besides; all parties would be obliged to close with so good a work as this, for their own reputation: Neither is any expedient more likely to unite them. For the most

---

[1] The original edition omits here the words, "are said, I know not whether truly or not." All other editions give these words. [T. S.]
[2] "Carmina," iii. 6. 5.

violent party men, I have ever observed, are such, as in the conduct of their lives have discovered least sense of religion or morality; and when all such are laid aside, at least those among them as shall be found incorrigible, it will be a matter perhaps of no great difficulty to reconcile the rest.

The many corruptions at present in every branch of business are almost inconceivable. I have heard it computed by skilful persons, that of six millions raised every year for the service of the public, one third, at least, is sunk and intercepted through the several classes and subordinations of artful men in office, before the remainder is applied to the proper use. This is an accidental ill effect of our freedom. And while such men are in trust, who have no check from within, nor any views but toward their interest, there is no other fence against them, but the certainty of being hanged upon the first discovery, by the arbitrary will of an unlimited monarch, or his vizier. Among us, the only danger to be apprehended is the loss of an employment; and that danger is to be eluded a thousand ways. Besides, when fraud is great, it furnishes weapons to defend itself: And at worst, if the crimes be so flagrant, that a man is laid aside out of perfect shame, (which rarely happens) he retires loaded with the spoils of the nation; *et fruitur diis iratis.* I could name a commission, where several persons, out of a salary of five hundred pounds, without other visible revenues, have always lived at the rate of two thousand, and laid out forty or fifty thousand upon purchases of lands or annuities. A hundred other instances of the same kind might easily be produced. What remedy, therefore, can be found against such grievances, in a constitution like ours, but to bring religion into countenance, and encourage those, who, from the hope of future reward, and dread of future punishment, will be moved to act with justice and integrity?

This is not to be accomplished any other way, but by introducing religion, as much as possible, to be the turn and fashion of the age; which only lies in the power of the administration; the prince with utmost strictness regulating the court, the ministry, and other persons in great employment; and these, by their example and authority, reforming all who have dependence on them.

It is certain, that a reformation successfully carried on in this great town, would in time spread itself over the whole kingdom; since most of the considerable youth pass here that season of their lives, wherein the strongest impressions are made, in order to improve their education, or advance their fortune; and those among them, who return into their several counties, are sure to be followed and imitated, as the greatest patterns of wit and good breeding.

And if things were once in this train, that is, if virtue and religion were established as the necessary titles to reputation and preferment; and if vice and infidelity were not only loaded with infamy, but made the infallible ruin of all men's pretensions; our duty, by becoming our interest, would take root in our natures, and mix with the very genius of our people; so that it would not be easy for the example of one wicked prince to bring us back to our former corruptions.

I have confined myself (as it is before observed) to those methods for the advancement of piety, which are in the power of a prince, limited like ours, by a strict execution of the laws already in force. And this is enough for a project, that comes without any name or recommendation; I doubt, a great deal more than will suddenly be reduced into practice. Though, if any disposition should appear towards so good a work, it is certain, that the assistance of the legislative power would be necessary to make it more complete. I will instance only a few particulars.

In order to reform the vices of this town, which, as we have said, hath so mighty an influence on the whole kingdom, it would be very instrumental to have a law made, that all taverns and alehouses should be obliged to dismiss their company at twelve at night, and shut up their doors; and that no woman should be suffered to enter any tavern or alehouse, upon any pretence whatsoever. It is easy to conceive what a number of ill consequences such a law would prevent; the mischiefs of quarrels, and lewdness, and thefts, and midnight brawls, the diseases of intemperance and venery, and a thousand other evils needless to mention. Nor would it be amiss, if the masters of those public-houses were obliged, upon the severest penalties, to give only a proportioned quantity of drink to every company; and when he found his guests disordered with excess, to refuse them any more.

I believe there is hardly a nation in Christendom, where all kind of fraud is practised in so unmeasurable a degree as with us. The lawyer, the tradesman, the mechanic, have found so many arts to deceive in their several callings, that they far outgrow the common prudence of mankind, which is in no sort able to fence against them. Neither could the legislature in anything more consult the public good, than by providing some effectual remedy against this evil, which, in several cases, deserves greater punishment than many crimes that are capital among us. The vintner, who, by mixing poison with his wines, destroys more lives than any one disease in the bill of mortality; the lawyer, who persuades you to a purchase which he knows is mortgaged for more than the worth, to the ruin of you and your family; the goldsmith or scrivener, who takes all your fortune to dispose of, when he has beforehand resolved to break the following day, do surely deserve the gallows much better than the wretch who is carried thither for stealing a horse.

It cannot easily be answered to God or man, why a law is not made for limiting the press; at least so far as to prevent the publishing of such pernicious books, as, under pretence of freethinking, endeavour to overthrow those tenets in religion which have been held inviolable, almost in all ages, by every sect that pretend to be Christian; and cannot, therefore, with any colour of reason, be called points in controversy, or matters of speculation, as some would pretend. The Doctrine of the Trinity, the Divinity of Christ, the Immortality of the Soul, and even the truth of all revelation, are daily exploded and denied in books openly printed; though it is to be supposed neither party will avow such principles, or own the supporting of them to be any way necessary to their service.[1]

It would be endless to set down every corruption or defect which requires a remedy from the legislative power. Senates are like to have little regard for any proposals that come from without doors; though, under a due sense of my own inabilities, I am fully convinced, that the unbiassed thoughts of an honest and wise man, employed on the good of his country, may be better digested than the results of a

---

[1] This passage refers to the deistical publications of Asgill, Toland, Tindal, and Collins, already noted. [T. S.]

multitude, where faction and interest too often prevail; as a single guide may direct the way better than five hundred, who have *contrary views*, or *look asquint*, or *shut their eyes*.

I shall therefore mention but one more particular, which I think the Parliament ought to take under consideration; whether it be not a shame to our country, and a scandal to Christianity, that in many towns, where there is a prodigious increase in the number of houses and inhabitants, so little care should be taken for the building of churches, that five parts in six of the people are absolutely hindered from hearing divine service? Particularly here in London, where a single minister, with one or two sorry curates, hath the care sometimes of above twenty thousand souls incumbent on him. A neglect of religion so ignominious, in my opinion, that it can hardly be equalled in any civilized age or country.[1]

But, to leave these airy imaginations of introducing new laws for the amendment of mankind; what I principally insist on is, a due execution of the old, which lies wholly in the crown, and in the authority derived from thence. I return, therefore, to my former assertion; that if stations of power, trust, profit, and honour, were constantly made the rewards of virtue and piety, such an administration must needs have a mighty influence on the faith and morals of the whole kingdom: And men of great abilities would then endeavour to excel in the duties of a religious life, in order to qualify themselves for public service. I may possibly be wrong in some of the means I prescribe towards this end; but that is no material objection against the design itself. Let those who are at the helm contrive it better, which, perhaps, they may easily do. Everybody will agree that the disease is manifest, as well as dangerous; that some remedy is necessary, and that none yet applied hath been effectual, which is a sufficient excuse for any man who wishes well to his country, to offer his thoughts, when he can have no other end in view but the public good. The present Queen is a princess of as many and great virtues as ever filled a

---

[1] This paragraph is known to have given the first hint to certain bishops, particularly to Bishop Atterbury, to procure a fund for building fifty new churches in London. [T. S.]

throne: How would it brighten her character to the present and after ages, if she would exert her utmost authority to instil some share of those virtues into her people, which they are too degenerate to learn only from her example! And, be it spoke with all the veneration possible for so excellent a sovereign, her best endeavours in this weighty affair are a most important part of her duty, as well as of her interest and her honour.

But, it must be confessed, that as things are now, every man thinks that he has laid in a sufficient stock of merit, and may pretend to any employment, provided he has been loud and frequent in declaring himself hearty for the government. 'Tis true, he is a man of pleasure, and a freethinker, that is, in other words, he is profligate in his morals, and a despiser of religion; but in point of party, he is one to be confided in; he is an assertor of liberty and property; he rattles it out against Popery and Arbitrary Power, and Priestcraft and High Church. 'Tis enough: He is a person fully qualified for any employment, in the court or the navy, the law or the revenue; where he will be sure to leave no arts untried, of bribery, fraud, injustice, oppression, that he can practise with any hope of impunity. No wonder such men are true to a government where liberty runs high, where property, however attained, is so well secured, and where the administration is at least so gentle: 'Tis impossible they could choose any other constitution, without changing to their loss.

Fidelity to a present establishment is indeed the principal means to defend it from a foreign enemy, but without other qualifications, will not prevent corruptions from within; and states are more often ruined by these than the other.

To conclude. Whether the proposals I have offered toward a reformation, be such as are most prudent and convenient, may probably be a question; but it is none at all, whether some reformation be absolutely necessary; because the nature of things is such, that if abuses be not remedied, they will certainly increase, nor ever stop, till they end in the subversion of a commonwealth. As there must always of necessity be some corruptions, so, in a well-instituted state, the executive power will be always contending against them, by *reducing things* (as Michiaevel speaks) *to their first principles;* never letting abuses grow inveterate, or multiply so far, that it will be hard to find remedies, and perhaps impossible to apply them. As he that would keep his house in repair, must attend every little breach or flaw, and supply it immediately; else time alone will bring all to ruin; how much more the common accidents of storms and rain? He must live in perpetual danger of his house falling about his ears; and will find it cheaper to throw it quite down, and build it again from the ground, perhaps upon a new foundation, or at least in a new form, which may neither be so safe, nor so convenient, as the old.

# THE SENTIMENTS

OF A

## CHURCH OF ENGLAND MAN,

WITH RESPECT TO

RELIGION AND GOVERNMENT.

WRITTEN IN THE YEAR 1708.

## NOTE.

THE writing of this tract, as has been already observed, placed Swift in a position where allegiance to party was not easy to maintain. It amounted to a warning to Whigs as well as Tories. To the former he urged that the Church of England was wide enough for the highest principles of civil liberty; to the latter he tried to show that to be a religious and God-fearing man it was not absolutely necessary to be a Tory in politics. "Whoever has examined the conduct and proceedings of both parties for some years past, whether in or out of power, cannot well conceive it possible to go far towards the extremes of either, without offering some violence to his integrity or understanding." It is true that Whiggism and "fanatical genius" were almost synonymous terms for Swift; but that was because the Church was of prime consideration with him, and the Whigs numbered in their ranks the great army of Dissent. Swift, in his famous letter to Pope, dated Dublin, January 10th, 1720-21, reviews his political opinions of 1708 to justify himself against the misrepresentations of "the virulence of libellers: whose malice has taken the same train in both, by fathering dangerous principles in government upon me, which I never maintained, and insipid productions, which I am not capable of writing." That review is but a summary of what is given fully in this tract. No appeal was ever better intentioned. "I only wish," he says to Pope, "my endeavours had succeeded better in the great point I had at heart, which was that of reconciling the ministers to each other." But High Church and Low Church were cries which had divided politicians as if they did not belong to one nation. To Swift it was easy enough to be a staunch Churchman and at the same time expose the fallacies underlying the faith in the sovereign power; but then Swift was here no party fanatic who would use the "Church in danger" cry for party purposes. "If others," he writes twelve years later, "who had more concern and more influence, would have acted their parts," his appeal had not been made in vain. As it was it failed in its intended purpose, and Swift lost what hold he had on Somers, Godolphin, and the rest. It remains, however, to testify to Swift's principles in a manner least expected by those who have set him down as intemperate and inconsistent. Certainly, no principles were ever more moderately expressed; and, assuredly, no expression of principles found fitter realization in conduct.

The text of this edition is based on that given in the "Miscellanies" of 1711. I have not succeeded in obtaining a copy of the original issue; but I have collated the various texts given in the re-issues by Faulkner, Hawkesworth, Scott, and the "Miscellanies" of 1728 (vol. i.) and 1747 (vol. i.).

[T. S.]

# THE SENTIMENTS OF A CHURCH OF ENGLAND MAN, WITH RESPECT TO RELIGION AND GOVERNMENT.

WHOEVER hath examined the conduct and proceedings of both parties for some years past, whether in or out of power, cannot well conceive it possible to go far towards the extremes of either, without offering some violence to his integrity or understanding. A wise and a good man may indeed be sometimes induced to comply with a number whose opinion he generally approves, though it be perhaps against his own. But this liberty should be made use of upon very few occasions, and those of small importance, and then only with a view of bringing over his own side another time to something of greater and more public moment. But to sacrifice the innocency of a friend, the good of our country, or our own conscience to the humour, or passion, or interest of a party, plainly shews that either our heads or our hearts are not as they should be: Yet this very practice is the fundamental law of each faction among us, as may be obvious to any who will impartially, and without engagement, be at the pains to examine their actions, which however is not so easy a task: For it seems a principle in human nature, to incline one way more than another, even in matters where we are wholly unconcerned. And it is a common observation, that in reading a history of facts done a thousand years ago, or standing by at play among those who are perfect strangers to us, we are apt to find our hopes and wishes engaged on a sudden in favour of one side more than another. No wonder then, we are all so ready to interest ourselves in the course of public affairs, where the most inconsiderable have some *real* share, and by the wonderful importance which every man is of to himself, a very great *imaginary* one.

And indeed, when the two parties that divide the whole commonwealth, come once to a rupture, without any hopes left of forming a third with better principles, to balance the others; it seems every man's duty to choose a side,[1] though he cannot entirely approve of either; and all pretences to neutrality are justly exploded by both, being too stale and obvious, only intending the safety and ease of a few individuals while the public is embroiled. This was the opinion and practice of the latter Cato, whom I esteem to have been the wisest and best of all the Romans. But before things proceed to open violence, the truest service a private man may hope to do his country, is, by unbiassing his mind as much as possible, and then endeavouring to moderate between the rival powers; which must needs be owned a fair proceeding with the world, because it is of all others the least consistent with the common design, of making a fortune by the merit of an opinion.

I have gone as far as I am able in qualifying myself to be such a moderator: I believe I am no bigot in religion, and I am sure I am none in government. I converse in full freedom with many considerable men of both parties, and if not in equal number, it is purely accidental and personal, as happening to be near the court, and to have made acquaintance there, more under one ministry than another. Then, I am not under the necessity of declaring myself by the prospect of an employment. And lastly, if all this be not sufficient, I industriously conceal my name, which wholly exempts me from any hopes and fears in delivering my opinion.

In consequence of this free use of my reason, I cannot possibly think so well or so ill of either party, as they would endeavour to persuade the world of each other, and of themselves. For instance; I do not charge it upon the body of the Whigs or the Tories, that their several principles lead them to introduce Presbytery, and the religion of the Church of Rome, or a commonwealth and arbitrary power. For, why should any party be accused of a principle which

---

[1] Faulkner and Scott have "one of the two sides." [T. S.]

they solemnly disown and protest against? But, to this they have a mutual answer ready; they both assure us, that their adversaries are not to be believed, that they disown their principles out of fear, which are manifest enough when we examine their practices. To prove this, they will produce instances, on one side, either of avowed Presbyterians, or persons of libertine and atheistical tenets, and on the other, of professed Papists, or such as are openly in the interest of the abdicated family. Now, it is very natural for all subordinate sects and denominations in a state, to side with some general party, and to choose that which they find to agree with themselves in some general principle. Thus at the restoration, the Presbyterians, Anabaptists, Independents, and other sects, did all with very good reason unite and solder up their several schemes to join against the Church, who without regard to their distinctions, treated them all as equal adversaries. Thus, our present dissenters do very naturally close in with the Whigs, who profess moderation, declare they abhor all thoughts of persecution, and think it hard that those who differ only in a few ceremonies and speculations, should be denied the privilege and profit of serving their country in the highest employments of state. Thus, the atheists, libertines, despisers of religion and revelation in general, that is to say, all those who usually pass under the name of freethinkers, do properly join with the same body; because they likewise preach up moderation, and are not so overnice to distinguish between an unlimited liberty of conscience, and an unlimited freedom of opinion. Then on the other side, the professed firmness of the Tories for Episcopacy as an apostolical institution: Their aversion to those sects who lie under the reproach of having once destroyed their constitution, and who they imagine, by too indiscreet a zeal for reformation have defaced the primitive model of the Church: Next, their veneration for monarchical government in the common course of succession, and their hatred to republican schemes: These, I say, are principles which not only the nonjuring zealots profess, but even Papists themselves fall readily in with. And every extreme here mentioned flings a general scandal upon the whole body it pretends to adhere to.

But surely no man whatsoever ought in justice or good manners to be charged with principles he actually disowns, unless his practices do openly and without the least room for doubt contradict his profession: Not upon small surmises, or because he has the misfortune to have ill men sometimes agree with him in a few general sentiments. However, though the extremes of Whig and Tory seem with little justice to have drawn religion into their controversies, wherein they have small concern; yet they both have borrowed one leading principle from the abuse of it; which is, to have built their several systems of political faith, not upon enquiries after truth, but upon opposition to each other, upon injurious appellations, charging their adversaries with horrid opinions, and then reproaching them for the want of charity; *et neuter falso*.

In order to remove these prejudices, I have thought nothing could be more effectual than to describe the sentiments of a Church of England man with respect to religion and government. This I shall endeavour to do in such a manner as may not be liable to least objection from either party, and which I am confident would be assented to by great numbers in both, if they were not misled to those mutual misrepresentations, by such motives as they would be ashamed to own.

I shall begin with religion.

And here, though it makes an odd sound, yet it is necessary to say, that whoever professes himself a member of the Church of England, ought to believe a God and his providence, together with revealed religion, and the divinity of Christ. For beside those many thousands, who (to speak in the phrase of divines) do practically deny all this by the immorality of their lives; there is no small number, who in their conversation and writings directly or by consequence endeavour to overthrow it; yet all these place themselves in the list of the National Church, though at the same time (as it is highly reasonable) they are great sticklers for liberty of conscience.

To enter upon particulars: A Church of England man hath a true veneration for the scheme established among us of ecclesiastic government; and though he will not determine whether Episcopacy be of divine right, he is sure it is most agreeable to primitive institution, fittest of all others for preserving order and purity, and under its present regulations best calculated for our civil state: He should therefore think the abolishment of that order among us would prove a mighty scandal and corruption to our faith, and manifestly dangerous to our monarchy; nay, he would defend it by arms against all the powers on earth, except our own legislature; in which case he would submit as to a general calamity, a dearth, or a pestilence.

As to rites and ceremonies, and forms of prayer; he allows there might be some useful alterations, and more, which in the prospect of uniting Christians might be very supportable, as things declared in their own nature indifferent; to which he therefore would readily comply, if the clergy, or, (though this be not so fair a method) if the legislature should direct: Yet at the same time he cannot altogether blame the former for their unwillingness to consent to any alteration; which beside the trouble, and perhaps disgrace, would certainly never produce the good effects intended by it. The only condition that could make it prudent and just for the clergy to comply in altering the ceremonial or any other indifferent part, would be, a firm resolution in the legislature to interpose by some strict and effectual laws to prevent the rising and spreading of new sects how plausible soever, for the future; else there must never be an end: And it would be to act like a man who should pull down and change the ornaments of his house, in compliance to every one who was disposed to find fault as he passed by, which besides the perpetual trouble and expense, would very much damage, and perhaps in time destroy the building. Sects in a state seem only tolerated with any reason because they are already spread; and because it would not be agreeable with so mild a government, or so pure a religion as ours, to use violent methods against great numbers of mistaken people, while they do not manifestly endanger the constitution of either. But the greatest advocates for general liberty of conscience, will allow that they ought to be checked in their beginnings, if they will allow them to be an evil at all, or which is the same thing, if they will only grant, it were better for the peace of the state, that there should be none. But while the clergy consider the natural temper of mankind in general, or of our own country in particular, what assurances can they have, that any compliances they shall make, will remove the evil of dissension, while the liberty still continues of professing whatever new opinion we please? Or how can it be imagined that the body of dissenting teachers, who must be all undone by such a revolution, will not cast about for some new objections to withhold their flocks, and draw in fresh proselytes by some further innovations or refinements?

Upon these reasons he is for tolerating such different forms in religious worship as are already admitted, but by no means for leaving it in the power of those who are tolerated, to advance their own models upon the ruin of what is already established, which it is natural for all sects to desire, and which they cannot justify by any consistent principles if they do not endeavour; and yet, which they cannot succeed in without the utmost danger to the public peace.

To prevent these inconveniences, he thinks it highly just, that all rewards of trust, profit, or dignity, which the state leaves in the disposal of the administration, should be given only to those whose principles direct them to preserve the constitution in all its parts. In the late affair of Occasional Conformity, the general argument of those who were against it, was not, to deny it an evil in itself, but that the remedy proposed was violent, untimely, and improper, which is the Bishop of Salisbury's opinion in the speech he made and published against the bill: But, however just their fears or complaints might have been upon that score, he thinks it a little too gross and precipitate to employ their writers already in arguments for repealing the sacramental test, upon no wiser a maxim, than that no man should on the account of conscience be deprived the liberty of serving his country; a topic which may be equally applied to admit Papists, Atheists, Mahometans, Heathens, and Jews. If the Church wants members of its own to employ in the service of the public; or be so unhappily contrived as to exclude from its communion such persons who are likeliest to have great abilities, it is time it should be altered and reduced into some more perfect, or at least more popular form: But in the meanwhile, it is not altogether improbable, that when those who dislike the constitution, are so very zealous in their offers for the service of their country, they are not wholly unmindful of their party or of themselves.

The Dutch whose practice is so often quoted to prove and celebrate the great advantages of a general liberty of conscience, have yet a national religion professed by all who bear office among them: But why should they be a precedent for us either in religion or government? Our country differs from theirs, as well in situation, soil, and productions of nature, as in the genius and complexion of inhabitants. They are a commonwealth founded on a sudden by a desperate attempt in a desperate condition, not formed or digested into a regular system by mature thought and reason, but huddled up under the pressure of sudden exigencies; calculated for no long duration, and hitherto subsisting by accident in the midst of contending powers, who cannot yet agree about sharing it among them. These difficulties do indeed preserve them from any great corruptions, which their crazy constitution would extremely subject them to in a long peace. That confluence of people in a persecuting age, to a place of refuge nearest at hand, put them upon the necessity of trade, to which they wisely gave all ease and encouragement: And if we could think fit to imitate them in this last particular, there would need no more to invite foreigners among us; who seem to think no further than how to secure their property and conscience, without projecting any share in that government which gives them protection, or calling it persecution if it be denied them. But I speak it for the honour of our administration, that although our sects are not so numerous as those in Holland, which I presume is not our fault, and I hope is not our misfortune, we much excel them and all Christendom besides in our indulgence to tender consciences.[1] One single compliance with the national form of receiving the sacrament, is all we require to qualify any sectary among us for the greatest employments in the state, after which he is at liberty to rejoin his own assemblies for the rest of his life. Besides, I will suppose any of the numerous sects in Holland, to have so far prevailed as to have raised a civil war, destroyed their

[1] When this was written there was no law against Occasional Conformity. [Faulkner, 1735.]

government and religion, and put their administrators to death; after which I will suppose the people to have recovered all again, and to have settled on their old foundation. Then I would put a query, whether that sect which was the unhappy instrument of all this confusion, could reasonably expect to be entrusted for the future with the greatest employments, or indeed to be hardly tolerated among them?

To go on with the sentiments of a Church of England man: He does not see how that mighty passion for the Church which some men pretend, can well consist with those indignities and that contempt they bestow on the persons of the clergy.[1] 'Tis a strange mark whereby to distinguish High Churchmen, that they are such who imagine the clergy can never be too low. He thinks the maxim these gentlemen are so fond of, that they are for an humble clergy, is a very good one; and so is he, and for an humble laity too, since humility is a virtue that perhaps equally benefits and adorns every station of life.

But then, if the scribblers on the other side freely speak the sentiments of their party, a divine of the Church of England cannot look for much better quarter thence. You shall observe nothing more frequent in their weekly papers than a way of affecting to confound the terms of Clergy and High Church, of applying both indifferently, and then loading the latter with all the calumny they can invent. They will tell you they honour a clergyman; but talk, at the same time, as if there were not three in the kingdom, who could fall in with their definition.[2] After the like manner they insult the universities, as poisoned fountains, and corrupters of youth.

Now, it seems clear to me, that the Whigs might easily have procured and maintained a majority among the clergy, and perhaps in the universities, if they had not too much

---

[1] "I observed very well with what insolence and haughtiness some lords of the High-Church party treated, not only their own chaplains, but all other clergy whatsoever, and thought this was sufficiently recompensed by their professions of zeal to the church."

[2] "I had likewise observed how the Whig lords took a direct contrary measure, treated the persons of particular clergymen with great courtesy, but shewed much ill-will and contempt for the order in general."

encouraged or connived at this intemperance of speech and virulence of pen, in the worst and most prostitute of their party; among whom there has been for some years past such a perpetual clamour against the ambition, the implacable temper, and the covetousness of the priesthood: Such a cant of High Church, and persecution, and being priest-ridden; so many reproaches about narrow principles, or terms of communion: Then such scandalous reflections on the universities, for infecting the youth of the nation with arbitrary and Jacobite principles, that it was natural for those, who had the care of religion and education, to apprehend some general design of altering the constitution of both. And all this was the more extraordinary, because it could not easily be forgot, that whatever opposition was made to the usurpations of King James, proceeded altogether from the Church of England, and chiefly from the clergy, and one of the universities. For, if it were of any use to recall matters of fact, what is more notorious than that prince's applying himself first to the Church of England? And upon their refusal to fall in with his measures, making the like advances to the dissenters of all kinds, who readily and almost universally complied with him, affecting in their numerous addresses and pamphlets, the style of Our Brethren the Roman Catholics, whose interests they put on the same foot with their own: And some of Cromwell's officers took posts in the army raised against the Prince of Orange.[1] These proceedings of theirs they can only extenuate by urging the provocations they had met from the Church in King Charles's reign, which though perhaps excusable upon the score of human infirmity, are not by any means a plea of merit equal to the constancy and sufferings of the bishops and clergy, or of the head and fellows of Magdalen College, that furnished the Prince of Orange's declaration with such powerful arguments to justify and promote the Revolution.

Therefore a Church of England man abhors the humour of the age in delighting to fling scandals upon the clergy in general; which besides the disgrace to the Reformation, and

[1] De Foe's "History of Addresses" contains some humbling instances of the applause with which the sectaries hailed their old enemy, James II., when they saw him engaged in hostility with the established Church. [S.]

to religion itself, casts an ignominy upon the kingdom that it does not deserve. We have no better materials to compound the priesthood of, than the mass of mankind, which corrupted as it is, those who receive orders must have some vices to leave behind them when they enter into the Church, and if a few do still adhere, it is no wonder, but rather a great one that they are no worse. Therefore he cannot think ambition, or love of power more justly laid to their charge than to other men, because, that would be to make religion itself, or at least the best constitution of Church-government, answerable for the errors and depravity of human nature.

Within these last two hundred years all sorts of temporal power have been wrested from the clergy, and much of their ecclesiastic, the reason or justice of which proceeding I shall not examine; but, that the remedies were a little too violent with respect to their possessions, the legislature hath lately confessed by the remission of their First Fruits.[1] Neither do the common libellers deny this, who in their invectives only tax the Church with an insatiable desire of power and wealth (equally common to all bodies of men as well as individuals) but thank God, that the laws have deprived them of both. However, it is worth observing the justice of parties: The sects among us are apt to complain, and think it hard usage to be reproached now after fifty years for overturning the state, for the murder of a king, and the indignity of a usurpation; yet these very men and their partisans, are continually reproaching the clergy, and laying to their charge the pride, the avarice, the luxury, the ignorance, and superstition, of Popish times for a thousand years past.

He thinks it a scandal to government that such an unlimited liberty should be allowed of publishing books against those doctrines in religion, wherein all Christians have agreed, much more to connive at such tracts as reject

[1] The first fruits were the first year's income of ecclesiastical benefices. In the middle ages they were taken by the Pope as a right; but were handed over to the English crown in 1534. Anne in 1703 gave them back to the Church by letters patent, an act confirmed by Parliament in 1704. The "Bounty" of Queen Anne, however, did not extend to Ireland; and one of Swift's missions in London was to obtain this remission of the first fruits for the Irish clergy also. [T. S.]

all revelation, and by their consequences often deny the very being of a God. Surely 'tis not a sufficient atonement for the writers, that they profess much loyalty to the present government, and sprinkle up and down some arguments in favour of the dissenters; that they dispute as strenuously as they can for liberty of conscience, and inveigh largely against all ecclesiastics, under the name of High Church; and, in short, under the shelter of some popular principles in politics and religion, undermine the foundations of all piety and virtue.

As he doth not reckon every schism of that damnable nature which some would represent, so he is very far from closing with the new opinion of those who would make it no crime at all, and argue at a wild rate, that God Almighty is delighted with the variety of faith and worship, as He is with the varieties of nature. To such absurdities are men carried by the affectation of freethinking, and removing the prejudices of education, under which head they have for some time begun to list morality and religion. It is certain that before the rebellion in 1642, though the number of Puritans (as they were then called) was as great as it is with us, and though they affected to follow pastors of that denomination, yet those pastors had episcopal ordination, possessed preferments in the Church, and were sometimes promoted to bishoprics themselves.[1] But, a breach in the general form of worship was in those days reckoned so dangerous and sinful in itself, and so offensive to Roman Catholics at home and abroad, and that it was too unpopular to be attempted; neither, I believe, was the expedient then found out of maintaining separate pastors out of private purses.

When a schism is once spread in a nation, there grows at length a dispute which are the schismatics. Without entering on the arguments, used by both sides among us, to fix the guilt on each other; 'tis certain, that, in the sense of the law, the schism lies on that side which opposes itself to the religion of the state. I leave it among the divines to dilate upon the danger of schism, as a spiritual evil, but

---

[1] In the reign of Elizabeth, and even in that of James, the Puritans were not, properly speaking, Dissenters; but, on the contrary, formed a sort of Low Church party in the national establishment. Archbishop Abbot himself has been considered as a Puritan. [S.]

I would consider it only as a temporal one. And I think it clear that any great separation from the established worship, though to a new one that is more pure and perfect, may be an occasion of endangering the public peace, because it will compose a body always in reserve, prepared to follow any discontented heads upon the plausible pretext of advancing true religion, and opposing error, superstition, or idolatry. For this reason Plato lays it down as a maxim, that, *men ought to worship the gods according to the laws of the country*, and he introduces Socrates in his last discourse utterly disowning the crime laid to his charge, of teaching new divinities or methods of worship. Thus the poor Huguenots of France were engaged in a civil war, by the specious pretences of some, who under the guise of religion sacrificed so many thousand lives to their own ambition and revenge. Thus was the whole body of Puritans in England drawn to be instruments, or abettors of all manner of villainy, by the artifices of a few men whose[1] designs from the first were levelled to destroy the constitution both of religion and government. And thus, even in Holland itself, where it is pretended that the variety of sects live so amicably together, and in such perfect obedience to the magistrate, it is notorious how a turbulent party joining with the Arminians, did in the memory of our fathers attempt to destroy the liberty of that republic. So that upon the whole, where sects are tolerated in a state, 'tis fit they should enjoy a full liberty of conscience, and every other privilege of freeborn subjects to which no power is annexed. And to preserve their obedience upon all emergencies, a government cannot give them too much ease, nor trust them with too little power.

The clergy are usually charged with a persecuting spirit, which they are said to discover by an implacable hatred to all dissenters; and this appears to be more unreasonable, because they suffer less in their interests by a toleration than any of the conforming laity: For while the Church remains in its present form, no dissenter can possibly have any share in its dignities, revenues, or power; whereas, by once receiving the sacrament, he is rendered capable of the highest

[1] Lord Clarendon's History; but see also Gardiner's "History of England." [T. S.]

employments in the state. And it is very possible, that a narrow education, together with a mixture of human infirmity, may help to beget among some of the clergy in possession such an aversion and contempt for all innovators, as physicians are apt to have for empirics, or lawyers for pettifoggers, or merchants for pedlars: But since the number of sectaries doth not concern the clergy either in point of interest or conscience, (it being an evil not in their power to remedy) 'tis more fair and reasonable to suppose their dislike proceeds from the dangers they apprehend to the peace of the commonwealth, in the ruin whereof they must expect to be the first and greatest sufferers.

To conclude this section, it must be observed, there is a very good word, which hath of late suffered much by both parties, and that is, MODERATION, which the one side very justly disowns, and the other as unjustly pretends to. Beside what passeth every day in conversation; any man who reads the papers published by Mr Lesley[1] and others of his stamp, must needs conclude, that if this author could make the nation see his adversaries under the colours he paints them in, we have nothing else to do, but rise as one man and destroy such wretches from the face of the earth. On the other side, how shall we excuse the advocates for moderation? among whom, I could appeal to a hundred papers of universal approbation by the cause they were writ for, which lay such principles to the whole body of the Tories, as, if they were true, and believed; our next business should in prudence be, to erect gibbets in every parish, and hang them out of the way. But I suppose it is presumed, the common people understand raillery, or at least, rhetoric, and will not take hyperboles in too literal a sense; which however in some junctures might prove a desperate experi-

[1] This was Charles Leslie, the second son of the Bishop of Clogher (1650-1722). He was educated for the bar, but forsook that, and entered into holy orders. In his zeal for the established Church he persecuted the Catholics; but this did not interfere with his adhesion to Jacobite political principles. He settled in London, and wrote a weekly paper called "The Rehearsal, or a Review of the Times," in which he attacked Locke and Hoadly. He did all he could for the cause of the exiled James, but he gave up the work when he found it hopeless, and died in Ireland. He wrote many virulent theological works, as well as a host of political tracts. [T. S.]

ment. And this is moderation in the modern sense of the word, to which, speaking impartially, the bigots of both parties are equally entitled.

## SECTION II.

### *The Sentiments of a Church of England Man with respect to Government.*

We look upon it as a very just reproach, though we cannot agree where to fix it, that there should be so much violence and hatred in religious matters, among men who agree in all fundamentals, and only differ in some ceremonies, or at most mere speculative points. Yet is not this frequently the case between contending parties in a state? For instance: Do not the generality of Whigs and Tories among us, profess to agree in the same fundamentals, their loyalty to the Queen, their abjuration of the Pretender, the settlement of the crown in the protestant line, and a revolution principle? Their affection to the Church established, with toleration of dissenters? Nay sometimes they go further, and pass over into each other's principles; the Whigs become great assertors of the prerogative, and the Tories of the people's liberty; these crying down almost the whole set of bishops, and those defending them; so that the differences fairly stated, would be much of a sort with those in religion among us, and amount to little more than, *who should take place*, or *go in and out first*, or *kiss the Queen's hand;* and what are these but a few court ceremonies? Or, *who should be in the ministry?* And what is that to the body of the nation, but a mere speculative point? Yet I think it must be allowed, that no religious sects ever carried their aversions for each other to greater heights than our state-parties have done, who the more to inflame their passions have mixed religious and civil animosities together; borrowing one of their appellations from the Church, with the addition of High and Low, how little soever their disputes relate to the term as it is generally understood.

I now proceed to deliver the sentiments of a Church of England man with respect to government.

He doth not think the Church of England so narrowly

calculated, that it cannot fall in with any regular species of government; nor does he think any one regular species of government more acceptable to God than another. The three generally received in the schools have all of them their several perfections, and are subject to their several depravations. However, few states are ruined by any defect in their institution, but generally by the corruption of manners, against which the best institution is no long security, and without which a very ill one may subsist and flourish: Whereof there are two pregnant instances now in Europe. The first is the aristocracy of Venice, which founded upon the wisest maxims, and digested by a great length of time, hath in our age admitted so many abuses through the degeneracy of the nobles, that the period of its duration seems to approach. The other is the united republics of the States-general, where a vein of temperance, industry, parsimony, and a public spirit, running through the whole body of the people, hath preserved an infant commonwealth of an untimely birth and sickly constitution, for above an hundred years, through so many dangers and difficulties, as a much more healthy one could never have struggled against, without those advantages.

Where security of person and property are preserved by laws which none but the Whole can repeal, there the great ends of government are provided for whether the administration be in the hands of One, or of Many. Where any one person or body of men, who do not represent the Whole, seize into their hands the power in the last resort, there is properly no longer a government, but what Aristotle and his followers call the abuse and corruption of one. This distinction excludes arbitrary power in whatever numbers; which notwithstanding all that Hobbes, Filmer[1] and others

---

[1] Hobbes, Thomas (1588-1679), the English philosopher, and author of "De Cive" (1642), "Treatise on Human Nature" (1650), "De Corpore Politico" (1650), "Leviathan" (1651), and other works. Swift is here combating Hobbes's advocacy for a sovereign power, as vested in a single person.

Filmer, Sir Robert (died 1647), author of "The Anarchy of a limited and mixed Monarchy," "Patriarcha," and "The Freeholder's Grand Inquest." In the "Patriarcha" Filmer attempted to prove that absolute government by a monarch was a patriarchal institution. Locke replied to this work in his "Two Treatises on Government." [T. S.]

have said to its advantage, I look upon as a greater evil than anarchy itself; as much as a savage is in a happier state of life than a slave at the oar.

It is reckoned ill manners, as well as unreasonable, for men to quarrel upon difference in opinion; because that is usually supposed to be a thing which no man can help in himself; which however I do not conceive to be an universal infallible maxim, except in those cases where the question is pretty equally disputed among the learned and the wise; where it is otherwise, a man of tolerable reason, small experience, and willing to be instructed, may apprehend he is got into a wrong opinion, though the whole course of his mind and inclination would persuade him to believe it true: He may be convinced that he is in error though he does not see where it lies, by the bad effects of it in the common conduct of his life, and by observing those persons for whose wisdom and goodness he has the greatest deference, to be of a contrary sentiment. According to Hobbes's comparison of reasoning with casting up accounts, whoever finds a mistake in the sum total, must allow himself out, though, after repeated trials he may not see in which article he has misreckoned. I will instance in one opinion, which I look upon every man obliged in conscience to quit, or in prudence to conceal; I mean, that whoever argues in defence of absolute power in a single person, though he offers the old plausible plea, that, *it is his opinion, which he cannot help unless he be convinced,* ought, in all free states to be treated as the common enemy of mankind. Yet this is laid as a heavy charge upon the clergy of the two reigns before the Revolution, who under the terms of Passive Obedience and Non-Resistance are said to have preached up the unlimited power of the prince, because they found it a doctrine that pleased the Court, and made way for their preferment. And I believe there may be truth enough in this accusation, to convince us, that human frailty will too often interpose itself among persons of the holiest function. However, it may be offered in excuse for the clergy, that in the best societies there are some ill members, which a corrupted court and ministry will industriously find out and introduce. Besides, it is manifest that the greater number of those who held and preached this doctrine, were misguided by equivocal terms, and by perfect ignorance in the principles of government, which they had not made any part of their study. The question originally put, and as I remember to have heard it disputed in public schools, was this; *Whether under any pretence whatsoever, it may be lawful to resist the supreme magistrate?* which was held in the negative; and this is certainly the right opinion. But many of the clergy, and other learned men, deceived by dubious expression, mistook the object to which passive obedience was due. By the supreme magistrate is properly understood the legislative power, which in all government must be absolute and unlimited. But the word magistrate seeming to denote a single person, and to express the executive power, it came to pass, that the obedience due to the legislature was for want of knowing or considering this easy distinction, misapplied to the administration. Neither is it any wonder, that the clergy or other well-meaning people should fall into this error, which deceived Hobbes himself so far, as to be the foundation of all the political mistakes in his book, where he perpetually confounds the executive with the legislative power, though all well-instituted states have ever placed them in different hands, as may be obvious to those who know anything of Athens, Sparta, Thebes, and other republics of Greece, as well as the greater ones of Carthage and Rome.

Besides, it is to be considered that when these doctrines began to be preached among us, the kingdom had not quite worn out the memory of that unhappy rebellion, under the consequences of which it had groaned almost twenty years. And a weak prince in conjunction with a succession of most prostitute ministers, began again to dispose the people to new attempts, which it was, no doubt, the clergy's duty to endeavour to prevent, if some of them had not for want of knowledge in temporal affairs, and others perhaps from a worse principle, proceeded upon a topic that strictly followed would enslave all mankind.

Among other theological arguments made use of in those times, in praise of monarchy, and justification of absolute obedience to a prince, there seemed to be one of a singular nature: It was urged that Heaven was governed by a monarch, who had none to control his power, but was absolutely obeyed: Then it followed, that earthly governments were the more perfect, the nearer they imitated the government in Heaven. All which I look upon as the strongest argument against despotic power that ever was offered; since no reason can possibly be assigned why it is best for the world that God Almighty hath such a power, which doth not directly prove that no mortal man should ever have the like.

But though a Church of England man thinks every species of government equally lawful, he does not think them equally expedient; or for every country indifferently. There may be something in the climate, naturally disposing men toward one sort of obedience, as is manifest all over Asia, where we never read of any commonwealth, except some small ones on the western coasts established by the Greeks. There may be a great deal in the situation of a country, and in the present genius of the people. It hath been observed, that the temperate climates usually run into moderate governments, and the extremes into despotic power. 'Tis a remark of Hobbes, that the youth of England are corrupted in their principles of government, by reading the authors of Greece and Rome who writ under commonwealths. But it might have been more fairly offered for the honour of liberty, that while the rest of the known world was overrun with the arbitrary government of single persons; arts and sciences took their rise, and flourished only in those few small territories were the people were free. And though learning may continue after liberty is lost, as it did in Rome, for a while, upon the foundations laid under the commonwealth, and the particular patronage of some emperors; yet it hardly ever began under a tyranny in any nation: Because slavery is of all things the greatest clog and obstacle to speculation. And indeed, arbitrary power is but the first natural step from anarchy or the savage life; the adjusting of power and freedom being an effect and consequence of maturer thinking: And this is nowhere so duly regulated as in a limited monarchy: Because I believe it may pass for a maxim in state, that the administration cannot be placed in too few hands, nor the legislature in too many. Now in this material point, the constitution of the English government far exceeds all others at this time on the earth, to which the present establishment of the Church doth so happily agree, that I think, whoever is an enemy to either, must of necessity be so to both.

He thinks, as our monarchy is constituted, a hereditary right is much to be preferred before election. Because the government here, especially by some late amendments, is so regularly disposed in all its parts, that it almost executes itself. And therefore upon the death of a prince among us, the administration goes on without any rub or interruption. For the same reasons we have little to apprehend from the weakness or fury of our monarchs, who have such wise councils to guide the first, and laws to restrain the other. And therefore this hereditary right should be kept so sacred, as never to break the succession, unless where the preserving of it may endanger the constitution; which is not from any intrinsic merit, or unalienable right in a particular family, but to avoid the consequences that usually attend the ambition of competitors, to which elective kingdoms are exposed; and which is the only obstacle to hinder them from arriving at the greatest perfection that government can possibly reach. Hence appears the absurdity of that distinction between a king *de facto*, and one *de jure*, with respect to us. For every limited monarch is a king *de jure*, because he governs by the consent of the whole, which is authority sufficient to abolish all precedent right. If a king come in by conquest, he is no longer a limited monarch, if he afterward consent to limitations, he becomes immediately king *de jure* for the same reason.

The great advocates for succession, who affirm it ought not to be violated upon any regard or consideration whatsoever, do insist much upon one argument that seems to carry little weight. They would have it, that a crown is a prince's birthright, and ought at least to be as well secured to him and his posterity as the inheritance of any private man: In short, that he has the same title to his kingdom which every individual has to his property. Now the consequence of this doctrine must be, that as a man may find several ways to waste, misspend, or abuse his patrimony, without being answerable to the laws; so a king may in like manner do what he will with his own, that is, he may squander and misapply his revenues, and even alienate the crown, without being called to an account by his subjects. They allow such a prince to be guilty indeed of much folly and wickedness, but for those he is to answer to God, as every private man must do that is guilty of mismanagement in his own concerns. Now the folly of this reasoning will best appear, by applying it in a parallel case. Should any man argue, that a physician is supposed to understand his own art best; that the law protects and encourages his profession; and therefore although he should manifestly prescribe poison to all his patients, whereof they should immediately die, he cannot be justly punished, but is answerable only to God: Or should the same be offered in behalf of a divine, who would preach against religion and moral duties; in either of these two cases everybody would find out the sophistry, and presently answer, that although common men are not exactly skilled in the composition or application of medicines, or in prescribing the limits of duty; yet the difference between poisons and remedies is easily known by their effects, and common reason soon distinguishes between virtue and vice: And it must be necessary to forbid both these the further practice of their professions, because their crimes are not purely personal to the physician or the divine, but destructive to the public. All which is infinitely stronger in respect to a prince, with whose good or ill conduct the happiness or misery of a whole nation is included; whereas it is of small consequence to the public, farther than examples, how any private person manages his property.

But granting that the right of a lineal successor to a crown were upon the same foot with the property of a subject, still it may at any time be transferred by the legislative power, as other properties frequently are. The supreme power in a state can do no wrong, because whatever that doth, is the action of all; and when the lawyers apply this maxim to the king, they must understand it only in that sense as he is administrator of the supreme power, otherwise it is not universally true, but may be controlled in several instances easy to produce.

And these are the topics we must proceed upon to justify our exclusion of the young Pretender in France; that of his suspected birth being merely popular, and therefore not made use of as I remember, since the Revolution in any speech, vote, or proclamation where there was occasion to mention him.

As to the abdication of King James, which the advocates on that side look upon to have been forcible and unjust, and consequently void in itself, I think a man may observe every article of the English Church, without being in much pain about it. 'Tis not unlikely that all doors were laid open for his departure, and perhaps not without the privity of the Prince of Orange, as reasonably concluding that the kingdom might be settled in his absence: But to affirm he had any cause to apprehend the same treatment with his father, is an improbable scandal flung upon the nation by a few bigotted French scribblers, or the invidious assertion of a ruined party at home, in the bitterness of their souls: Not one material circumstance agreeing with those in 1648; and the greatest part of the nation having preserved the utmost horror for that ignominious murder: But whether his removal were caused by his own fears or other men's artifices, 'tis manifest to me, that supposing the throne to be vacant, which was the foot they went upon, the body of the people were thereupon left at liberty, to choose what form of government they pleased, by themselves or their representatives.

The only difficulty of any weight against the proceedings at the Revolution, is an obvious objection, to which the writers upon that subject have not yet given a direct or sufficient answer, as if they were in pain at some consequences which they apprehend those of the contrary opinion might draw from it. I will repeat this objection as it was offered me some time ago, with all its advantages, by a very pious, learned, and worthy gentleman [1] of the nonjuring party.

The force of his argument turned upon this; that the laws made by the supreme power, cannot otherwise than by the supreme power be annulled: That this consisting in England of a King, Lords, and Commons, whereof each have a negative voice, no two of them can repeal or enact a law without consent of the third; much less may any one of them be entirely excluded from its part of the legislature by a vote of the other two. That all these maxims were openly violated at the Revolution; where an assembly of the nobles and people, not summoned by the king's writ

---

[1] Mr. Nelson, author of "The Feasts and Fasts of the Church of England."

(which was an essential part of the constitution) and consequently no lawful meeting, did merely upon their own authority, declare the king to have abdicated, the throne vacant, and gave the crown by a vote to a nephew, when there were three children to inherit; though by the fundamental laws of the realm the next heir is immediately to succeed. Neither does it appear how a prince's abdication can make any other sort of vacancy in the throne, than would be caused by his death, since he cannot abdicate for his children (who claim their right of succession by act of parliament) otherwise than by his own consent in form to a bill from the two houses.

And this is the difficulty that seems chiefly to stick with the most reasonable of those, who from a mere scruple of conscience refuse to join with us upon the revolution principle; but for the rest, are I believe as far from loving arbitrary government, as any others can be, who are born under a free constitution, and are allowed to have the least share of common good sense.

In this objection there are two questions included: First, whether upon the foot of our constitution, as it stood in the reign of the late King James, a king of England may be deposed? The second is, whether the people of England convened by their own authority, after the king had withdrawn himself in the manner he did, had power to alter the succession?

As for the first; it is a point I shall not presume to determine, and shall therefore only say, that to any man who holds the negative, I would demand the liberty of putting the case as strongly as I please. I will suppose a prince limited by laws like ours, yet running into a thousand caprices of cruelty like Nero or Caligula. I will suppose him to murder his mother and his wife, to commit incest, to ravish matrons, to blow up the senate, and burn his metropolis, openly to renounce God and Christ, and worship the devil. These and the like exorbitances are in the power of a single person to commit without the advice of a ministry, or assistance of an army. And if such a king as I have described, cannot be deposed but by his own consent in parliament, I do not well see how he can be resisted, or what can be meant by a limited monarchy; or what signifies the people's consent in making and repealing laws, if the person who administers hath no tie but conscience, and is answerable to none but God. I desire no stronger proof that an opinion must be false, than to find very great absurdities annexed to it; and there cannot be greater than in the present case: For it is not a bare speculation that kings may run into such enormities as are above-mentioned; the practice may be proved by examples not only drawn from the first Cæsars or later emperors, but many modern princes of Europe; such as Peter the Cruel, Philip the Second of Spain, John Basilovitz[1] of Muscovy, and in our own nation, King John, Richard the Third, and Henry the Eighth. But there cannot be equal absurdities supposed in maintaining the contrary opinion; because it is certain, that princes have it in their power to keep a majority on their side, by any tolerable administration; till provoked by continual oppressions, no man indeed can then answer where the madness of the people will stop.

As to the second part of the objection; whether the people of England convened by their own authority, upon King James's precipitate departure, had power to alter the succession?

In answer to this, I think it is manifest from the practice of the wisest nations, and who seem to have had the truest notions of freedom, that when a prince was laid aside for mal-administration, the nobles and people, if they thought it necessary for the public weal, did resume the administration of the supreme power (the power itself having been always in them) and did not only alter the succession, but often the very form of government too; because they believed there was no natural right in one man to govern another, but that all was by institution, force, or consent. Thus, the cities of Greece, when they drove out their tyrannical kings, either chose others from a new family, or abolished the kingly government, and became free states. Thus the Romans upon the expulsion of Tarquin found it inconvenient for them to be subject any longer to the pride, the lust, the cruelty and arbitrary will of single persons, and therefore by

---

[1] Peter the Cruel is Peter the Great. Ivan Basilovitz was the first emperor of Russia who assumed the title of Czar. He was born in 1529, and died in 1584.

general consent entirely altered the whole frame of their government. Nor do I find the proceedings of either, in this point, to have been condemned by any historian of the succeeding ages.

But a great deal hath been already said by other writers upon this invidious and beaten subject; therefore I shall let it fall, though the point is commonly mistaken, especially by the lawyers; who of all others seem least to understand the nature of government in general; like under-workmen, who are expert enough at making a single wheel in a clock, but are utterly ignorant how to adjust the several parts, or regulate the movements.

To return therefore from this digression: It is a Church of England man's opinion, that the freedom of a nation consists in an absolute unlimited legislative power, wherein the whole body of the people are fairly represented, and in an executive duly limited; because on this side likewise there may be dangerous degrees, and a very ill extreme. For when two parties in a state are pretty equal in power, pretensions, merit, and virtue, (for these two last are with relation to parties and a court, quite different things) it hath been the opinion of the best writers upon government, that a prince ought not in any sort to be under the guidance or influence of either, because he declines by this means from his office of presiding over the whole, to be the head of a party; which besides the indignity, renders him answerable for all public mismanagements and the consequences of them; and in whatever state this happens, there must either be a weakness in the prince or ministry, or else the former is too much restrained by the legislature.[1]

To conclude: A Church of England man may with prudence and a good conscience approve the professed principles of one party more than the other, according as he thinks they best promote the good of Church and State; but he will never be swayed by passion or interest, to advance an opinion merely because it is that of the party he most approves; which one single principle he looks upon as the root of all our civil animosities. To enter into a party as into an order of friars with so resigned an obedience to

---

[1] This is as given in the "Miscellanies" (1711). Scott and Faulkner print "by the nobles, or those who represent the people." [T. S.]

superiors, is very unsuitable both with the civil and religious liberties we so zealously assert. Thus the understandings of a whole senate are often enslaved by three or four leaders on each side; who instead of intending the public weal, have their hearts wholly set upon ways and means how to get or to keep employments. But to speak more at large, how has this spirit of faction mingled itself with the mass of the people, changed their nature and manners, and the very genius of the nation; broke all the laws of charity, neighbourhood, alliance and hospitality; destroyed all ties of friendship, and divided families against themselves! And no wonder it should be so, when in order to find out the character of a person, instead of inquiring whether he be a man of virtue, honour, piety, wit, good sense, or learning; the modern question is only, whether he be a Whig or a Tory, under which terms all good and ill qualities are included.

Now, because it is a point of difficulty to choose an exact middle between two ill extremes, it may be worth enquiring in the present case, which of these, a wise and good man would rather seem to avoid: Taking therefore their own good and ill characters with due abatements and allowances for partiality and passion; I should think that in order to preserve the constitution entire in Church and State, whoever has a true value for both, would be sure to avoid the extremes of Whig for the sake of the former, and the extremes of Tory on account of the latter.

I have now said all that I could think convenient upon so nice a subject, and find I have the ambition common with other reasoners, to wish at least that both parties may think me in the right, which would be of some use to those who have any virtue left, but are blindly drawn into the extravagancies of either, upon false representations, to serve the ambition or malice of designing men, without any prospect of their own. But if that is not to be hoped for, my next wish should be, that both might think me in the wrong; which I would understand as an ample justification of myself, and a sure ground to believe, that I have proceeded at least with impartiality, and perhaps with truth.

# REMARKS
## UPON A
# BOOK,
### INTITULED,
## "THE RIGHTS OF THE CHRISTIAN CHURCH, &c."
#### WRITTEN IN THE YEAR 1708, BUT LEFT UNFINISHED.

# NOTE.

Dr. Matthew Tindal, of whom a short account has already been given (see note, p. 9), issued his "Rights of the Christian Church" in 1706. In 1707 it had already gone through three editions. The full title of the work is: "The Rights of the Christian Church asserted, against the Romish and all other Priests, who claim an independent Power over it: with a Preface concerning the Government of the Church of England, as by law established." Ostensibly the book was an attack on the Roman Catholic Church, but the attack was so cleverly veiled that it included in its criticisms the Church of England also; and must take its place among the works of the deistical writers of the time who aimed at subverting the foundations of the relationships between the Church and the State. According to Dr. Hicks, who wrote several works in reply to Tindal's book, Tindal told a gentleman, who found him at work on it, that "he was writing a book which would make the clergy mad." If so, he did not fall short of his intention; for not only the clergy, but even learned laymen became "mad." In addition to Dr. Hicks of Oxford, the Church of England found champions in Dr. William Wotton, Samuel Hill, Conyers-Place, Mr. Oldisworth, and Swift. Swift delayed the preparation of the materials for his reply, or else he found other matters to occupy his time—the Sacheverel business came on soon after, and the Tindal controversy lost interest in this more immediate and more important affair. So that Swift's criticism remained unfinished, and was only published when his editors came to search among his papers. In 1710 Tindal's work was ordered, by a vote of the House of Commons, to be publicly burned by the hangman. The grand jury of Middlesex were presented that the author, printer, and publisher of "The Rights of the Christian Church" to be dangerous and disaffected persons, and promoters of sedition and profaneness; and this charge was grounded on the following extracts. I take these from Scott's note, and I find that the page references are to the second edition of Tindal's work issued in 1706.

"The church is a private society, and no more power belonging to it than to other private companies and clubs, and, consequently, all the right anyone has to be an ecclesiastical officer, and the power he is entrusted with, depends on the consent of the parties concerned, and is no greater than they can bestow." Preface, p. xxx.

"The Scriptures nowhere make the receiving the Lord's Supper from the hands of a priest necessary." p. 104.

"The remembrance of Christ's sufferings a mere grace-cup delivered to be handed about." p. 105.

"Among Christians, one no more than another can be reckoned a priest from Scripture"—"And the clerk has as good a title to the priesthood as the parson . . . Every one, as well as the minister, rightly consecrateth the elements to himself . . . Anything farther than this, may rather be called Conjuration than Consecration." p. 108.

"The absurdities of bishops being by divine appointment, governors of the Christian Church, and no others are capable of being of that number, who derive not their right by an uninterrupted succession of bishops in the Catholic Church." p. 313.

"The supreme powers had no way to escape the heavier oppressions, and more insupportable usurpations of their own clergy, than by submitting to the Pope's milder yoke and gentler authority." p. 255.

"One grand cause of mistake is, not considering when God acts as governor of the universe, and when as prince of a particular nation. The Jews, when they came out of the land of bondage, were under no settled government, till God was pleased to offer himself to be their king, to which all the people expressly consented . . . God's laws bound no nation, except those that agreed to the Horeb contract." p. 151.

"Not only an independent power of excommunication, but of ordination in the clergy, is inconsistent with the magistrate's right to protect the commonwealth." p. 87.

"Priests, no better than spiritual make-baits, baraters, boute-feux, and incendiaries, and who make churches serve to worse purposes than bear gardens." p. 118.

"It is a grand mistake to suppose the magistrate's power extends to indifferent things . . . Men have liberty as they please, and a right . . . to form what clubs, companies, or meetings, they think fit, either for business or pleasure, which the magistrate . . . cannot hinder, without manifest injustice." p. 15.

"God . . . interposed not among the Jews, until they had chosen him for their king." p. 312.

For a full account of Tindal and his work, see the "Memoirs of the Life and Writings of Matthew Tindal, with a History of the Controversies wherein he was engaged," published in 1733. The text of the present reprint of Swift's "Remarks" is based on that given in "Works," vol. vii. of the 4to edition of 1764. It has also been collated with the 8vo edition of same date (vol. xiii.) and with that of 1762 (vol. xiii.).

[T. S.]

# REMARKS UPON A BOOK INTITULED "THE RIGHTS OF THE CHRISTIAN CHURCH, &c."

BEFORE I enter upon a particular examination of this treatise, it will be convenient to do two things:

*First*, To give some account of the author, together with the motives, that might probably engage him in such a work. And,

*Secondly*, to discover the nature and tendency in general, of the work itself.

The first of these, although it hath been objected against, seems highly reasonable, especially in books that instil pernicious principles. For, although a book is not intrinsically much better or worse, according to the stature or complexion of the author, yet, when it happens to make a noise, we are apt, and curious, as in other noises, to look about from whence it cometh. But however, there is something more in the matter.

If a theological subject be well handled by a layman, it is better received than if it came from a divine; and that for reasons obvious enough, which, although of little weight in themselves, will ever have a great deal with mankind.

But, when books are written with ill intentions, to advance dangerous opinions, or destroy foundations; it may be then of real use to know from what quarter they come, and go a good way towards their confutation. For instance, if any man should write a book against the lawfulness of punishing felony with death; and, upon enquiry, the author should be found in Newgate under condemnation for robbing a house; his arguments would not very unjustly lose much of their force, from the circumstances he lay under. So, when

Milton writ his book of divorces, it was presently rejected as an occasional treatise; because every body knew, he had a shrew for his wife. Neither can there be any reason imagined, why he might not, after he was blind, have writ another upon the danger and inconvenience of eyes. But, it is a piece of logic which will hardly pass on the world; that because one man hath a sore nose, therefore all the town should put plasters upon theirs. So, if this treatise about the rights of the church should prove to be the work of a man steady in his principles, of exact morals, and profound learning, a true lover of his country, and a hater of Christianity, as what he really believes to be a cheat upon mankind, whom he would undeceive purely for their good; it might be apt to check unwary men, even of good dispositions towards religion. But if it be found the production of a man soured with age and misfortunes, together with the consciousness of past miscarriages; of one, who, in hopes of preferment, was reconciled to the Popish religion;[1] of one wholly prostitute in life and principles, and only an enemy to religion, because it condemns them: In this case, and this last I find is the universal opinion, he is like to have few proselytes, beside those, who, from a sense of their vicious lives, require to be perpetually supplied by such amusements as this; which serve to flatter their wishes, and debase their understandings.

I know there are some who would fain have it, that this discourse was written by a club of freethinkers, among whom the supposed author only came in for a share. But, sure, we cannot judge so meanly of any party, without

---

[1] Dr. Matthew Tindal became a convert to the Romish religion during the reign of James II. What share interest had in his conversion may be easily imagined; but it is uncertain whether it was the disappointment of his expectations, or conviction, that, in 1687, induced him to reconcile himself to the Church of England, and become a decided favourer of those doctrines which produced the Revolution. He often sat as a judge in the Court of Delegates, but did not practise much as an advocate in Doctor's Commons. His chief means of support was a pension from government of £200. Tindal died in 1733, three years after publication of his grand deistical work, "Christianity as Old as the Creation." His effects, amounting to £2,000 and upwards, were appropriated by the noted Eustace Budgell, to the prejudice of the heir at law, under a will attended with circumstances of great suspicion. [S.]

affronting the dignity of mankind. If this be so, and if here be the product of all their quotas and contributions, we must needs allow, that freethinking is a most confined and limited talent. It is true indeed, the whole discourse seemeth to be a motley, inconsistent composition, made up of various shreds of equal fineness, although of different colours. It is a bundle of incoherent maxims and assertions, that frequently destroy one another. But still there is the same flatness of thought and style; the same weak advances towards wit and raillery; the same petulancy and pertness of spirit; the same train of superficial reading; the same thread of threadbare quotations: the same affectation of forming general rules upon false and scanty premises. And, lastly, the same rapid venom sprinkled over the whole; which, like the dying impotent bite of a trodden benumbed snake, may be nauseous and offensive, but cannot be very dangerous.

And, indeed, I am so far from thinking this libel to be born of several fathers, that it hath been the wonder of several others, as well as myself; how it was possible for any man, who appeareth to have gone the common circle of academical education;[1] who hath taken so universal a liberty, and hath so entirely laid aside all regards, not only of Christianity, but common truth and justice; one who is dead to all sense of shame, and seemeth to be past the getting or losing a reputation, should, with so many advantages, and upon so unlimited a subject, come out with so poor, so jejune a production. Should we pity or be amazed at so perverse a talent, which, instead of qualifying an author to give a new turn to old matter, disposeth him quite contrary to talk in an old beaten trivial manner upon topics wholly new. To make so many sallies into pedantry without a call, upon a subject the most alien, and in the very moments he is declaiming against it, and in an age too, where it is so violently exploded, especially among those readers he proposeth to entertain.

I know it will be said, that this is only to talk in the common style of an answerer; but I have not so little policy. If there were any hope of reputation or merit from

[1] See note, p. 9, where it will be seen that Tindal was an Oxford man. [T. S.]

such victory, I should be apt like others to cry up the courage and conduct of an enemy. Whereas to detect the weakness, the malice, the sophistry, the falsehood, the ignorance of such a writer, requireth little more than to rank his perfections in such an order, and place them in such a light, that the commonest reader may form a judgment of them.

It may still be a wonder how so heavy a book, written upon a subject in appearance so little instructive or diverting, should survive to three editions, and consequently find a better reception than is usual with such bulky spiritless volumes; and this, in an age that pretendeth so soon to be nauseated with what is tedious and dull. To which I can only return, that, as burning a book by the common hangman, is a known expedient to make it sell; so, to write a book that deserveth such treatment, is another: And a third, perhaps as effectual as either, is to ply an insipid, worthless tract with grave and learned answers, as Dr. Hickes, Dr. Potter,[1] and Mr. Wotton have done. Design and performances, however commendable, have glanced a reputation upon the piece; which oweth its life to the strength of those hands and weapons, that were raised to destroy it; like flinging a mountain upon a worm, which, instead of being bruised, by the advantage of its littleness, lodgeth under it unhurt.

But neither is this all. For the subject, as unpromising as it seemeth at first view, is no less than that of Lucretius, to free men's minds from the bondage of religion; and this not by little hints and by piecemeal, after the manner of

[1] George Hickes, D.D. (1642-1715), born at Newsham, Yorks, and educated at Oxford. He visited Scotland with his patron, the Duke of Lauderdale, in 1677, and was presented by the St. Andrews University with the degree of LL.D. Became Dean of Worcester in 1683, but lost that office at the Revolution, for not taking the oaths. The nonjuring prelates, in 1693, consecrated him Bishop of Thetford. Dr. Hickes was a profound scholar, and well versed in northern literature. Among his works may be named, "Institutiones Grammaticæ Anglo-Saxonicæ et Mæso-Gothicæ," "Antiquæ Literaturæ Septentrionalis Thesaurus."

John Potter, D.D. (1674-1747), born at Wakefield, and educated at Oxford. In 1707 he published a "Discourse on Church Government," and eight years later became Bishop of Oxford. On the death of Wake, in 1737, he was appointed to the Archbishopric of Canterbury. [T. S.]

those little atheistical tracts that steal into the world, but in a thorough wholesale manner; by making religion, church, Christianity, with all their concomitants, a perfect contrivance of the civil power. It is an imputation often charged on this sort of men, that, by their invectives against religion, they can possibly propose no other end than that of fortifying themselves and others against the reproaches of a vicious life; it being necessary for men of libertine practices to embrace libertine principles, or else they cannot act in consistence with any reason, or preserve any peace of mind. Whether such authors have this design, (whereof I think they have never gone about to acquit themselves) thus much is certain; that no other use is made of such writings: Neither did I ever hear this author's book justified by any person, either Whig or Tory, except such who are of that profligate character. And, I believe, whoever examineth it, will be of the same opinion; although indeed such wretches are so numerous, that it seemeth rather surprising, why the book hath had no more editions, than why it should have so many.

Having thus endeavoured to satisfy the curious with some account of this author's character, let us examine what might probably be the motives to engage him in such a work. I shall say nothing of the principal, which is a sum of money; because that is not a mark to distinguish him from any other trader with the press. I will say nothing of revenge and malice, from resentment of the indignities and contempt he hath undergone for his crime of apostasy. To this passion he has thought fit to sacrifice order, propriety, discretion, and common sense, as may be seen in every page of his book: But, I am deceived, if there were not a third motive as powerful as the other two; and that is, vanity. About the latter end of King James's reign he had almost finished a learned discourse in defence of the Church of Rome, and to justify his conversion: All which, upon the Revolution, was quite out of season. Having thus prostituted his reputation, and at once ruined his hopes, he had no course left, but to shew his spite against religion in general; the false pretensions to which, had proved so destructive to his credit and fortune: And, at the same time, loth to employ the speculations of so many years to no purpose; by an easy turn, the same arguments he had made use of to advance Popery, were full as properly levelled by him against Christianity itself; like the image, which, while it was new and handsome, was worshipped for a saint, and when it came to be old and broken, was still good enough to make a tolerable devil. And, therefore every reader will observe, that the arguments for Popery are much the strongest of any in his book, as I shall further remark when I find them in my way.

There is one circumstance in his title-page, which I take to be not amiss, where he calleth his book, " Part the First." This is a project to fright away answerers, and make the poor advocates for religion believe, he still keepeth further vengeance in *petto*. It must be allowed, he hath not wholly lost time, while he was of the Romish communion. This very trick he learned from his old father, the Pope; whose custom it is to lift up his hand, and threaten to fulminate, when he never meant to shoot his bolts; because the princes of Christendom had learned the secret to avoid or despise them. Dr. Hickes knew this very well, and therefore, in his answer to this "Book of Rights," where a second part is threatened, like a rash person he desperately crieth, "Let it come." But I, who have not too much phlegm to provoke angry wits of his standard, must tell the author, that the doctor plays the wag, as if he were sure, it were all grimace. For my part, I declare, if he writeth a second part, I will not write another answer; or, if I do, it shall be published, before the other part cometh out.[1]

There may have been another motive, although it be hardly credible, both for publishing this work, and threatening a second part: It is not soon conceived how far the sense of a man's vanity will transport him. This man must have somewhere heard, that dangerous enemies have been often bribed to silence with money or preferment: And, therefore, to shew how formidable he is, he hath published

---

[1] Tindal did, however, attempt to maintain his ground against his numerous opponents, in "A Defence of the Rights of the Christian Church, against a late Visitation Sermon, 8vo. 1707;" and also in "A Second Defence of the Rights of the Christian Church considered, in two late Indictments against a Bookseller and his Servant, for selling one of the said Books, 1707." [S.]

his first essay; and, in hopes of hire to be quiet, hath frighted us with his design of another. What must the clergy do in these unhappy circumstances? If they should bestow this man bread enough to stop his mouth, it will but open those of a hundred more, who are every whit as well qualified to rail as he. And truly, when I compare the former enemies to Christianity, such as Socinus,[1] Hobbes, and Spinosa,[2] with such of their successors, as Toland, Asgil, Coward, Gildon,[3] this author of the "Rights," and some others; the church appeareth to me like the sick old lion in the fable, who, after having his person outraged by the bull, the elephant, the horse, and the bear, took nothing so much to heart, as to find himself at last insulted by the spurn of an ass.

I will now add a few words to give the reader some general notion of the nature and tendency of the work itself.

I think I may assert, without the least partiality, that it is a treatise wholly devoid of wit or learning, under the most violent and weak endeavours and pretences to both. That it is replenished throughout with bold, rude, improbable falsehoods, and gross misinterpretations; and supported by the most impudent sophistry and false logic I have anywhere observed. To this he hath added a paltry, traditional cant of "priestrid" and "priestcraft," without reason or pretext as he applyeth it. And when he raileth at those doctrines in Popery (which no Protestant was ever supposed to believe) he leads the reader, however, by the hand, to

---

[1] Lælius Socinus (1525-1562), born at Siena. He studied at Bologna, and in 1546 became a member of a secret freethinking society in Venice. The society, however, was broken up, and Socinus left Italy for Switzerland and Poland. He died at Zurich. His papers were published by his nephew, Faustus Socinus, who founded a sect on the tenets they taught.

[2] Benedict or Baruch Spinoza (1632-1677), born at Amsterdam, of a Portuguese Jewish family. He was excommunicated by his people for atheism. He retired to the Hague and took to making lenses, and the study of philosophy. His "Ethics" and "Tractatus Theologico-Politicus" constitute a system of philosophy which has had no little influence on modern thought. See Pollock's "Spinoza."

[3] Charles Gildon (1665-1723-4) was educated at Douay. He printed a book called "The Deist's Manual." For accounts of Coward, Toland, and Asgil, see note, p. 9.

make applications against the English clergy, and then he never faileth to triumph, as if he had made a very shrewd and notable stroke. And because the court and kingdom seemeth disposed to moderation with regard to Dissenters, more perhaps than is agreeable to the hot unreasonable temper of some mistaken men among us; therefore under the shelter of that popular opinion, he ridiculeth all that is sound in religion, even Christianity itself, under the names of Jacobite, Tackers, High Church, and other terms of factious jargon. All which, if it were to be first rased from his book (as just so much of nothing to the purpose) how little would remain to give the trouble of an answer! To which let me add, that the spirit or genius, which animates the whole, is plainly perceived to be nothing else but the abortive malice of an old neglected man,[1] who hath long lain under the extremes of obloquy, poverty and contempt; that have soured his temper, and made him fearless. But where is the merit of being bold, to a man that is secure of impunity to his person, and is past apprehension of anything else? He that hath neither reputation nor bread hath very little to lose, and hath therefore as little to fear. And, as it is usually said, "Whoever values not his own life, is master of another man's;" so there is something like it in reputation: He that is wholly lost to all regards of truth or modesty, may scatter so much calumny and scandal, that some part may perhaps be taken up before it fall to the ground; because the ill talent of the world is such, that those who will be at pains enough to inform themselves in a malicious story, will take none at all to be undeceived, nay, will be apt with some reluctance to admit a favourable truth.

To expostulate, therefore, with this author for doing mischief to religion, is to strew his bed with roses; he will reply in triumph, that this was his design; and I am loth to mortify him, by asserting he hath done none at all. For I never yet saw so poor an atheistical scribble, which would not serve as a twig for sinking libertines to catch at. It must be allowed in their behalf, that the faith of Christians is not as a grain of mustard seed in comparison of theirs, which can remove such mountains of absurdities, and submit

---

[1] Tindal was not an old man at the time Swift wrote, certainly not older than was Swift himself. [T. S.]

with so entire a resignation to such apostles. If these men had any share of that reason they pretend to, they would retire into Christianity, merely to give it ease. And therefore men can never be confirmed in such doctrines, until they are confirmed in their vices; which last, as we have already observed, is the principal design of this and all other writers against revealed religion.

I am now opening the book which I propose to examine. An employment, as it is entirely new to me, so it is that to which, of all others, I have naturally the greatest antipathy. And, indeed, who can dwell upon a tedious piece of insipid thinking, and false reasoning, so long as I am likely to do, without sharing the infection?

But, before I plunge into the depths of the book itself, I must be forced to wade through the shallows of a long preface.

This preface, large as we see it, is only made up of such supernumerary arguments against an independent power in the church, as he could not, without nauseous repetition, scatter into the body of his book: And it is detached, like a forlorn hope, to blunt the enemy's sword that intendeth to attack him. Now, I think, it will be easy to prove, that the opinion of *imperium in imperio*, in the sense he chargeth it upon the clergy of England, is what no one divine of any reputation, and very few at all, did ever maintain; and, that their universal sentiment in this matter is such as few Protestants did ever dispute. But, if the author of the "Regale," or two or three more obscure writers, have carried any points further than Scripture and reason will allow, (which is more than I know, or shall trouble myself to enquire) the clergy of England is no more answerable for those, than the laity is for all the folly and impertinence of this treatise. And, therefore, that people may not be amused, or think this man is somewhat, that he hath advanced or defended any oppressed truths, or overthrown any growing dangerous errors, I will set in as clear a light as I can, what I conceive to be held by the established clergy and all reasonable Protestants in this matter.

Everybody knows and allows, that in all government there is an absolute, unlimited, legislative power, which is originally in the body of the people, although, by custom, conquest, usurpation, or other accidents, sometimes fallen into the hands of one or a few. This in England is placed in the three estates (otherwise called the two Houses of Parliament) in conjunction with the King. And whatever they please to enact or to repeal in the settled forms, whether it be ecclesiastical or civil, immediately becometh law or nullity. Their decrees may be against equity, truth, reason and religion, but they are not against law; because law is the will of the supreme legislature, and that is, themselves. And there is no manner of doubt, but the same authority, whenever it pleaseth, may abolish Christianity, and set up the Jewish, Mahometan, or heathen religion. In short, they may do anything within the compass of human power. And, therefore, who will dispute that the same law, which deprived the church not only of lands, misapplied to superstitious uses, but even the tithes and glebes, (the ancient and necessary support of parish priests) may take away all the rest, whenever the lawgivers please, and make the priesthood as primitive, as this writer, or others of his stamp, can desire.

But as the supreme power can certainly do ten thousand things more than it ought, so there are several things which some people may think it can do, although it really cannot. For, it unfortunately happens, that edicts which cannot be executed, will not alter the nature of things. So, if a king and parliament should please to enact, that a woman who hath been a month married, is *virgo intacta*, would that actually restore her to her primitive state? If the supreme power should resolve a corporal of dragoons to be a doctor of divinity, law or physic, few, I believe, would trust their souls, fortunes, or bodies to his direction; because that power is neither fit to judge or teach those qualifications which are absolutely necessary to the several professions. Put the case that walking on the slack rope were the only talent required by act of parliament for making a man a bishop; no doubt, when a man had done his feat of activity in form, he might sit in the House of Lords, put on his robes and his rochet, go down to his palace, receive and spend his rents; but it requireth very little Christianity to believe this tumbler to be one whit more a bishop than he was before; because the law of God hath otherwise decreed;

which law, although a nation may refuse to receive it, cannot alter in its own nature.

And here lies the mistake of this superficial man, who is not able to distinguish between what the civil power can hinder, and what it can do. "If the parliament can annul ecclesiastical laws, they must be able to make them, since no greater power is required for one than the other." See pref., p. viii. This consequence he repeateth above twenty times, and always in the wrong. He affecteth to form a few words into the shape and size of a maxim, then trieth it by his ear, and, according as he likes the sound or cadence, pronounceth it true. Cannot I stand over a man with a great pole, and hinder him from making a watch, although I am not able to make one myself. If I have strength enough to knock a man on the head, doth it follow I can raise him to life again? The parliament may condemn all the Greek and Roman authors; can it therefore create new ones in their stead? They may make laws, indeed, and call them canon and ecclesiastical laws, and oblige all men to observe them under pain of high treason. And so may I, who love as well as any man to have in my own family the power in the last resort, take a turnip, then tie a string to it, and call it a watch, and turn away all my servants, if they refuse to call it so too.

For my own part, I must confess that this opinion of the independent power of the Church, or *imperium in imperio*, wherewith this writer raiseth such a dust, is what I never imagined to be of any consequence, never once heard disputed among divines, nor remember to have read, otherwise than as a scheme in one or two authors of middle rank, but with very little weight laid on it. And I dare believe, there is hardly one divine in ten that ever once thought of this matter. Yet to see a large swelling volume written only to encounter this doctrine, what could one think less than that the whole body of the clergy were perpetually tiring the press and the pulpit with nothing else?

I remember some years ago, a virtuoso writ a small tract about worms, proved them to be in more places than was generally observed, and made some discoveries by glasses. This having met with some reception, presently the poor man's head was full of nothing but worms; all we eat and drink, all the whole consistence of human bodies, and those of every other animal, the very air we breathe, in short, all nature throughout was nothing but worms: And, by that system, he solved all difficulties, and from thence all causes in philosophy. Thus it hath fared with our author, and his independent power. The attack against occasional conformity, the scarcity of coffee, the invasion of Scotland, the loss of kerseys and narrow cloths, the death of King William, the author's turning Papist for preferment, the loss of the battle of Almanza, with ten thousand other misfortunes, are all owing to this *imperium in imperio.*

It will be therefore necessary to set this matter in a clear light, by enquiring whether the clergy have any power independent of the civil, and of what nature it is.

Whenever the Christian religion was embraced by the civil power in any nation, there is no doubt but the magistrates and senates were fully instructed in the rudiments of it. Besides, the Christians were so numerous, and their worship so open before the conversion of princes, that their discipline, as well as doctrine, could not be a secret: They saw plainly a subordination of ecclesiastics, bishops, priests, and deacons: That these had certain powers and employments different from the laity: That the bishops were consecrated, and set apart for that office by those of their own order: That the presbyters and deacons were differently set apart, always by the bishops: That none but the ecclesiastics presumed to pray or preach in places set apart for God's worship, or to administer the Lord's Supper: That all questions relating either to discipline or doctrine, were determined in ecclesiastical conventions. These and the like doctrines and practices, being most of them directly proved, and the rest by very fair consequences deduced from the words of our Saviour and His apostles, were certainly received as a divine law by every prince or state which admitted the Christian religion: and, consequently, what they could not justly alter afterwards, any more than the common laws of nature. And, therefore, although the supreme power can hinder the clergy or Church from making any new canons, or executing the old; from consecrating bishops, or refuse those that they do consecrate; or, in short, from performing any ecclesiastical office, as they may from eating, drinking, and sleeping; yet they cannot themselves perform those offices, which are assigned to the clergy by our Saviour and His apostles; or, if they do, it is not according to the divine institution, and, consequently, null and void. Our Saviour telleth us, "His kingdom is not of this world;" and therefore, to be sure, the world is not of His kingdom, nor can ever please Him by interfering in the administration of it, since He hath appointed ministers of His own, and hath empowered and instructed them for that purpose: So that, I believe, the clergy, who, as he sayeth, are good at distinguishing, would think it reasonable to distinguish between their power, and the liberty of exercising this power. The former they claim immediately from Christ, and the latter from the permission, connivance, or authority of the civil government; with which the clergy's power, according to the solution I have given, cannot possibly interfere.

But this writer, setting up to form a system upon stale, scanty topics, and a narrow circle of thought, falleth into a thousand absurdities. And for a further help, he hath a talent of rattling out phrases, which seem to have sense, but have none at all: the usual fate of those who are ignorant of the force and compass of words, without which it is impossible for a man to write either pertinently or intelligibly upon the most obvious subjects.

So, in the beginning of his preface, page iv, he says, "The Church of England being established by acts of parliament, is a perfect creature of the civil power; I mean the polity and discipline of it, and it is that which maketh all the contention; for as to the doctrines expressed in the articles, I do not find high church to be in any manner of pain; but they who lay claim to most orthodoxy can distinguish themselves out of them." It is observable in this author, that his style is naturally harsh and ungrateful to the ear, and his expressions mean and trivial; but whenever he goeth about to polish a period, you may be certain of some gross defect in propriety or meaning: So the lines just quoted seem to run easily over the tongue: and, upon examination, they are perfect nonsense and blunder: To speak in his own borrowed phrase, what is contained in the idea of established? Surely, not existence. Doth establishment give being to a thing? He might have said the same thing of Christianity in general, or the existence of God, since both are confirmed by acts of parliament. But, the best is behind: for, in the next line, having named the church half a dozen times before, he now says, he meaneth only "the polity and discipline of it": As if, having spoke in praise of the art of physic, a man should explain himself, that he meant only the institution of a college of physicians into a president and fellows. And it will appear, that this author, however versed in the practice, hath grossly transgressed the rules of nonsense, (whose property it is neither to affirm nor deny) since every visible assertion gathered from those few lines is absolutely false: For where was the necessity of excepting the doctrines expressed in the articles, since these are equally creatures of the civil power, having been established by acts of parliament as well as the others. But the Church of England is no creature of the civil power, either as to its polity or doctrines. The fundamentals of both were deduced from Christ and His apostles, and the instructions of the purest and earliest ages, and were received as such by those princes or states who embraced Christianity, whatever prudential additions have been made to the former by human laws, which alone can be justly altered or annulled by them.

What I have already said, would, I think, be a sufficient answer to his whole preface, and indeed to the greatest part of his book, which is wholly turned upon battering down a sort of independent power in the clergy; which few or none of them ever claimed or defended. But there being certain peculiarities in this preface, that very much set off the wit, the learning, the raillery, reasoning and sincerity of the author; I shall take notice of some of them, as I pass.

But here, I hope, it will not be expected, that I should bestow remarks upon every passage in this book, that is liable to exception for ignorance, falsehood, dulness, or malice. Where he is so insipid, that nothing can be struck out for the reader's entertainment, I shall observe Horace's rule:

  "Quæ desperes tractata nitescere posse, relinquas."

Upon which account I shall say nothing of that great instance of his candour and judgment in relation to Dr. Stillingfleet,[1] who (happening to lie under his displeasure upon the fatal test of *imperium in imperio*) is High Church and Jacobite, took the oaths of allegiance to save him from the gallows,[2] and subscribed the articles only to keep his preferment: Whereas the character of that prelate is universally known to have been directly the reverse of what this writer gives him.

But before he can attempt to ruin this damnable opinion of two independent powers, he telleth us; page vi., "It will be necessary to shew what is contained in the idea of government." Now, it is to be understood, that this refined way of speaking was introduced by Mr. Locke; after whom the author limpeth as fast as he is able. All the former philosophers in the world, from the age of Socrates to ours, would have ignorantly put the question, *Quid est imperium?* But now it seemeth we must vary our phrase; and, since our modern improvement of human understanding, instead of desiring a philosopher to describe or define a mouse-trap, or tell me what it is; I must gravely ask, what is contained in the idea of a mouse-trap? But then to observe how deeply this new way of putting questions to a man's self, maketh him enter into the nature of things; his present business is to show us, what is contained in the idea of government. The company knoweth nothing of the matter, and would gladly be instructed; which he doth in the following words, p. 5.

"It would be in vain for one intelligent being to pretend to set rules to the actions of another, if he had it not in his

---

[1] Edward Stillingfleet (1635-1699), educated at Cambridge, wrote in 1659 his "Irenicum, or Weapon Salve for the Church's Wounds." He also published a "Rational Account of the Protestant Religion" in 1664. He occupied successively the important clerical offices of Prebendary of St. Paul's, Archdeaconry of London, Deanery of St. Paul's, and Bishopric of Worcester. The later years of his life were occupied in a controversy with Locke on that writer's "Essay on the Human Understanding." [T. S.]

[2] Page v, he quotes Bishop Stillingfleet's "Vindication of the Doctrine of the Trinity," where the bishop says, that a man might be very right in the belief of an article, though mistaken in the explication of it. Upon which Tindal observes: "These men treat the articles, as they do the oath of allegiance, which, they say, obliges them not actually to assist the government, but to do nothing against it; that is, nothing that would bring 'em to the gallows." [Note in edition 1764, 4to.]

power to reward the compliance with, or punish the deviations from, his rules by some good, or evil, which is not the natural consequence of those actions; since the forbidding men to do or forbear an action on the account of that convenience or inconvenience which attendeth it, whether he who forbids it will or no, can be no more than advice."

I shall not often draw such long quotations as this, which I could not forbear to offer as a specimen of the propriety and perspicuity of this author's style. And, indeed, what a light breaketh out upon us all, as soon as we have read these words! How thoroughly are we instructed in the whole nature of government? What mighty truths are here discovered; and how clearly conveyed to our understandings? And therefore let us melt this refined jargon into the old style for the improvement of such, who are not enough conversant in the new.

If the author were one who used to talk like one of us, he would have spoke in this manner: "I think it necessary to give a full and perfect definition of government, such as will shew the nature and all the properties of it; and my definition is thus: One man will never cure another of stealing horses, merely by minding him of the pains he hath taken, the cold he hath got, and the shoe-leather he hath lost in stealing that horse; nay, to warn him, that the horse may kick or fling him, or cost him more than he is worth in hay and oats, can be no more than advice. For the gallows is not the natural effect of robbing on the highway, as heat is of fire: and therefore, if you will govern a man, you must find out some other way of punishment, than what he will inflict upon himself."

Or, if this will not do, let us try it in another case (which I instanced before) and in his own terms. Suppose he had thought it necessary (and I think it was as much so as the other) to shew us what is contained in the idea of a mouse-trap, he must have proceeded in these terms. "It would be in vain for an intelligent being, to set rules for hindering a mouse from eating his cheese, unless he can inflict upon that mouse some punishment, which is not the natural consequence of eating the cheese. For, to tell her, it may lie heavy on her stomach; that she will grow too big to get back into her hole, and the like, can be no more than advice:

therefore, we must find out some way of punishing her, which hath more inconveniences than she will ever suffer by the mere eating of cheese." After this, who is so slow of understanding, as not to have in his mind a full and complete idea of a mouse-trap? Well.—The Free thinkers may talk what they please of pedantry, and cant, and jargon of schoolmen, and insignificant terms in the writings of the clergy, if ever the most perplexed and perplexing follower of Aristotle from Scotus to Suarez[1] could be a match for this author.

But the strength of his arguments is equal to the clearness of his definitions. For, having most ignorantly divided government into three parts, whereof the first contains the other two; he attempteth to prove that the clergy possess none of these by a divine right. And he argueth thus, p. vii. "As to a legislative power, if that belongs to the clergy by a divine right, it must be when they are assembled in convocation: but the 25 Hen. VIII. c. 19 is a bar to any such divine right, because that act makes it no less than a *præmunire* for them, so much so as to meet without the king's writ, &c." So that the force of his argument lieth here; if the clergy had a divine right, it is taken away by the 25th of Henry the Eighth. And as ridiculous as this argument is, the preface and book are founded upon it.

Another argument against the legislative power in the clergy of England, is, p. viii. that Tacitus telleth us; that in great affairs, the Germans consulted the whole body of the people. "*De minoribus rebus principes consultant, de majoribus omnes: Ita tamen, ut ea quoque, quorum penes plebem arbitrium est, apud principes pertractentur.*"—*Tacitus de Moribus et Populis Germaniæ.* Upon which Tindal observeth thus: "*De majoribus omnes*, was a fundamental amongst

---

[1] Duns Scotus flourished in the thirteenth century. He studied at Oxford and Paris, and his learning and acumen in reasoning earned for him the title *The Subtle Doctor.* He died at Cologne in 1308. He was a strong upholder of the doctrine of the Immaculate Conception. His works are published in twelve volumes folio.

Francis Suarez (1548-1617) was a Spanish Jesuit who wrote a work by command of the Pope against the English Reformation. He published some very able religio-philosophical treatises, from the Roman Catholic point of view; but, indeed, his writings altogether were enormous, so far as their number are concerned. [T. S.]

our ancestors long before they arrived in Great Britain, and matters of religion were ever reckoned among their *majora.*" (See Pref. p. viii. and ix.) Now it is plain, that our ancestors, the Saxons, came from Germany: It is likewise plain, that religion was always reckoned by the heathens among their *majora:* And it is plain, the whole body of the people could not be the clergy, and therefore, the clergy of England have no legislative power.

*Thirdly,* p. ix. They have no legislative power, because Mr. Washington, in his "Observations on the Ecclesiastical Jurisdiction of the Kings of England," sheweth, from "undeniable authorities, that in the time of William the Conqueror, and several of his successors, there were no laws enacted concerning religion, but by the great council of the kingdom." I hope, likewise, Mr. Washington observeth that this great council of the kingdom, as appeareth by undeniable authorities, was sometimes entirely composed of bishops and clergy, and called the parliament, and often consulted upon affairs of state, as well as church, as it is agreed by twenty writers of three ages; and if Mr. Washington says otherwise, he is an author just fit to be quoted by beaux.

*Fourthly,*—But it is endless to pursue this matter any further; in that, it is plain, the clergy have no divine right to make laws; because Henry VIII, Edward VI, and Queen Elizabeth, with their parliaments will not allow it them. Now, without examining what divine right the clergy have, or how far it extendeth; is it any sort of proof that I have no right, because a stronger power will not let me exercise it? Or doth all, that this author says through his preface, or book itself, offer any other sort of argument but this, or what he deduces the same way?

But his arguments and definitions are yet more supportable than the grossness of historical remarks, which are scattered so plentifully in his book, that it would be tedious to enumerate, or to shew the fraud and ignorance of them. I beg the reader's leave to take notice of one here just in my way; and, the rather, because I design for the future to let hundreds of them pass without further notice. "When," says he, p. x. "by the abolishing of the Pope's power, things were brought back to their ancient channel, the parliament's right in making ecclesiastical laws revived of course." What can possibly be meant by this "ancient channel?" Why, the channel that things ran in before the Pope had any power in England: that is to say, before Austin the monk converted England, before which time, it seems, the parliament had a right to make ecclesiastical laws. And what parliament could this be? Why, the Lords Spiritual and Temporal, and the Commons met at Westminster.

I cannot here forbear reproving the folly and pedantry of some lawyers, whose opinions this poor creature blindly followeth, and rendereth yet more absurd by his comments. The knowledge of our constitution can be only attained by consulting the earliest English histories, of which those gentlemen seem utterly ignorant, further than a quotation or an index. They would fain derive our government as now constituted, from antiquity: And, because they have seen Tacitus quoted for his *majoribus omnes;* and have read of the Goths' military institution in their progresses and conquests, they presently dream of a parliament. Had their reading reached so far, they might have deduced it much more fairly from Aristotle and Polybius, who both distinctly name the composition of *rex, seniores, et populus;* and the latter, as I remember particularly, with the highest approbation. The princes, in the Saxon Heptarchy, did indeed call their nobles sometimes together upon weighty affairs, as most other princes of the world have done in all ages. But they made war and peace, and raised money by their own authority: They gave or mended laws by their charters, and they raised armies by their tenures. Besides, some of those kingdoms fell in by conquests, before England was reduced under one head, and therefore could pretend no rights, but by the concessions of the conqueror.

Further, which is more material, upon the admission of Christianity, great quantities of land were acquired by the clergy, so that the great council of the nation was often entirely of churchmen, and ever a considerable part. But, our present constitution is an artificial thing, not fairly to be traced, in my opinion, beyond Henry I. Since which time it hath in every age admitted several alterations; and differeth now as much, even from what it was then, as almost any two species of government described by Aristotle.

And, it would be much more reasonable to affirm, that the government of Rome continued the same under Justinian, as it was in the time of Scipio, because the senate and consuls still remained, although the power of both had been several hundred years transferred to the emperors.

## REMARKS ON THE PREFACE.[1]

Page iv, v. "If men of opposite sentiments can subscribe the same articles, they are as much at liberty as if there were none." May not a man subscribe the whole articles, because he differs from another in the explication of one? How many oaths are prescribed, that men may differ in the explication of some part of them? Instance, &c.

Page vi. "Idea of Government." A canting pedantic way, learned from Locke; and how prettily he sheweth it. Instance—

Page vii, "25 Hen. VIII. c. 19 is a bar to any such divine right [of a legislative power in the clergy.]" Absurd to argue against the clergy's divine right, because of the statute of Henry VIII. How doth that destroy divine right? The sottish way of arguing; from what the parliament can do; from their power, &c.

Page viii. "If the parliament did not think they had a plenitude of power in this matter, they would not have damned all the canons of 1640." What doth he mean? A grave divine could not answer all his playhouse and Alsatia[2] cant, &c. He hath read Hudibras, and many plays.

*Ibid.* "If the parliament can annul ecclesiastical laws, they must be able to make them." Distinguish, and shew the silliness, &c.

*Ibid.* All that he saith against the discipline, he might say the same against the doctrine, nay, against the belief of

---

[1] References to Tindal's book, and remarks upon it, which the author left thus indigested, being hints for himself to use in answering the said book.

[2] Or Whitefriars, then a place of asylum, and frequented by sharpers, of whose gibberish there are several specimens in Shadwell's comedy, "The Squire of Alsatia." [S.]

## "THE RIGHTS OF THE CHRISTIAN CHURCH" 101

a God, *viz.* That the legislature might forbid it. The Church formeth and contriveth canons; and the civil power, which is compulsive, confirms them.

Page ix. "There were no laws enacted but by the great council of the kingdom." And that was very often, chiefly, only bishops.

*Ibid.* "Laws settled by parliament to punish the clergy." What laws were those?

Page x. "The people are bound to no laws but of their own choosing." It is fraudulent; for they may consent to what others choose, and so people often do.

Page xiv. paragraph 6. "The clergy are not supposed to have any divine legislature, because that must be superior to all worldly power; and then the clergy might as well forbid the parliament to meet but when and where they please, &c." No such consequence at all. They have a power exclusive from all others. Ordained to act as clergy, but not govern in civil affairs; nor act without leave of the civil power.

Page xxv. "The parliament suspected the love of power natural to churchmen." Truly, so is the love of pudding, and most other things desirable in this life; and in that they are like the laity, as in all other things that are not good. And, therefore, they are held not in esteem for what they are like in, but for their virtues. The true way to abuse them with effect, is to tell us some faults of theirs, that other men have not, or not so much of as they, &c. Might not any man speak full as bad of senates, diets, and parliaments, as he can do about councils; and as bad of princes, as he does of bishops?

Page xxxi. "They might as well have made Cardinals Campegi and de Chinuchii, Bishops of Salisbury and Worcester, as have enacted that their several sees and bishoprics were utterly void." No. The legislature might determine who should not be a bishop there, but not make a bishop.

*Ibid.* "Were not a great number deprived by parliament upon the Restoration?" Does he mean presbyters? What signifies that?

*Ibid.* "Have they not trusted this power with our princes?" Why, aye. But that argueth not right, but power. Have they not cut off a king's head, &c. The Church must do the best they can, if not what they would.

Page xxxvi. "If tithes and first-fruits are paid to spiritual persons as such, the king or queen is the most spiritual person, &c." As if the first-fruits, &c. were paid to the king, as tithes to a spiritual person.

Page xliii. "King Charles II. thought fit that the bishops in Scotland should hold their bishoprics during will and pleasure; I do not find that the High Church complained of this as an encroachment, &c." No; but as a pernicious counsel of Lord Loch.[1]

Page xliv. "The common law judges have a power to determine, whether a man has a legal right to the sacrament." They pretend it, but what we complain of as most abominable hardship, &c.

Page xlv. "Giving men thus blindly to the devil, is an extraordinary piece of complaisance to a lay chancellor." He is something in the right; and therefore it is a pity there are any; and I hope the Church will provide against it. But if the sentence be just, it is not the person, but the contempt. And, if the author attacketh a man on the highway, and taketh but twopence, he shall be sent to the gallows, more terrible to him than the devil, for his contempt of the law, &c. Therefore he need not complain of being sent to hell.

Page xliv. Mr. Leslie may carry things too far, as it is natural, because the other extreme is so great. But what he says of the king's losses, since the Church lands were given away, is too great a truth, &c.

Page lxxvi. "To which I have nothing to plead, except the zeal I have for the Church of England." You will see some pages further, what he meaneth by the Church; but it is not fair not to begin with telling us what is contained in the idea of a Church, &c.

Page lxxxiii. "They will not be angry with me for thinking better of the Church than they do, &c." No, but they will differ from you; because the worse the Queen is pleased, you think her better. I believe the Church will not concern themselves much about your opinion of them, &c.

Page lxxxiv. "But the Popish, Eastern, Presbyterian and Jacobite clergy, &c." This is like a general pardon,

---

[1] Scott thinks this refers to Lord Lauderdale. [T. S.]

with such exceptions as make it useless, if we compute it, &c.

Page lxxxvii. "Misapplying of the word church, &c." This is cavilling. No doubt his project is for exempting the people: But that is not what in common speech we usually mean by the Church. Besides, who doth not know that distinction?

*Ibid.* "Constantly apply the same ideas to them." This is, in old English, meaning the same thing.

Page lxxxix. "Demonstrates I could have no design but the promoting of truth, &c." Yes, several designs, as money, spleen, atheism, &c. What? will any man think truth was his design, and not money and malice? Doth he expect the House will go into a committee for a bill to bring things to his scheme, to confound everything, &c.

Some deny Tindal to be the author, and produce stories of his dulness and stupidity. But what is there in all this book, that the dullest man in England might not write, if he were angry and bold enough, and had no regard to truth?


## REMARKS UPON THE BOOK, &c.

Page 4. "Whether Lewis XIV. has such a power over Philip V?" He speaketh here of the unlimited, uncontrollable authority of fathers. A very foolish question; and his discourse hitherto, of government, weak and trivial, and liable to objections.

*Ibid.* "Whom he is to consider not as his own, but the Almighty's workmanship." A very likely consideration for the ideas of the state of nature. A very wrong deduction of paternal government; but that is nothing to the dispute, &c.

Page 12. "And as such might justly be punished by every one in the state of nature." False; he doth not seem to understand the state of nature, although he hath borrowed it from Hobbes, &c.

Page 14. "Merely speculative points, and other indifferent things, &c." And why are speculative opinions so insignificant? Do not men proceed in their practice according to their speculations? So, if the author were a chancellor, and one of his speculations were, that the poorer the clergy the better; would not that be of great use, if a cause came before him of tithes or Church lands?

*Ibid.* "Which can only be known by examining whether men had any power in the state of nature over their own, or others' actions in these matters." No, that is a wrong method, unless where religion hath not been revealed; in natural religion.

*Ibid.* "Nothing at first sight can be more obvious, than that in all religious matters, none could make over the right of judging for himself, since that would cause his religion to be absolutely at the disposal of another." At his rate of arguing (I think I do not misrepresent him, and I believe he will not deny the consequence) a man may profess Heathenism, Mahometism, &c. and gain as many proselytes as he can; and they may have their assemblies, and the magistrate ought to protect them, provided they do not disturb the state: And they may enjoy all secular preferments, be lords chancellors, judges, &c. But there are some opinions in several religions, which, although they do not directly make men rebel, yet lead to it. Instance some. Nay we might have temples for idols, &c. A thousand such absurdities follow from his general notions, and ill-digested schemes. And we see in the Old Testament, that kings were reckoned good or ill, as they suffered or hindered image-worship and idolatry, &c. which was limiting conscience.

Page 15. "Men may form what clubs, companies, or meetings they think fit, &c. which the magistrate, as long as the public sustains no damage, cannot hinder, &c." This is false; although the public sustain no damage, they will forbid clubs, where they think danger may happen.

Page 16. "The magistrate is as much obliged to protect them in the way they choose of worshipping Him, as in any other indifferent matter."—Page 17. "The magistrate to treat all his subjects alike, how much soever they differ from him or one another in these matters." This shews, that although they be Turks, Jews, or Heathens, it is so. But we are sure Christianity is the only true religion, &c. and therefore it should be the magistrate's chief care to propagate it; and that God should be worshipped in that form, that those who are the teachers think most proper, &c.

Page 18. "So that persecution is the most comprehensive of all crimes, &c." But he hath not told us what is concluded in the idea of persecution. State it right.

*Ibid.* "But here it may be demanded, If a man's conscience make him do such acts, &c." This doth not answer the above objection: For, if the public be not disturbed with atheistical principles preached, nor immoralities, all is well. So that still, men may be Jews, Turks, &c.

Page 22. 'The same reason which obliges them to make statutes of mortmain, and other laws, against the people's giving estates to the clergy, will equally hold for their taking them away when given." A great security for property! Will this hold to any other society in the state, as merchants, &c. or only to ecclesiastics? A pretty project: Forming general schemes requires a deeper head than this man's.

*Ibid.* "But the good of the society being the only reason of the magistrate's having any power over men's properties, I cannot see why he should deprive his subjects of any part thereof, for the maintenance of such opinions as have no tendency that way, &c." Here is a paragraph (*vide* also *infra*) which has a great deal in it. The meaning is, that no man ought to pay tithes, who doth not believe what the minister preacheth. But how came they by this property? When they purchased the land, they paid only for so much; and the tithes were exempted. It is an older title than any man's estate is, and if it were taken away to-morrow, it could not without a new law belong to the owners of the other nine parts, any more than impropriations do.

*Ibid.* "For the maintenance of such opinions, as no ways contribute to the public good." By such opinions as the public receive no advantage by, he must mean Christianity.

Page 23. "Who by reason of such articles are divided into different sects." A pretty cause of sects! &c.

Page 24. "So the same reason as often as it occurs, will oblige him to leave that Church." This is an excuse for his turning Papist.

*Ibid.* "Unless you suppose churches like traps, easy to admit one; but when once he is in, there he must always stick, either for the pleasure or profit of the trap-setters." Remark his wit.

Page 29. "Nothing can be more absurd than maintaining there must be two independent powers in the same society." This is abominably absurd; shew it.

Page 33. "The whole hierarchy as built on it, must necessarily fall to the ground, and great will be the fall of this spiritual Babylon." I will do him justice, and take notice, when he is witty, &c.

Page 36. "For if there may be two such [independent powers] in every society on earth, why may there not be more than one in heaven?" A delicate consequence.

Page 37. "Without having the less, he could not have the greater, in which that is contained." Sophistical; instance wherein.

Page 42. "Some since, subtler than the Jews, have managed commutations more to their own advantage, by enriching themselves, and beggaring, if Fame be not a liar, many an honest dissenter." It is fair to produce witnesses, is she a liar or not? The report is almost impossible. Commutations were contrived for roguish registers and proctors, and lay chancellors, but not for the clergy.

Page 43. "Kings and people, who (as the Indians do the Devil) adored the Pope out of fear." I am in doubt, whether I shall allow that for wit or no, &c. Look you, in these cases, preface it thus: If one may use an old saying.

Page 44. "One reason why the clergy make what they call schism, to be so heinous a sin." There it is now; because he hath changed churches, he ridiculeth schism; as Milton wrote for divorces, because he had an ill wife. For ten pages on, we must give the true answer, that makes all these arguments of no use.

Page 60. "It possibly will be said, I have all this while been doing these gentlemen a great deal of wrong." To do him justice, he sets forth the objections of his adversaries with great strength, and much to their advantage. No doubt those are the very objections we would offer.

Page 68. "Their executioner." He is fond of this word in many places, yet there is nothing in it further than it is the name for the hangman, &c.

Page 69. "Since they exclude both from having anything in the ordering of Church matters." Another part of his scheme: For by this the people ought to execute ecclesiastical offices without distinction, for he brings the other opinion as an absurd one.

Page 72. "They claim a judicial power, and, by virtue of it the government of the Church, and thereby (pardon the expression) become traitors both to God and man." Who doth he desire to pardon him? or is this meant of the English clergy? So it seemeth. Doth he desire them to pardon him? They do it as Christians. Doth he desire the government to do it? But then how can they make examples? He says, the clergy do so, &c. so he means all.

Page 74. "I would gladly know what they mean by giving the Holy Ghost." Explain what is really meant by giving the Holy Ghost, like a king empowering an ambassador.[1]

Page 76. "The Popish clergy make very bold with the Three Persons of the Trinity." Why then, don't mix them, but we see whom this glanceth on most. As to the *Congé d'élire*, and *Nolo episcopari*, not so absurd; and, if omitted, why changed.

Page 78. "But not to digress"—Pray, doth he call scurrility upon the clergy, a digression? The apology needless, &c.

*Ibid.* "A clergyman, it is said, is God's ambassador." But you know an ambassador may have a secretary, &c.

*Ibid.* "Call their pulpit speeches, the word of God." That is a mistake.

Page 79. "Such persons to represent Him." Are not they that own His power, fitter to represent Him than others? Would the author be a fitter person?

*Ibid.* "Puffed up with intolerable pride and insolence." Not at all; for where is the pride to be employed by a prince, whom so few own, and whose being is disputed by such as this author?

*Ibid.* "Perhaps from a poor servitor, &c. to be a prime minister in God's kingdom." That is right. God taketh

---

[1] See Hooker's "Eccl. Pol.," book v. § 77.

notice of the difference between poor servitors, &c. Extremely foolish—shew it. The argument lieth strongly against the apostles, poor fishermen; and St. Paul, a tent-maker. So gross and idle!

Page 80. "The formality of laying hand over head on a man." A pun; but an old one. I remember, when Swan[1] made that pun first, he was severely checked for it.

*Ibid.* "What more is required to give one a right, &c." Here shew, what power is in the church, and what in the state to make priests.

Page 85. "To bring men into, and not turn them out of the ordinary way of salvation." Yes; but as one rotten sheep doth mischief—and do you think it reasonable, that such a one as this author, should converse with Christians, and weak ones.

Page 86. See his fine account of spiritual punishment.

Page 87. "The clergy affirm, that if they had not the power to exclude men from the Church, its unity could not be preserved." So to expel an ill member from a college, would be to divide the college; as in All-Souls, &c. Apply it to him.[2]

Page 88. "I cannot see but it is contrary to the rules of charity, to exclude men from the Church, &c." All this turns upon the falsest reasoning in the world. So, if a man be imprisoned for stealing a horse, he is hindered from other duties: And, you might argue, that a man who doth ill, ought to be more diligent in minding other duties, and not to be debarred from them. It is for contumacy and rebellion against that power in the church, which the law hath confirmed. So a man is outlawed for a trifle, upon contumacy.

Page 92. "Obliging all by penal laws to receive the sacrament." This is false.

Page 93. "The want of which means can only harden a man in his impenitence." It is for his being hardened that he is excluded. Suppose a son robbeth his father on the highway, and his father will not see him till he restoreth the

---

[1] Captain Swan was a celebrated low humorist and punster who frequented Will's Coffee-house when it was the fashionable resort of men of wit and pleasure. [S.]

[2] Tindal was a fellow of All Souls College. [T. S.]

money and owneth his fault. It is hard to deny him paying his duty in other things, &c. How absurd this!

Page 95. "And that only *they* had a right to give it." Another part of his scheme, that the people have a right to give the sacrament. See more of it, pp. 135 and 137.

Page 96. "Made familiar to such practices by the heathen priests." Well; and this shews the necessity of it for peace' sake. A silly objection of this and other enemies to religion, to think to disgrace it by applying heathenism, which only concerns the political part wherein they were as wise as others, and might give rules. Instance in some, &c.

Page 98. "How differently from this do the great pretenders to primitive practice act, &c." This is a remarkable passage. Doth he condemn or allow this mysterious way? It seems the first—and therefore these words are a little turned, but infallibly stood in the first draught as a great argument for Popery.

Page 100. "They dress them up in a *sanbenito*." So, now we are to answer for the inquisition. One thing is, that he makes the fathers guilty of asserting most of the corruptions about the power of priests.

Page 104. "Some priests assume to themselves an arbitrary power of excluding men from the Lord's Supper." His scheme; that any body may administer the sacraments, women or children, &c.

Page 108. "One no more than another can be reckoned a priest." See his scheme. Here he disgraces what the law enacts, about the manner of consecrating, &c.

Page 118. "Churches serve to worse purposes than beargardens." This from Hudibras.

Page 119. "In the time of that wise heathen Ammianus Marcellinus."[1] Here he runs down all Christianity in general.

Page 120. "I shall, in the following part of my discourse, shew that this doctrine is so far from serving the ends of religion, that, 1. It prevents the spreading of the gospel, &c." This independent power in the church is like the worms; being the cause of all diseases.

---

[1] Ammianus Marcellinus (died *c*. 390) wrote a history of Rome in thirty-one books, of which Gibbon thought rather highly. The history may be taken as a continuation of Tacitus and Suetonius. [T. S.]

Page 124. "How easily could the Roman emperors have destroyed the Church?" Just as if he had said; how easily could Herod kill Christ whilst a child, &c.

Page 125. "The people were set against bishops by reason of their tyranny." Wrong. For the bishops were no tyrants: Their power was swallowed up by the Popes, and the people desired they should have more. It were the regulars that tyrannized and formed priestcraft. *He is ignorant.

Page 139. "He is not bound by the laws of Christ to leave his friends in order to be baptized, &c." This directly against the Gospel.—One would think him an emissary, by his preaching schism.

Page 142. "Then will the communion of saints be practicable, to which the principles of all parties, the occasional conformists only excepted, stand in direct opposition, &c." So that all are wrong but they. The Scripture is fully against schism. Tindal promoteth it and placeth in it all the present and future happiness of man.

Page 144. All he has hitherto said on this matter, with a very little turn, were arguments for Popery: For, it is certain, that religion had share in very few wars for many hundred years before the Reformation, because they were all of a mind. It is the ambition of rebels, preaching upon the discontents of sectaries, that they are not supreme, which hath caused wars for religion. He is mistaken altogether. His little narrow understanding and want of learning.

Page 145. "Though some say the high-fliers' lives might serve for a very good rule, if men would act quite contrary to them." Is he one of those some? Beside the new turn of wit, &c. all the clergy in England come under his notion of high-fliers, as he states it.

Page 147. "None of them (Churchmen) could be brought to acknowledge it lawful upon any account whatever, to exclude the Duke of York." This account false in fact.

*Ibid.* "And the body-politic, whether ecclesiastical or civil, must be dealt with after the same manner, as the body-natural." What, because it is called a body, and is a simile, must it hold in all circumstances?

Page 148. "We find all wise legislators have had regard to the tempers, inclinations, and prejudices, &c." This paragraph false.—It was directly contrary in several, as Lycurgus, &c.

Page 152. "All the skill of the prelatists is not able to discover the least distinction between bishop and presbyter." Yet, God knows, this hath been done many a time.

Page 158. "The Epistle to the Philippians is directed to the bishops and deacons, I mean in due order after the people, *viz.* to the saints with their bishops and deacons." I hope he would argue from another place, that the people precede the king, because of these words: "Ye shall be destroyed both you and your king."

Page 167. "The Pope and other great Church dons." I suppose, he meaneth bishops: But I wish, he would explain himself, and not be so very witty in the midst of an argument; it is like two mediums; not fair in disputing.

Page 168. "Clemens Romanus blames the people not for assuming a power, but for making a wrong use of it, &c." His great error all along is, that he doth not distinguish between a power, and a liberty of exercising that power, &c. I would appeal to any man, whether the clergy have not too little power, since a book like this, that unsettleth foundations and would destroy all, goes unpunished, &c.

Page 171. "By this or some such method the bishops obtained their power over their fellow presbyters, and both over the people. The whole tenor of the Gospel directly contrary to it." Then it is not an allowable means: This carries it so far as to spoil his own system; it is a sin to have bishops as we have them.

Page 172. "The preservation of peace and unity, and not any divine right, was the reason of establishing a superiority of one of the presbyters over the rest. Otherwise there would, as they say, have been as many schismatics as Presbyters. No great compliment to the clergy of those days." Why so? It is the natural effect of a worse independency, which he keepeth such a clatter about; an indepency of churches on each other, which must naturally create schism.

Page 183. "How could the Christians have asserted the disinterestedness of those who first preached the Gospel, particularly their having a right to the tenth part." Yes, that would have passed easy enough; for they could not imagine teachers could live on air; and their heathen priests were much more unreasonable.

Page 184. "Men's suffering for such opinions is not sufficient to support the weight of them." This is a glance against Christianity. State the case of converting infidels; the converters are supposed few; the bulk of the priests must be of the converted country. It is their own people therefore they maintain. What project or end can a few converters propose? they can leave no power to their families, &c. State this, I say, at length, and give it a true turn. Princes give corporations power to purchase lands.

Page 187. "That it became an easy prey to the barbarous nations." Ignorance in Tindal. The empire long declined before Christianity was introduced. This a wrong cause, if ever there was one.

Page 190. "It is the clergy's interest to have religion corrupted." Quite the contrary; prove it. How is it the interest of the English clergy to corrupt religion? The more justice and piety the people have, the better it is for them; for that would prevent the penury of farmers, and the oppression of exacting covetous landlords, &c. That which hath corrupted religion, is the liberty unlimited of professing all opinions. Do not lawyers render law intricate by their speculations, &c. And physicians, &c.

Page 209. "The spirit and temper of the clergy, &c." What does this man think the clergy are made of? Answer generally to what he says against councils in the ten pages before. Suppose I should bring quotations in their praise.

Page 211. "As the clergy, though few in comparison of the laity, were the inventors of corruptions." His scheme is, that the fewer and poorer the clergy the better, and the contrary among the laity. A noble principle; and delicate consequences from it.

Page 207. "Men are not always condemned for the sake of opinions, but opinions sometimes for the sake of men." And so, he hopes, that if his opinions are condemned, people will think, it is a spite against him, as having been always scandalous.

Page 210. "The meanest layman as good a judge as the greatest priest, for the meanest man is as much interested in the truth of religion as the greatest priest." As if one should say, the meanest sick man hath as much interest in health as a physician, therefore is as good a judge of physic as a physician, &c.

*Ibid.* "Had synods been composed of laymen, none of those corruptions which tend to advance the interest of the clergy, &c." True, but the part the laity had in reforming, was little more than plundering. He should understand, that the nature of things is this, that the clergy are made of men, and, without some encouragement, they will not have the best, but the worst.

Page 215. "They who gave estates to, rather than they who took them from, the clergy, were guilty of sacrilege." Then the people are the Church, and the clergy not; another part of his scheme.

Page 219. "The clergy, as they subsisted by the alms of the people, &c." This he would have still. Shew the folly of it. Not possible to shew any civilized nation ever did it. Who would be clergymen then? The absurdity appears by putting the case, that none were to be statesmen, lawyers, or physicians, but who were to subsist by alms.

Page 222. "These subtle clergymen work their designs, who lately cut out such a tacking job for them, &c." He is mistaken—Everybody was for the bill almost: though not for the tack. The Bishop of Sarum was for it, as appears by his speech against it. But it seems, the tacking is owing to metaphysical speculations. I wonder whether is most perplexed, this author in his style, or the writings of our divines. In the judgment of all people our divines have carried practical preaching and writing to the greatest perfection it ever arrived to; which shews, that we may affirm in general, our clergy is excellent, although this or that man be faulty. As if an army be constantly victorious, regular, &c. we may say, it is an excellent victorious army: But Tindal, to disparage it, would say, such a serjeant ran away; such an ensign hid himself in a ditch; nay, one colonel turned his back, therefore, it is a corrupt, cowardly army, &c.

Page 224. "They were as apprehensive of the works of Aristotle, as some men are of the works of a late philosopher, which, they are afraid, will let too much light into the world." Yet just such another; only a commentator on Aristotle. People are likely to improve their understanding much with Locke; It is not his "Human Understanding," but other works that people dislike, although in that there are some dangerous tenets, as that of [no] innate ideas.

Page 226. "Could they, like the popish priests, add to this a restraint on the press, their business would be done." So it ought: For example, to hinder his book, because it is written to justify the vices and infidelity of the age. There can be no other design in it. For, is this a way or manner to do good? Railing doth but provoke. The opinion of the whole parliament is, the clergy are too poor.

*Ibid.* "When some nations could be no longer kept from prying into learning, this miserable gibberish of the schools was contrived." We have exploded schoolmen as much as he, and in some people's opinion too much, since the liberty of embracing any opinion is allowed. They following Aristotle, who is doubtless the greatest master of arguing in the world: But it hath been a fashion of late years to explode Aristotle, and therefore this man hath fallen into it like others, for that reason, without understanding him. Aristotle's poetry, rhetoric, and politics, are admirable, and therefore, it is likely, so are his logics.

Page 230. "In these freer countries, as the clergy have less power, so religion is better understood, and more useful and excellent discourses are made on that subject, &c." Not generally. Holland not very famous, Spain hath been, and France is. But it requireth more knowledge, than his, to form general rules, which people strain (when ignorant) to false deductions to make them out.

Page 232. Chap. VII. "That this hypothesis of an independent power in any set of clergymen, makes all reformation unlawful, except where those who have this power, do consent." The title of this chapter, A Truism.

Page 234. "If God has not placed mankind in respect to civil matters under an absolute power, but has permitted them in every society to act as they judge best for their own safety, &c." Bad parallels; bad politics; want of due distinction between teaching and government. The people may know when they are governed well, but not be wiser than their instructors. Shew the difference.

*Ibid.* "If God has allowed the civil society these privileges can we suppose He hath less kindness for His church, &c." Here they are distinguished, then, here it makes for him. It is a sort of turn of expression, which is scarce with him, and he contradicts himself to follow it.

Page 235. "This cursed hypothesis had, perhaps, never been thought on with relation to civils, had not the clergy (who have an inexhaustible magazine of oppressive doctrines) contrived first in ecclesiasticals, &c." The seventh paragraph furious and false. Were there no tyrants before the clergy, &c.?

Page 236. "Therefore in order to serve them, though I expect little thanks, &c." And, why so? Will they not, as you say, follow their interest? I thought you said so. He has three or four sprightly turns of this kind, that look, as if he thought he had done wonders, and had put all the clergy in a ferment. Whereas, I do assure him, there are but two things wonderful in his book: First, how any man in a Christian country could have the boldness and wickedness to write it: And, how any government would neglect punishing the author of it, if not as an enemy of religion, yet a profligate trumpeter of sedition. These are hard words, got by reading his book.

*Ibid.* "The light of nature as well as the Gospel, obliges people to judge of themselves, &c. to avoid false prophets, seducers, &c." The legislature can turn out a priest, and appoint another ready-made, but not make one; as you discharge a physician, and may take a farrier; but he is no physician, unless made as he ought to be.

*Ibid.* "Since no more power is required for the one than the other." That is, I dislike my physician, and can turn him off, therefore I can make any man a physician, &c. "*Cujus est destruere*, &c." Jest on it: Therefore because he lays schemes for destroying the Church, we must employ him to raise it again. See, what danger lies in applying maxims at random. So, because it is the soldiers' business to knock men on the head, it is theirs likewise to raise them to life, &c.

Page 237. "It can belong only to the people to appoint their own ecclesiastical officers." This word "people" is so delicious in him, that I cannot tell what is included in the idea of the "people." Doth he mean the rabble or the legislature, &c. In this sense it may be true, that the legislature giveth leave to the bishops to appoint, and they appoint themselves; I mean, the executive power appoints, &c. He sheweth his ignorance in government. As to High Church he carrieth it a prodigious way, and includeth, in the idea of it, more than others will allow.

Page 239. "Though it be customary to admit none to the ministry who are not approved by the bishops or priests, &c." One of his principles to expose.

*Ibid.* "If every one has not an inherent right to choose his own guide, then a man must be either of the religion of his guide, or, &c." That would make delicate work in a nation: What would become of all our churches? They must dwindle into conventicles. Show what would be the consequence of this scheme in several points. This great reformer, if his projects were reduced to practice, how many thousand sects, and consequently tumults, &c. Men must be governed in speculation, at least not suffered to vent them, because opinions tend to actions, which are most governed by opinions, &c. If those who write for the church writ no better, they would succeed but scurvily. But to see whether he be a good writer, let us see when he hath published his second part.

Page 253. "An excellent author in his preface to the Account of Denmark." This man judgeth and writeth much of a level. Molesworth's preface full of stale profligate topics. That author wrote his book in spite to a nation, as this doth to religion, and both perhaps on poor personal piques.[1]

*Ibid.* "By which means, and not by any difference in speculative matters, they are more rich and populous." As if ever anybody thought that a difference in speculative opinions made men richer or poorer; for example, &c.

Page 258. "Play the Devil for God's sake." If this is meant for wit, I would be glad to observe it; but in such cases I first look whether there be common sense, &c.

Page 261. "Christendom has been the scene of perpetual

---

[1] This was Robert, Viscount Molesworth (1656-1725), who was born in Dublin, and educated at Trinity College there. He was ambassador at Copenhagen, but had to resign on account of a dispute with the Danish king. The "Account of Denmark," which he wrote on his return, was answered by Dr. King. [T. S.]

wars, massacres, &c." He doth not consider that most religious wars have been caused by schisms, when the dissenting parties were ready to join with any ambitious discontented man. The national religion always desireth peace, even in her notions, for its interests.

Page 270. "Some have taken the liberty to compare a high church priest in politics to a monkey in a glass-shop, where, as he can do no good, so he never fails of doing mischief enough." That is his modesty, it is his own simile, and it rather fits a man that does so and so, (meaning himself.) Besides the comparison is foolish: So it is with *men*, as with *stags*.

Page 276. "Their interest obliges them directly to promote tyranny." The matter is, that Christianity is the fault, which spoils the priests, for they were like other men, before they were priests. Among the Romans, priests did not do so; for they had the greatest power during the republic. I wonder he did not prove they spoiled Nero.

Page 277. "No princes have been more insupportable and done greater violence to the commonwealth than those the clergy have honoured for saints and martyrs." For example in our country, the princes most celebrated by our clergy are, &c. &c. &c. And the quarrels since the Conquest were nothing at all of the clergy, but purely of families, &c. wherein the clergy only joined like other men.

Page 279. "After the Reformation,[1] I desire to know whether the conduct of the clergy was anyways altered for the better, &c." Monstrous misrepresentation. Does this man's spirit of declaiming let him forget all truth of fact, as here, &c.? Shew it. Or doth he flatter himself, a time will come in future ages, that men will believe it on his word? In short, between declaiming, between misrepresenting, and falseness, and charging Popish things, and independency huddled together, his whole book is employed.

Set forth at large the necessity of union in religion, and the disadvantage of the contrary, and answer the contrary in Holland, where they have no religion, and are the worst constituted government in the world to last. It is ignorance of causes and appearances which makes shallow people judge

---

[1] "Reformation" in 4to and 8vo editions, but Tindal's word is "Restoration." [T. S.]

so much to their advantage. They are governed by the administration and almost legislature of Holland through advantage of property; nor are they fit to be set in balance with a noble kingdom, &c. like a man that gets a hundred pounds a year by hard labour, and one that has it in land.

Page 280. "It may be worth enquiring, whether the difference between the several sects in England, &c." A noble notion started, that union in the Church must enslave the kingdom: reflect on it. This man hath somewhere heard, that it is a point of wit to advance paradoxes, and the bolder the better. But the wit lies in maintaining them, which he neglecteth, and formeth imaginary conclusions from them, as if they were true and uncontested.

He adds, "That in the best constituted Church, the greatest good which can be expected of the ecclesiastics, is from their divisions." This is a maxim deduced from a gradation of false suppositions. If a man should turn the tables, and argue that all the debauchery, atheism, licentiousness, &c. of the times, were owing to the poverty of the clergy, &c. what would he say? There have been more wars of religion since the ruin of the clergy, than before, in England. All the civil wars before were from other causes.

Page 283. "Prayers are made in the loyal university of Oxford, to continue the throne free from the contagion of schism. See Mather's sermon on the 29th of May, 1705." Thus he ridicules the university while he is eating their bread. The whole university comes with the most loyal addresses, yet that goes for nothing. If one indiscreet man drops an indiscreet word, all must answer for it.

Page 286. "By allowing all, who hold no opinions prejudicial to the state, and contribute equally with their fellow-subjects to its support, equal privileges in it." But who denies that of the dissenters? The Calvinist scheme, one would not think, proper for monarchy. Therefore, they fall in with the Scotch, Geneva, and Holland; and when they had strength here, they pulled down the monarchy. But I will tell an opinion they hold prejudicial to the state in his opinion; and that is, that they are against toleration, of which, if I do not shew him ten times more instances from their greatest writers, than he can do of passive obedience among the clergy, I have done.

"Does not justice demand, that they who alike contribute to the burden, should alike receive the advantage?" Here is another of his maxims closely put without considering what exceptions may be made. The Papists have contributed doubly (being so taxed) therefore by this rule they ought to have double advantage. Protection in property, leave to trade and purchase, &c. are enough for a government to give. Employments in a state are a reward for those who entirely agree with it, &c. For example, a man, who upon all occasions declared his opinion of a commonwealth to be preferable to a monarchy, would not be a fit man to have employments; let him enjoy his opinion, but not be in a capacity of reducing it to practice, &c.

Page 287. "There can be no alteration in the established mode of Church discipline, which is not made in a legal way." Oh, but there are several methods to compass this legal way, by cunning, faction, industry. The common people, he knows, may be wrought upon by priests; these may influence the faction, and so compass a very pernicious law, and in a legal way ruin the state; as King Charles I. began to be ruined in a legal way, by passing bills, &c.

Page 288. "As everything is persecution, which puts a man in a worse condition than his neighbours." It is hard to think sometimes whether this man is hired to write for or against dissenters and the sects. This is their opinion, although they will not own it so roundly. Let this be brought to practice: Make a quaker lord chancellor, who thinketh paying tithes unlawful. And bring other instances to shew that several employments affect the Church.

*Ibid.* "Great advantage which both Church and state have got by the kindness already shewn to dissenters." Let them then be thankful for that. We humour children for their good sometimes, but too much may hurt. Observe that this 64th paragraph just contradicts the former. For, if we have advantage by kindness shewn dissenters, then there is no necessity of banishment, or death.

Page 290. "Christ never designed the holy Sacrament should be prostituted to serve a party. And that people should be bribed by a place to receive unworthily." Why, the business is, to be sure, that those who are employed are of the national church; and the way to know it is by receiving the sacrament, which all men ought to do in their own church; and if not, are hardly fit for an office; and if they have those moral qualifications he mentioneth, joined to religion, no fear of receiving unworthily. And for this there might be a remedy: To take an oath, that they are of the same principles, &c. for that is the end of receiving; and that it might be no bribe, the bill against occasional conformity would prevent entirely.

*Ibid.* "Preferring men not for their capacity, but their zeal to the Church." The misfortune is, that if we prefer dissenters to great posts, they will have an inclination to make themselves the national church, and so there will be perpetual struggling; which case may be dangerous to the state. For men are naturally wishing to get over others to their own opinion: Witness this writer, who hath published as singular and absurd notions as possible, yet hath a mighty zeal to bring us over to them, &c.

Page 292. Here are two pages of scurrilous faction, with a deal of reflections on great persons. Under the notion of High-Churchmen, he runs down all uniformity and church government. Here is the whole Lower House of Convocation, which represents the body of the clergy and both universities, treated with rudeness by an obscure, corrupt member, while he is eating their bread.

Page 294. "The reason why the middle sort of people retain so much of their ancient virtue &c. is because no such pernicious notions are the ingredients of their education; which 'tis a sign are infinitely absurd, when so many of the gentry and nobility can, notwithstanding their prepossession, get clear of them." Now the very same argument lies against religion, morality, honour, and honesty, which are, it seems, but prejudices of education, and too many get clear of them. The middle sort of people have other things to mind than the factions of the age. He always assigneth many causes, and sometimes with reason, since he maketh imaginary effects. He quarrels at power being lodged in the clergy: When there is no reasonable Protestant, clergy, or laity, who will not readily own the inconveniences by too great power and wealth, in any one body of men, ecclesiastics, or seculars: But on that account to weed up the wheat with the tares; to banish all religion, because it is capable of being corrupted; to give unbounded licence to all sects, &c.—And if heresies had not been used with some violence in the primitive age, we should have had, instead of true religion, the most corrupt one in the world.

Page 316. "The Dutch, and the rest of our presbyterian allies, &c." The Dutch will hardly thank him for this appellation. The French Huguenots, and Geneva Protestants themselves, and others, have lamented the want of episcopacy, and approved ours, &c. In this and the next paragraph, the author introduceth the arguments he formerly used, when he turned papist in King James's time; and loth to lose them, he gives them a new turn; and they are the strongest in his book, at least have most artifice.

Page 333. "'Tis plain, all the power the bishops have, is derived from the people, &c." In general the distinction lies here. The permissive power of exercising jurisdiction, lies in the people, or legislature, or administrator of a kingdom; but not of making him a bishop. As a physician that commenceth abroad, may be suffered to practise in London or be hindered; but they have not the power of creating him a doctor, which is peculiar to a university. This is some allusion; but the thing is plain, as it seemeth to me, and wanteth no subterfuge, &c.

Page 338. "A journeyman bishop to ordain for him." Doth any man think, that writing at this rate, does the author's cause any service? Is it his wit or his spleen that he cannot govern?

Page 364. "Can any have a right to an office without having a right to do those things in which the office consists?" I answer, the ordination is valid. But a man may prudentially forbid to do some things. As a clergyman may marry without licence or banns; the marriage is good; yet he is punishable for it.

Page 368. "A choice made by persons who have no right to choose, is an error of the first concoction." That battered simile again; this is hard. I wish the physicians had kept that a secret, it lieth so ready for him to be witty with.

Page 370. "If prescription can make mere nullities to become good and valid, the laity may be capable of all manner of ecclesiastical power, &c." There is a difference; for here the same way is kept, although there might be breaches; but it is quite otherwise, if you alter the whole method from what it was at first. We see bishops: There always were bishops: It is the old way still. So a family is still held the same, although we are not sure of the purity of every one of the race.

Page 380. "It is said, That every nation is not a complete body politic within itself as to ecclesiasticals. But the whole church, say they, composes such a body, and Christ is the head of it. But Christ's headship makes Christians no more one body politic with respect to ecclesiasticals than to civils." Here we must shew the reason and necessity of the Church being a corporation all over the world: To avoid heresies, and preserve fundamentals, and hinder corrupting of Scripture, &c. But there are no such necessities in government, to be the same everywhere, &c. It is something like the colleges in a university; they all are independent, yet, joined, are one body. So a general council consisteth of many persons independent of one another, &c.

However there is such a thing as *jus gentium*, &c. And he that is doctor of physic, or law, is so in any university of Europe, like the *Respublica Literaria*. Nor to me does there seem anything contradicting, or improper in this notion of the Catholic Church; and for want of such a communion, religion is so much corrupted, and would be more, if there were [not] more communion in this than in civils. It is of no import to mankind how nations are governed; but the preserving the purity of religion is best held up by endeavouring to make it one body over the world. Something like as there is in trade. So to be able to communicate with all Christians we come among, is at least to be wished and aimed at as much as we can.

Page 384. "In a word, if the bishops are not supreme, &c." Here he reassumeth his arguments for Popery, that there cannot be a body politic of the Church through the whole world, without a visible head to have recourse to. These were formerly writ to advance Popery, and now to put an absurdity upon the hypothesis of a Catholic Church. As they say in Ireland, in King James's time, they built masshouses, which we make very good barns of.

Page 388. "Bishops are, under a *premunire*, obliged to confirm and consecrate the person named in the *congé d'élire*." This perhaps is complained of. He is permitted to do it. We allow the legislature may hinder if they please; as they may turn out Christianity, if they think fit.

Page 389. "It is the magistrate who empowers them to do more for other bishops than they can for themselves, since they cannot appoint their own successors." Yes they could, if the magistrate would let them. Here is an endless splutter, and a parcel of perplexed distinctions upon no occasion. All that the clergy pretend to, is a right of qualifying men for the ministry, something like what a university doth with degrees. This power they claim from God, and that the civil power cannot do it as pleasing to God without them; but they may choose whether they will suffer it or no. A religion cannot be crammed down a nation's throat against their will; but when they receive a religion, it is supposed they receive as their converters give it; and, upon that foot, they cannot justly mingle their own methods, that contradict that religion, &c.

Page 390. "With us the bishops act only ministerially and by virtue of the regal commission, by which the prince firmly enjoins and commands them to proceed in choosing, confirming, and consecrating, &c." Suppose we held it unlawful to do so: How can we help it? but does that make it rightful, if it be not so? Suppose the author lived in a heathen country, where a law would be made to call Christianity idolatrous; would that be a topic for him to prove it so by, &c.? And why do the clergy incur a *premunire*;—To frighten them—Because the law understandeth, that, if they refuse, the chosen cannot be a bishop: But, if the clergy had an order to do it otherwise than they have prescribed, they ought and would incur an hundred rather.

Page 402. "I believe the Catholic Church, &c." Here he ridicules the Apostles' Creed.—Another part of his scheme.—By what he says in these pages, it is certain, his design is either to run down Christianity, or set up Popery; the latter it is more charitable to think, and, from his past life, highly probable.

Page 405. "That which gave the Papists so great advantage was, clergymen's talking so very inconsistent with themselves, &c." State the difference here between our separation from Rome, and the dissenters from us, and shew the falseness of what he sayeth. I wish he would tell us what he leaveth for a clergyman to do, if he may not instruct the people in religion, and if they should not receive his instructions.

Page 411. "The restraint of the press a badge of Popery." Why is that a badge of Popery? Why not restrain the press to those who would confound religion, as in civil matters? But this toucheth himself. He would starve, perhaps, &c. Let him get some honester livelihood then. It is plain, all his arguments against constraint, &c. favour the papists as much as dissenters; for both have opinions that may affect the peace of the state.

Page 413. "Since this discourse, &c." And must we have another volume on this one subject of independency? Or, is it to fright us? I am not of Dr. Hickes's mind, *Qu'il venge*. I pity the readers, and the clergy that must answer it, be it ever so insipid. Reflect on his sarcastic conclusion, &c.

# A PREFACE

TO THE

## B——P OF S——M'S

# INTRODUCTION, &c.

# NOTE.

AT the time of writing this scathing piece of invective, Swift was busy dealing out to an old friend a similar specimen of his terrible power of rejoinder. Steele, in the newly established "Guardian," as Mr. Churton Collins well puts it, "drunk with party spirit, had so far forgotten himself as to insert . . . a coarse and ungenerous reflection on Swift." Swift sought an explanation through Addison, but Steele's egotism was stronger than the feeling of friendship, and the insult remained for Swift to wipe out in "The Importance of the 'Guardian' Considered." Probably this severance from his friend, due to political differences—for Steele glowed in Whiggism—deepened, if possible, his hatred to Whigs of whatever degree; and in Burnet he found another object for his wit. But apart from such a suggestion, there was enough in the Bishop's attitude towards the Tories to rouse Swift to his task. It was not enough that Burnet should accuse his political opponents of sympathy with the French, Jacobitism, and Popery, but he must needs flaunt his vanity in issuing, in advance, for purposes of advertisement, the introduction to a work which was to come later. This was enough for Swift, and the prelate who "could smell popery at five hundred miles distance better than fanaticism under his nose," became the recipient of one of the most amusing and yet most virulent attacks which even that controversial age produced. "The whole pamphlet," Mr. Collins truly says, "is inimitable. Its irony, its humour, its drollery, are delicious."

It must not, however, be imagined that Swift's opinion of Burnet is only that which can be gathered from this "Preface." He fully appreciated the sterling qualities of scholarship and good nature, since in his "Remarks" on Burnet's "History of My Own Time," he says: "after all he was a man of generosity and good nature, and very communicative; but in his last ten years was absolutely party-mad, and fancied he saw Popery under every bush." Lord Dartmouth has left an excellent sketch of Burnet's character in a note to the "History of My Own Time": "Bishop Burnet was a man of the most extensive knowledge I ever met with; had read and seen a great deal, with a prodigious memory, and a very indifferent judgment: he was extremely partial, and readily took everything for granted that he heard to the prejudice of those he did not like: which made him pass for a man of less truth than he really was. I do not think he designedly published anything he believed to be false. He had a boisterous, vehement manner of expressing himself, which often made him ridiculous, especially in the House of Lords, when what he said would not have been thought so, delivered in a lower voice, and a calmer behaviour. His vast knowledge occasioned his frequent rambling from the point he was speaking to, which ran him into discourses of so universal a nature, that there was no end to be expected but from a failure of his strength and spirits, of both which he had a larger share than most men; which were accompanied with a most invincible assurance." (Note to the Preface of Burnet's "History of My Own Time," vol. i. p. xxxiii, Oxford, 1897.)

It may not be altogether out of place to give here a short biographical sketch of Bishop Burnet.

Gilbert Burnet was born at Edinburgh in 1643. He studied first at Aberdeen and then in Holland. In 1665, after he was elected a Fellow of the Royal Society, he entered holy orders, became vicar of Saltoun, and, in 1669, professor of divinity at Glasgow. The year 1673 found him in London, engaged on his "History of the Reformation," and fulfilling the duties of chaplain to the king, preacher to the Rolls, and lecturer of St. Clement's. The "Reformation" appeared in three folio volumes; the first in 1679, the second in 1681, and the third in 1714. He had already written the "Lives of the Dukes of Hamilton," the "Life of Sir Matthew Hale," and a "Life of the Earl of Rochester." Getting into some political trouble he was deprived of his offices, and left England for the continent. After travelling in France he settled in Holland, and married a Dutch lady. When the Prince of Orange came to England to assume the government of the country, Burnet accompanied him, and in 1689 was installed into the bishopric of Salisbury. Evidently he had too zealous a sentiment for William and Mary, for his pastoral letter to the clergy of his diocese, commenting on the new sovereign, was condemned by the parliament, and ordered to be burnt by the common hangman. He married again, on the death of his Dutch wife, a rich widow, Mrs. Berkeley, who was his third spouse —hence Swift's caustic reference. He died March 17th, 1714-15. In addition to his histories of the Reformation and his own times, he wrote an "Exposition of the Thirty-Nine Articles" (1699), the "Life of Bishop Bedell" and the other lives already named, and several sermons and controversial pieces.

The text of this pamphlet is that of the first edition, collated with those given by Faulkner, Hawkesworth, the "Miscellanies" of 1745, and Scott. It was originally published in 1713.

[T. S.]

# A PREFACE

TO THE

# B----p of *S--r--m*'s

INTRODUCTION

To the Third Volume of the

Hiftory of the Reformation

OF THE

Church of *England*.

By *GREGORY MISOSARUM*.

―――*Spargere voces*
*In vulgum ambiguas*; & *quærere confcius arma*.

𝕮𝖍𝖊 𝖘𝖊𝖈𝖔𝖓𝖉 𝕰𝖉𝖎𝖙𝖎𝖔𝖓.

LONDON:
Printed for *John Morphew*, near *Stationers Hall*. 1713. Price 6*d*.

# A PREFACE[1] TO THE B——P OF S——M'S INTRODUCTION, &c.

## THE PREFACE.[2]

MR. MORPHEW,

*Y*OUR *care in putting an advertisement in the* EXAMINER *has been of great use to me. I do now send you my Preface to the B—p of S—r—m's* INTRODUCTION *to his third volume, which I desire you to print in such a form, as in the bookseller's phrase will make a sixpenny touch; hoping it will give such a public notice of my design, that it may come into the hands of those who perhaps look not into the B—p's* Introduction. *I desire you will prefix to this a passage out of* Virgil, *which does so perfectly agree with my present thoughts of his L—dsh—p, that I cannot express them better, nor more truly, than those words do.*

*I am, Sir,*
*Your most humble servant,*
G. MISOSARUM.

THIS way of publishing introductions to books that are, God knows when, to come out, is either wholly new, or so long unpractised, that my small reading cannot trace it. However we are to suppose, that a person of his Lordship's great age and experience, would hardly act such a piece of singularity without some extraordinary motives. I cannot but observe, that his fellow-labourer, the author of the paper

---

[1] Mr. Nichols quotes from the "Speculum Sarisburianum," "That the frequent and hasty repetitions of such prefaces and introductions, no less than three new ones in about one year's time, beside an old serviceable one republished concerning persecution—are preludes to other practical things, beside pastoral cares, sermons, and histories." [S.]

[2] This preface "to the bookseller" is in imitation of the bishop's own preface to the bookseller in the "Introduction," which was signed "G. Sarum." [T. S.]

called *The Englishman*,[1] seems, in some of his late performances, to have almost transcribed the notions of the Bishop: these notions, I take to have been dictated by the same masters, leaving to each writer that peculiar manner of expressing himself, which the poverty of our language forces me to call their style. When the *Guardian* changed his title, and professed to engage in faction, I was sure the word was given, that grand preparations were making against next sessions; that all advantages would be taken of the little dissensions reported to be among those in power; and that the *Guardian* would soon be seconded by some other piqueerers[2] from the same camp. But I will confess, my suspicions did not carry me so far as to conjecture that this venerable champion would be in such mighty haste to come into the field, and serve in the quality of an *enfant perdu*,[3] armed only with a pocket pistol, before his great blunderbuss could be got ready, his old rusty breastplate scoured, and his cracked headpiece mended.

I was debating with myself, whether this hint of producing a small pamphlet to give notice of a large folio, was not borrowed from the ceremonial in Spanish romances, where a dwarf is sent out upon the battlements to signify to all passengers, what a mighty giant there is in the castle; or whether the Bishop copied this proceeding from the *fanfarronade* of Monsieur Boufflers, when the Earl of Portland and that general had an interview. Several men were appointed at certain periods to ride in great haste toward the English camp, and cry out, *Monseigneur vient, Monseigneur vient:* Then, small parties advanced with the same speed and the same cry, and this foppery held for many hours, until the mareschal himself arrived. So here, the Bishop (as we find by his dedication to Mr Churchill the bookseller) has for a long time sent warning of his arrival by advertisements in *Gazettes*, and now his Introduction advances to tell us again, *Monseigneur vient:* In the mean time, we must gape and wait and gaze the Lord knows how long, and keep our

---

[1] Steele.

[2] Piqueerer = pickeerer (modern) = a marauder, a skirmisher in advance of an army. From French *picorer* = to maraud. [T. S.]

[3] *Enfant perdu*, one of the advanced guard; or, as Hawkesworth notes it, "one of the forlorn hope." [T.S.]

spirits in some reasonable agitation, until his Lordship's rea self shall think fit to appear in the habit of a folio.

I have seen the same sort of management at a puppet-show. Some puppets of little or no consequence appeared several times at the window to allure the boys and the rabble: The trumpeter sounded often, and the doorkeeper cried a hundred times till he was hoarse, that they were just going to begin; yet after all, we were forced sometimes to wait an hour before Punch himself in person made his entry.

But why this ceremony among old acquaintance? The world and he have long known one another: Let him appoint his hour and make his visit, without troubling us all day with a succession of messages from his laqueys and pages.

With submission, these little arts of getting off an edition, do ill become any author above the size of Marten[1] the surgeon. My Lord tells us, that "many thousands of the two former parts of his History are in the kingdom,"[2] and now he perpetually advertises in the gazette, that he intends to publish the third: This is exactly in the method and style of Marten: "The seventh edition (many thousands of the former editions having been sold off in a small time) of Mr Marten's book concerning secret diseases," &c.

Does his Lordship intend to publish his great volume by subscription, and is this Introduction only by way of specimen? I was inclined to think so, because, in the prefixed letter to Mr Churchill, which introduces this Introduction, there are some dubious expressions: He says, "the advertisements he published were in order to move people to furnish him with materials, which might help him to finish his work with great advantage." If he means half-a-guinea upon the subscription, and t'other half at the delivery, why does he not tell us so in plain terms?

---

[1] This is John Marten, the author of two treatises on the gout, and a "Treatise of all the Degrees and Symptoms of the Venereal Disease" (1708?-9). His notoriety brought on him the ire of a "licens'd practitioner in physick and surgery," one J. Spinke, who, in a pamphlet entitled "Quackery Unmask'd" (1709), dealt Marten some most uncourteous blows. From the pamphlet, it is difficult to judge whether Spinke or Marten were the greater quack; we should judge the former. Certainly Marten deserves our sympathy, if only for Spinke's virulence. [T.S.]

[2] Page 26.

I am wondering how it came to pass, that this diminutive letter to Mr Churchill should understand the business of introducing better than the Introduction itself; or why the Bishop did not take it into his head to send the former into the world some months before the latter; which would have been a greater improvement upon the solemnity of the procession?

Since I writ these last lines, I have perused the whole pamphlet (which I had only dipped in before) and found I have been hunting upon a wrong scent; for the author hath in several parts of his piece, discovered the true motives which put him upon sending it abroad at this juncture; I shall therefore consider them as they come in my way.

My Lord begins his Introduction with an account of the reasons why he was guilty of so many mistakes in the first volume of his "History of the Reformation:" His excuses are just, rational, and extremely consistent. He says, "he wrote in haste,"[1] which he confirms by adding, "that it lay a year after he wrote it before it was put into the press:"[2] At the same time he mentioned a passage extremely to the honour of that pious and excellent prelate, Archbishop Sancroft, which demonstrates his Grace to have been a person of great sagacity, and almost a prophet. Dr. Burnet, then a private divine, "desired admittance to the Cotton library, but was prevented by the archbishop, who told Sir John Cotton, that the said doctor was no friend to the prerogative of the crown, nor to the constitution of the kingdom." This judgment was the more extraordinary, because the doctor had not long before published a book in Scotland, with his name prefixed, which carries the regal prerogative higher than any writer of the age:[3] however, the

---

[1] Page 6.  [2] Page 10.
[3] This was Burnet's "Vindication of the Authority, Constitution, and Laws of the Church and State of Scotland," dedicated to the Duke of Lauderdale, and published in 1672. The dedication contains an eulogium of the duke, and the work a defence of episcopacy and monarchy against Buchanan and his followers. At a later period, the author did not probably recollect this juvenile publication with much complacence. [S.]

It is somewhat remarkable to see the progress of this story. In the first edition of this "Introduction," it should seem, "he was prevented by the Archbishop," &c. When the "Introduction" was reprinted a

good archbishop lived to see his opinion become universal in the kingdom.

The Bishop goes on for many pages, with an account of certain facts relating to the publishing of his two former volumes of the Reformation, the great success of that work, and the adversaries who appeared against it. These are matters out of the way of my reading; only I observe that poor Mr Henry Wharton,[1] who has deserved so well of the commonwealth of learning, and who gave himself the trouble of detecting some hundreds of the Bishop's mistakes, meets with very ill quarter from his Lordship. Upon which I cannot avoid mentioning a peculiar method which this prelate takes to revenge himself upon those who presume to differ from him in print. The Bishop of Rochester[2] happened some years ago to be of this number. My Lord of Sarum in his reply ventured to tell the world, that the gentleman who had writ against him, meaning Dr Atterbury, was one upon whom he had conferred great obligations; which was a very generous Christian contrivance of charging

year after with the "History," it stands: "A great prelate had been beforehand and possessed him [Sir John Cotton] against me—That unless the Archbishop of Canterbury would recommend me—he desired to be excused—The Bishop of Worcester could not prevail on the Archbishop to interpose." This is somewhat less than preventing, unless the Archbishop be meant by the "great prelate." Which is not very probable. 1. Because in the Preface to this very third volume, p. 4, he says, "It was by Archbishop Sancroft's order he had the free use of everything that lay in the Lambeth Library." 2. Because the Author of "Speculum Sarisburianum" (p. 6), tells us, "His access to the Library was owing solely to the recommendation of Archbishop Sancroft, as I have been informed by some of the family." 3. Because Bishop Burnet, in his "History of My Own Times," vol. i. p. 396, says it was "Dolben, Bishop of Rochester (at the instigation of the Duke of Lauderdale), that diverted Sir John Cotton from suffering me to search his Library." ["Miscellanies," vol. viii. 1745.]

[1] Henry Wharton (1664-1694-5), a divine, born at Worstead, Norfolk, and educated at Cambridge. Became chaplain to Archbishop Sancroft in 1688, and then rector of Chartham. Wrote "A Treatise on the Celibacy of the Clergy;" "The Enthusiasm of the Church of Rome demonstrated in the Life of Ignatius Loyola;" "A Defence of Pluralities;" "Specimen of Errors in Burnet's 'History of the Reformation;'" "Anglia Sacra, sive Collectio Historiarum;" and "History of Archbishop Laud." The criticism on Burnet's "History" was written under the *nom de guerre* of Anthony Farmar. [T. S.]

[2] Dr. Atterbury.

his adversary with ingratitude. But it seems the truth happened to be on the other side; which the doctor made appear in such a manner as would have silenced his Lordship for ever, if he had not been writing proof. Poor Mr Wharton in his grave is charged with the same accusation, but with circumstances the most aggravating that malice and something else could invent;[1] and which I will no more believe than five hundred passages in a certain book of travels.[2] See the character he gives of a divine, and a scholar, who shortened his life in the service of God and the church. "Mr Wharton desired me to intercede with Tillotson for a prebend of Canterbury. I did so, but Wharton would not believe it; said he would be revenged, and so writ against me. Soon after he was convinced I had spoke for him, said he was set on to do what he did, and, if I would procure any thing for him, he would discover every thing to me."[3] What a spirit of candour, charity, and good nature, generosity, and truth, shines through this story, told of a most excellent and pious divine, twenty years after his death, without one single voucher![4]

[1] Page 22.      [2] Burnet's "Travels."      [3] Page 23.
[4] Burnet's account of this matter was reprinted in the Preface to his "History of the Reformation," and it contains also the bishop's rejoinder against Wharton's method of criticism in the "Specimen": "He had examined the dark ages before the Reformation with much diligence, and so knew many things relating to those times beyond any man of the age; he pretended that he had many more errors in reserve, and that this specimen was only a hasty collection of a few, out of many other discoveries he could make. This consisted of some trifling and minute differences in some dates and transactions of no importance, upon which nothing depended; so I cannot tell whether I took these too easily from printed books, or if I committed any errors in my notes taken in the several offices. He likewise follows me through the several recapitulations I had made of the state of things before the Reformation, and finds errors and omissions in most of these; he adds some things out of papers I had never seen. The whole was writ with so much malice, and such contempt, that I must give some account of the man, and of his motives. He had expressed great zeal against popery, in the end of King James's reign, being then chaplain to Archbishop Sancroft, who, as he said, had promised him the first of those prebends of Canterbury that should fall in his gift: for when he saw that the archbishop was resolved not to take the oaths, but to forsake the post, he made an earnest application to me, to secure that for him at Archbishop Tillotson's hands. I pressed him in it as much as was decent for me to do, but he said he would not encourage these aspiring men,

Come we now to the reasons, which moved his lordship to set about this work at this time. He "could delay it no longer, because the reasons of his engaging in it at first seem to return upon him."[1] He was then frightened with "the danger of a popish successor in view, and the dreadful apprehensions of the power of France. England has forgot these dangers, and yet is nearer to them than ever,"[2] and therefore he is resolved to "awaken them" with his third volume; but in the mean time, sends this Introduction to let them know they are asleep. He then goes on in describing the condition of the kingdom,[3] after such a manner as if destruction hung over us by a single hair; as if the Pope, the devil, the Pretender, and France, were just at our doors.

When the Bishop published his History, there was a popish plot on foot, the Duke of York a known papist was presumptive heir to the crown, the House of Commons would not hear of any expedient for securing their religion under a popish prince, nor would the King or Lords, consent to a bill of exclusion: The French King was in the height of his grandeur, and the vigour of his age. At this day the presumptive heir, with that whole illustrious family, are Protestants, the Popish Pretender excluded for ever by several acts of Parliament, and every person in the smallest employment, as well as the members in both Houses, obliged to abjure him. The French King is at the lowest ebb of life; his armies have been conquered and his towns

by promising any thing, before it should fall; as indeed none of them fell during his time. Wharton, upon this answer, thought I had neglected him, looking on it as a civil denial, and said he would be revenged; and so he published that specimen: upon which, I, in a letter that I printed, addressed to the present Bishop of Worcester, charged him again and again to bring forth all that he pretended to have reserved at that time, for, till that was done, I would not enter upon the examination of that specimen. It was received with contempt, and Tillotson justified my pressing him to take Wharton under his particular protection so fully, that he sent and asked me pardon. He said he was set on to it; and that, if I would procure any thing for him, he would discover any thing to me. I despised that offer, but said that I would at any price buy of him those discoveries that he pretended to have in reserve. But Mr Chiswell (at whose house he then lay) being sick, said he could draw nothing of that from him, and he believed he had nothing. He died about a year after."—BURNET'S *History of the Reformation*, III. vii. [T. S.]

[1] Page 27.  [2] Page 28.  [3] Page 28.

won from him for ten years together, and his kingdom is in danger of being torn by divisions during a long minority. Are these cases parallel? Or are we now in more danger of France and popery than we were thirty years ago? What can be the motive for advancing such false, such detestable assertions? What conclusions would his Lordship draw from such premises as these? If injurious appellations were of any advantage to a cause, (as the style of our adversaries would make us believe) what appellations would those deserve who thus endeavour to sow the seeds of sedition, and are impatient to see the fruits? "But," saith he,[1] "the deaf adder stops her ear let the charmer charm never so wisely." True, my Lord, there are indeed too many adders in this nation's bosom, adders in all shapes, and in all habits, whom neither the Queen nor parliament can charm to loyalty, truth, religion, or honour.

Among other instances produced by him of the dismal condition we are in, he offers one which could not easily be guessed. It is this: That the little factious pamphlets written about the end of King Charles II.'s reign, "lie dead in shops, are looked on as waste paper, and turned to pasteboard." How many are there of his Lordship's writings which could otherwise never have been of any real service to the public? Has he indeed so mean an opinion of our taste, to send us at this time of day into all the corners of Holborn, Duck Lane, and Moorfields, in quest after the factious trash published in those days by Julian Johnson, Hickeringil, Dr. Oates, and himself?[2]

His Lordship, taking it for a *postulatum*, that the Queen and ministry, both Houses of Parliament, and a vast

---

[1] Page 28.

[2] The Rev. Samuel Johnson, degraded from his clerical rank, scourged, and imprisoned, for a work called "Julian's Arts to undermine Christianity," in which he drew a parallel between that apostate and James, then Duke of York. [S.]

Edmund Hickeringil, a fanatic preacher at Colchester. He appears, from the various pamphlets which he wrote during the reigns of Charles II. and his brother, to have been a meddling crazy fool. [S.] He was born in Essex, 1630, and was educated at Cambridge. He entered the army, and went to Jamaica, of which place he wrote a very curious account. Afterwards he entered holy orders, and became rector of All Saints, Colchester. He was a most eccentric individual. [T. S.]

majority of the landed gentlemen throughout England are running headlong into Popery, lays hold on the occasion to describe "the cruelties in Queen Mary's reign, an inquisition setting up faggots in Smithfield, and executions all over the kingdom. Here is that" (says he) "which those that look toward a popish successor must look for."[1] And he insinuates through his whole pamphlet, that all who are not of his party, "look toward a popish successor." These he divides into two parts, the Tory laity, and the Tory clergy. He tells the former, though they have no religion at all, but "resolve to change with every wind and tide; yet they ought to have compassion on their countrymen and kindred."[2] Then he applies himself to the Tory clergy, assures them, that "the fires revived in Smithfield, and all over the nation, will have no amiable view; but least of all to them, who if they have any principle at all, must be turned out of their livings, leave their families, be hunted from place to place into parts beyond the seas, and meet with that contempt with which they treated foreigners who took sanctuary among us."

This requires a recapitulation, with some remarks. First, I do affirm, that of every hundred professed atheists, deists, and socinians in the kingdom, ninety-nine at least are staunch thorough-paced Whigs, entirely agreeing with his Lordship in politics and discipline; and therefore will venture all the fires of hell, rather than singe one hair of their beards in Smithfield. Secondly, I do likewise affirm, that those whom we usually understand by the appellation of Tory or high-church clergy, were the greatest sticklers against the exorbitant proceedings of King James, the best writers against popery, and the most exemplary sufferers for the established religion. Thirdly, I do pronounce it to be a most false and infamous scandal upon the nation in general, and on the clergy in particular, to reproach them for "treating foreigners with haughtiness and contempt:" The French Huguenots are many thousand witnesses to the contrary; and I wish they deserved a thousandth part of the good treatment they have received.[3]

Lastly, I observe that the author of the paper called *The*

---

[1] Page 36.   [2] Page 36.
[3] Swift's disparaging reference to the Huguenots must be put down to the fact that he included them among Dissenters, on account of their Calvinism. [T. S.]

*Englishman*, hath run into the same cant, gravely advising the whole body of the clergy not to bring in Popery, because that will put them under a necessity of parting with their wives, or losing their livings.

The bulk of the kingdom, both clergy and laity, happens to differ extremely from this prelate, in many principles both of politics and religion: Now I ask, whether if any man of them had signed his name to a system of atheism, or Popery, he could have argued with them otherwise than he does? Or, if I should write a grave letter to his Lordship with the same advice, taking it for granted that he was half an atheist, and half a papist, and conjuring him by all he held dear to have compassion upon all those who believed a God, "not to revive the fires in Smithfield," that he must either forfeit his bishopric, or not marry a fourth wife;[1] I ask whether he would not think I intended him the highest injury and affront?

But as to the Tory laity; he gives them up in a lump for abandoned atheists: They are a set of men so "impiously corrupted in the point of religion, that no scene of cruelty can fright them from leaping into it [Popery] and perhaps acting such a part in it, as may be assigned them."[2] He therefore despairs of influencing them by any topics drawn from religion or compassion, and advances the consideration of interest, as the only powerful argument to persuade them against Popery.

What he offers upon this head is so very amazing from a Christian, a clergyman, and a prelate of the Church of England, that I must in my own imagination strip him of those three capacities, and put him among the number of that set of men he mentions in the paragraph before; or else it will be impossible to shape out an answer.

His Lordship, in order to dissuade the Tories from their design of bringing in Popery, tells them, "how valuable a part of the whole soil of England, the abbey lands, the estates of the bishops, of the cathedrals, and the tithes are;"[3] how difficult such "a resumption would be to many families; yet all these must be thrown up; for sacrilege in the church of Rome, is a mortal sin." I desire it may be

---

[1] Bishop Burnet had already been married three times. [T. S.]
[2] Page 37.   [3] Page 38.

observed, what a jumble here is made of ecclesiastical revenues, as if they were all upon the same foot, were alienated with equal justice, and the clergy had no more reason to complain of the one than the other. Whereas the four branches mentioned by him are of very different consideration. If I might venture to guess the opinion of the clergy upon this matter, I believe they could wish that some small part of the abbey lands had been applied to the augmentation of poor bishoprics, and a very few acres to serve for glebes in those parishes where there are none; after which I think they would not repine that the laity should possess the rest. If the estates of some bishops and cathedrals were exorbitant before the Reformation, I believe the present clergy's wishes reach no further than that some reasonable temper had been used, instead of paring them to the quick: But as to the tithes, without examining whether they be of divine institution, I conceive there is hardly one of that sacred order in England, and very few even among the laity that love the Church, who will not allow the misapplying of those revenues to secular persons, to have been at first a most flagrant act of injustice and oppression: Though at the same time, God forbid they should be restored any other way than by gradual purchase, by the consent of those who are now the lawful possessors, or by the piety and generosity of such worthy spirits as this nation sometimes produceth. The Bishop knows very well that the application of tithes to the maintenance of monasteries, was a scandalous usurpation even in popish times: That the monks usually sent out some of their fraternity to supply the cures; and that when the monasteries were granted away by Henry VIII., the parishes were left destituted, or very meanly provided of any maintenance for a pastor: So that in many places, the whole ecclesiastical dues, even to mortuaries, Easter-offerings, and the like, are in lay hands, and the incumbent lies wholly at the mercy of his patron for his daily bread. By these means there are several hundred parishes in England under £20 a year, and many under ten. I take his Lordship's bishopric to be worth near £2,500 annual income; and I will engage at half a year's warning to find him above 200 beneficed clergymen who have not so much among them all to support themselves and their families; most of them orthodox, of good life and conversation, as loth to see the fires kindled in Smithfield, as his Lordship, and at least as ready to face them under a popish persecution. But nothing is so hard for those who abound in riches, as to conceive how others can be in want. How can the neighbouring vicar feel cold or hunger, while my Lord is seated by a good fire in the warmest room in his palace, with a dozen dishes before him? I remember one other prelate much of the same stamp; who when his clergy would mention their wishes that some act of parliament might be thought of for the good of the Church, would say, "Gentlemen, *we* are very well as *we* are; if they would let *us* alone, *we* should ask no more."[1]

"Sacrilege" (says my Lord) "in the church of Rome, is a mortal sin;"[2] and is it only so in the church of Rome? Or is it but a venial sin in the Church of England? Our litany calls fornication a deadly sin; and I would appeal to his Lordship for fifty years past, whether he thought that or sacrilege the deadliest? To make light of such a sin, at the same moment that he is frighting us from an idolatrous religion, should seem not very consistent. "*Thou* that sayest, a man should not commit adultery, dost *thou* commit adultery? *Thou* that abhorrest idols, dost *thou* commit sacrilege?"

To smooth the way for the return of Popery in Queen Mary's time, the grantees were confirmed by the Pope in the possession of the abbey lands. But the Bishop tells us, that "this confirmation was fraudulent and invalid." I shall believe it to be so, though I happen to read in his Lordship's history: But he adds, that although the confirmation had been good, the priests would have got their land again by these two methods; "first,[3] the Statute of Mortmain was repealed for 20 years, in which time no doubt they reckoned they would recover the best part of what they had lost; besides that, engaging the clergy to renew no leases, was a thing entirely in their own power, and this in forty years time would raise their revenues to be about ten times their

---

[1] Scott, in a note, thinks this reflection on Burnet to be unjust, because of that prelate's zeal "in forwarding a scheme in 1704 for improving the livings of the poorer clergy." [T. S.]
[2] Page 38.  [3] Page 39.

present value." These two expedients for increasing the revenues of the Church, he represents as pernicious designs, fit only to be practised in times of Popery, and such as the laity ought never to consent to: Whence, and from what he said before about tithes, his Lordship has freely declared his opinion, that the clergy are rich enough, and that the least addition to their subsistence would be a step toward Popery. Now it happens, that the two only methods, which could be thought on, with any probability of success, toward some reasonable augmentation of ecclesiastical revenues, are here rejected by a Bishop, as a means for introducing Popery, and the nation publicly warned against them. The continuance of the Statute of Mortmain in full force, after the Church had been so terribly stripped, appeared to Her Majesty and the kingdom a very unnecessary hardship; upon which account it was at several times relaxed by the legislature. Now as the relaxation of that statute is manifestly one of the reasons which gives the Bishop those terrible apprehensions of Popery coming on us; so I conceive another ground of his fears, is the remission of the first-fruits and tenths. But where the inclination to Popery lay, whether in Her Majesty who proposed this benefaction, the parliament which confirmed, or the clergy who accepted it, his Lordship hath not thought fit to determine.

The other popish expedient for augmenting church-revenues, is "engaging the clergy to renew no leases."[1] Several of the most eminent clergymen have assured me, that nothing has been more wished for by good men, than a law to prevent (at least) bishops from setting leases for lives. I could name ten bishoprics in England whose revenues one with another do not amount to £600 a-year for each; and if his lordship's, for instance, would be above ten times the value when the lives are expired, I should think the overplus would not be ill disposed toward an augmentation of such as are now shamefully poor. But I do assert, that such an expedient was not always thought popish and dangerous by this right reverend historian. I have had the honour formerly to converse with him; and he has told me several years ago, that he lamented

[1] Page 39.

extremely the power which bishops had of letting leases for lives, whereby, as he said, they were utterly deprived of raising their revenues, whatever alterations might happen in the value of money by length of time: I think the reproach of betraying private conversation will not upon this account be laid to my charge. Neither do I believe he would have changed his opinion upon any score, but to take up another, more agreeable to the maxims of his party; that "the least addition of property to the Church, is one step toward Popery."

The Bishop goes on with much earnestness and prolixity to prove that the Pope's confirmation of the church lands to those who held them by King Henry's donation, was null and fraudulent: Which is a point that I believe no Protestant in England would give threepence to have his choice whether it should be true or false: It might indeed serve as a passage in his history, among a thousand other instances, to detect the knavery of the court of Rome; but I ask, where could be the use of it in this Introduction? Or why all this haste in publishing it at this juncture; and so out of all method apart, and before the work itself? He gives his reasons in very plain terms; we are now, it seems, "in more danger of Popery than toward the end of King Charles II.'s reign. That set of men (the Tories) is so impiously corrupted in the point of religion, that no scene of cruelty can fright them from leaping into it, and perhaps from acting such a part in it as may be assigned them."[1] He doubts whether the High-Church clergy have any principles, and therefore will be ready to turn off their wives, and look on the fires kindled in Smithfield as an amiable view. These are the facts he all along takes for granted, and argues accordingly; therefore, in despair of dissuading the nobility and gentry of the land from introducing Popery by any motives of honour, religion, alliance or mercy, he assures them, that "the Pope has not duly confirmed their titles to the church lands in their possession," which therefore must infallibly be restored, as soon as that religion is established among us.

Thus, in his Lordship's opinion, there is nothing wanting

[1] Page 37.

to make the majority of the kingdom, both for number, quality and possession, immediately embrace Popery, except a "firm bull from the Pope," to secure the abbey and other church lands and tithes to the present proprietors and their heirs; if this only difficulty could now be adjusted, the Pretender would be restored next session, the two Houses reconciled to the church of Rome against Easter term, and the fires lighted in Smithfield by Midsummer. Such horrible calumnies against a nation are not the less injurious to decency, good-nature, truth, honour, and religion, because they may be vented with safety. And I will appeal to any reader of common understanding, whether this be not the most natural and necessary deduction from the passages I have cited and referred to.

Yet all this is but friendly dealing, in comparison with what he affords the clergy upon the same article. He supposes[1] all that reverend body, who differ from him in principles of church or state, so far from disliking Popery, upon the above-mentioned motives of perjury, "quitting their wives, or burning their relations;" that the hopes of "enjoying the abbey lands" would soon bear down all such considerations, and be an effectual incitement to their perversion; and so he goes gravely on, as with the only argument which he thinks can have any force, to assure them, that "the parochial priests in Roman Catholic countries are much poorer than in ours, the several orders of regulars, and the magnificence of their church, devouring all their treasure," and by consequence "their hopes are vain of expecting to be richer after the introduction of Popery."

But after all, his Lordship despairs, that even this argument will have any force with our abominable clergy, because, to use his own words, "They are an insensible and degenerate race, who are thinking of nothing but their present advantages; and so that they may now support a luxurious and brutal course of irregular and voluptuous practices, they are easily hired to betray their religion, to sell their country, and give up that liberty and those properties, which are the present felicities and glories of this

[1] Page 46.

nation."[1] He seems to reckon all these evils as matters fully determined on, and therefore falls into the last usual form of despair, by threatening the authors of these miseries with "lasting infamy, and the curses of posterity upon perfidious betrayers of their trust."[2]

Let me turn this paragraph into vulgar language for the use of the poor, and strictly adhere to the sense of the words. I believe it may be faithfully translated in the following manner: "The bulk of the clergy, and one-third of the bishops, are stupid sons of whores, who think of nothing but getting money as soon as they can: If they may but produce enough to supply them in gluttony, drunkenness, and whoring, they are ready to turn traitors to God and their country, and make their fellow-subjects slaves." The rest of the period, about threatening "infamy," and "the curses of posterity upon such dogs and villains," may stand as it does in the Bishop's own phrase, and so make the paragraph all of a piece.

I will engage, on the other side, to paraphrase all the rogues and rascals in the *Englishman*, so as to bring them up exactly to his Lordship's style: But, for my own part, I much prefer the plain Billingsgate way of calling names, because it expresses our meaning full as well, and would save abundance of time which is lost by circumlocution; so, for instance, John Dunton,[3] who is retained on the same side with the Bishop, calls my Lord-treasurer and Lord Bolingbroke, traitors, whoremasters, and Jacobites, which three words cost our right reverend author thrice as many lines to define them; and I hope his Lordship does not think there is any difference in point of morality, whether a man calls me traitor in one word, or says I am one "hired to betray my religion and sell my country."[4]

I am not surprised to see the Bishop mention with contempt all Convocations of the Clergy;[5] for Toland, Collins, Tindal,[6] and others of the fraternity, talk the very same language. His Lordship confesses he "is not" inclined "to expect much from the assemblies of clergymen." There lies

---

[1] Page 47.  [2] Page 47.
[3] See note on p. 50 of vol. i. of this edition of Swift's works. [T. S.]
[4] Page 51.  [5] Page 47.
[6] See note, p. 9. [T. S.]

the misfortune; for if he and some more of his order would correct their "inclinations," a great deal of good might be expected from such assemblies, as much as they are now cramped by that submission, which a corrupt clergy brought upon their innocent successors. He will not deny that his copiousness in these matters is, in his own opinion, one of the meanest parts of his new work. I will agree with him, unless he happens to be more "copious" in any thing else. However, it is not easy to conceive why he should be so "copious" upon a subject he so much despises, unless it were to gratify his talent of railing at the clergy, in the number of whom he disdains to be reckoned, because he is a Bishop. For it is a style I observe some prelates have fallen into of late years, to talk of clergymen as if themselves were not of the number: You will read in many of their speeches at Dr Sacheverel's[1] trial, expressions to this or the like effect: "My lords, if clergymen be suffered," &c. wherein they seem to have reason; and I am pretty confident, that a great majority of the clergy were heartily inclined to disown any relation they had to the managers in lawn. However, it was a confounding argument against Presbytery, that those who are most suspected to lean that way, treating their inferior brethren with haughtiness, rigour, and contempt: Although, to say the truth, nothing better could be hoped for; because, I believe, it may pass for a universal rule, that in every diocese governed by bishops of the Whig species, the clergy (especially the poorer sort) are under double discipline, and the laity left to themselves. The opinion of Sir Thomas More, which he produces to prove the ill consequences or insignificancy of

[1] Henry Sacheverell, D.D., was educated at Marlborough and Oxford. At Magdalen College he was a fellow-student with Addison, and obtained there his fellowship and doctor's degree. In 1709 he preached two sermons, one at the Derby Assizes, and the other at St. Paul's, in which he urged the imminent danger of the Church. For these sermons, which the parliament considered highly inflammatory, he was, by the House of Commons, at the instigation of Godolphin, impeached, and tried before the Lords in 1710. He was found guilty of a misdemeanour, and was suspended from preaching for three years. The trial made a great stir at the time, and served but to increase the popularity of a man who, had he been let alone, would, probably, never have been heard of. He died in 1724, holding the living of St. Andrew, Holborn, to which he was presented after the expiration of his sentence. [T. S.]

Convocations, advances no such thing, but says, "if the clergy assembled often, and might act as other assemblies of clergy in Christendom, much good might have come: but the misfortune lay in their long disuse, and that in his own and a good part of his father's time, they never came together, except at the command of the prince."[1]

I suppose his lordship thinks, there is some original impediment in the study of divinity, or secret incapacity in a gown and cassock without lawn, which disqualifies all inferior clergymen from debating upon subjects of doctrine or discipline in the church. It is a famous saying of his, that "he looks upon every layman to be an honest man, until he is by experience convinced to the contrary; and on every clergyman as a knave, till he finds him to be an honest man." What opinion then must we have of a Lower House of Convocation:[2] where I am confident he will hardly find three persons that ever convinced him of their honesty, or will ever be at the pains to do it? Nay, I am afraid they would think such a conviction might be no very advantageous bargain, to gain the character of an honest man with his Lordship, and lose it with the rest of the world.

In the famous Concordate that was made between Francis I. of France and Pope Leo X., the Bishop tells us, that "the king and pope came to a bargain, by which they divided the liberties of the Gallican Church between them, and indeed quite enslaved it."[3] He intends, in the third part of his History which he is going to publish, "to open this whole matter to the world." In the mean time, he mentions some ill consequences to the Gallican Church from that Concordate, which are worthy to be observed: "The church of France became a slave, and this change in their constitution put an end not only to national, but even to provincial synods in that kingdom. The assemblies of the

---

[1] See Sir Thomas More's "Apology," 1533, p. 241.
[2] It must not be forgotten, that, during the reign of Queen Anne, the body of the clergy were high-church men; but the bishops, who had chiefly been promoted since the Revolution, were Whiggish in politics, and moderate in their sentiments of church government. Hence the Upper and Lower Houses of Convocation rarely agreed in sentiment on affairs of church or state. [S.]
[3] Page 53.

clergy there, meet now only to give subsidies," &c. and he says, "our nation may see by that proceeding, what it is to deliver up the essential liberties of a free constitution to a court." ¹

All I can gather from this matter is, that our King Henry made a better bargain than his contemporary Francis, who divided the liberties of the church between himself and the Pope, while the King of England seized them all to himself. But how comes he to number the want of synods in the Gallican church among the grievances of that Concordate, and as a mark of their slavery, since he reckons all Convocations of the Clergy in England to be useless and dangerous? Or what difference in point of liberty was there between the Gallican Church under Francis, and the English under Harry? For, the latter was as much a papist as the former, unless in the point of obedience to the see of Rome; and in every quality of a good man, or a good prince, (except personal courage wherein both were equal) the French monarch had the advantage by as many degrees as is possible for one man to have over another.

Henry VIII. had no manner of intention to change religion in his kingdom; he still continued to persecute and burn Protestants after he had cast off the Pope's supremacy, and I suppose this seizure of ecclesiastical revenues (which Francis never attempted) cannot be reckoned as a mark of the church's liberty. By the quotation the Bishop sets down to show the slavery of the French church, he represents it as a grievance, that "bishops are not now elected there as formerly, but wholly appointed by the prince; and that those made by the court have been ordinarily the chief advancers of schisms, heresies, and oppressions of the church." ² He cites another passage from a Greek writer, and plainly insinuates, that it is justly applicable to Her Majesty's reign: "Princes choose such men to that charge [of a bishop] who may be their slaves, and in all things obsequious to what they prescribe; and may lie at their feet, and have not so much as a thought contrary to their commands." ³

These are very singular passages for his Lordship to set

---

¹ Page 53.    ² Page 55.    ³ Page 55.

down in order to show the dismal consequences of the French Concordate, by the slavery of the Gallican Church, compared with the freedom of ours. I shall not enter into a long dispute, whether it were better for religion that bishops should be chosen by the clergy, or people, or both together: I believe our author would give his vote for the second (which however would not have been of much advantage to himself, and some others that I could name). But I ask, Whether bishops are any more elected in England than in France? And the want of synods are in his own opinion rather a blessing than a grievance, unless he will affirm that more good can be expected from a popish synod than an English Convocation. Did the French clergy ever receive a greater blow to their liberties, than the submission made to Henry VIII., or so great a one as the seizure of their lands? The Reformation owed nothing to the good intentions of K. Henry: He was only an instrument of it, (as the logicians speak) by accident; nor doth he appear through his whole reign to have had any other views than those of gratifying his insatiable love of power, cruelty, oppression, and other irregular appetites. But this kingdom as well as many other parts of Europe, was, at that time, generally weary of the corruptions and impositions of the Roman court and church, and disposed to receive those doctrines which Luther and his followers had universally spread. Cranmer the archbishop, Cromwell, and others of the court, did secretly embrace the Reformation; and the King's abrogating the Pope's supremacy, made the people in general run into the new doctrines with greater freedom, because they hoped to be supported in it by the authority and example of their prince, who disappointed them so far that he made no other step than rejecting the Pope's supremacy as a clog upon his own power and passions, but retained every corruption beside, and became a cruel persecutor, as well of those who denied his own supremacy, as of all others who professed any Protestant doctrine. Neither hath any thing disgusted me more in reading the histories of those times, than to see one of the worst princes of any age or country, celebrated as an instrument in that glorious work of the Reformation.

The Bishop having gone over all the matters that properly fall within his Introduction, proceeds to expostulate with several sorts of people;[1] First with Protestants who are no Christians, such as atheists, deists, freethinkers, and the like enemies to Christianity. But these he treats with the tenderness of a friend, because they are all of them of sound Whig principles in church and state. However, to do him justice, he lightly touches some old topics for the truth of the Gospel; and concludes by " wishing that the freethinkers would consider well, if (*Anglice*, whether) they think it possible to bring a nation to be without any religion at all, and what the consequences of that may prove;[2] and in case they allow the negative, he gives it clearly for Christianity.

Secondly, he applies himself (if I take his meaning right) to Christian papists " who have a taste of liberty," and desires them to " compare the absurdities of their own religion with the reasonableness of the reformed:"[3] Against which, as good luck would have it, I have nothing to object.

Thirdly, he is somewhat rough against his own party, " who having tasted the sweets of Protestant liberty, can look back so tamely on Popery coming on them; it looks as if they were bewitched, or that the devil were in them, to be so negligent. It is not enough that they resolve not to turn papists themselves: They ought to awaken all about them, even the most ignorant and stupid, to apprehend their danger, and to exert themselves with their utmost industry to guard against it, and to resist it. If after all their endeavours to prevent it, the corruption of the age, and the art and power of our enemies, prove too hard for us, then, and not until then, we must submit to the will of God, and be silent, and prepare ourselves for all the extremity of suffering and of misery:"[4] with a great deal more of the same strain.

With due submission to the profound sagacity of this prelate, who can smell Popery at 500 miles distance, better than fanaticism just under his nose; I take leave to tell him, that this reproof to his friends, for want of zeal and clamour against Popery, slavery, and the Pretender, is what they have not deserved. Are the pamphlets and papers, daily published by the sublime authors of his party full

[1] Page 56.  [2] Page 59.
[3] Page 59.  [4] Pages 60, 61.

of any thing else? Are not the Queen, the ministers, the majority of Lords and Commons, loudly taxed in print with this charge against them at full length? Is it not the perpetual echo of every Whig coffeehouse and club? Have they not quartered Popery and the Pretender upon the peace, and treaty of commerce; upon the possessing, and quieting, and keeping, and demolishing of Dunkirk? Have they not clamoured because the Pretender continued in France, and because he left it? Have they not reported, that the town swarmed with many thousand papists, when upon search there were never found so few of that religion in it before? If a clergyman preaches obedience to the higher powers, is he not immediately traduced as a papist? Can mortal man do more? To deal plainly, my Lord, your friends are not strong enough yet to make an insurrection, and it is unreasonable to expect it from them, until their neighbours are ready.

My Lord, I have a little seriousness at heart upon this point, where your Lordship affects to show so much. When you can prove, that one single word has ever dropped from any minister of state, in public or private, in favour of the Pretender, or his cause; when you can make it appear, that in the course of this administration, since the Queen thought fit to change her servants, there hath one step been made toward weakening the Hanover title, or giving the least countenance to any other whatsoever; then, and not until then, go dry your chaff and stubble, give fire to the zeal of your faction, and reproach them with lukewarmness.

Fourthly, the Bishop applies himself to the Tories in general. Taking it for granted, after his charitable manner, that they are all ready prepared to introduce Popery, he puts an excuse into their mouths, by which they would endeavour to justify their change of religion. That "Popery is not what it was before the Reformation: Things are now much mended; and further corrections might be expected, if we would enter into a treaty with them: In particular, they see the error of proceeding severely with heretics; so that there is no reason to apprehend the returns of such cruelties as were practised an age and a half ago."[1]

[1] Page 62.

This, he assures us, is a plea offered by the Tories in defence of themselves, for going about at this juncture to establish the Popish religion among us : What argument does he bring to prove the fact itself ?

"Quibus indiciis, quo teste, probavit ?
Nil horum : verbosa et grandis epistola venit"[1]

Nothing but this tedious Introduction, wherein he supposes it all along as a thing granted. That there might be a perfect union in the whole Christian Church, is a blessing which every good man wishes, but no reasonable man can hope. That the more polite Roman Catholics have in several places given up some of their superstitious fopperies, particularly concerning legends, relics, and the like, is what nobody denies. But the material points in difference between us and them are universally retained and asserted, in all their controversial writings. And if his Lordship really thinks that every man who differs from him, under the name of a Tory in some church and state opinions, is ready to believe transubstantiation, purgatory the infallibility of pope or councils, to worship saints and angels, and the like ; I can only pray God to enlighten his understanding, or graft in his heart the first principles of charity ; a virtue which some people ought not by any means wholly to renounce, "because it covers a multitude of sins."

Fifthly, the Bishop applies himself to his own party in both Houses of Parliament, whom he exhorts to "guard their religion and liberty against all danger at what distance soever it may appear. If they are absent and remiss on critical occasions," that is to say, if they do not attend close next sessions, to vote upon all occasions whatsoever against the proceedings of the Queen and Her Ministry ; "or, if any views of advantage to themselves prevail on them."[2] In other words, if any of them vote for the Bill of Commerce, in hopes of a place or a pension, a title, or a garter ; "God may work a deliverance for us another way." That is to say, by inviting the Dutch. "But they and their families," (id est) those who are negligent or revolters, "shall perish." By

[1] Juvenal, "Sat.' x. 70-71. [T. S.]
[2] Pages 67, 68.

which is meant; they shall be hanged as well as the present ministry and their abettors, as soon as we recover our power. "Because they let in idolatry, superstition, and tyranny." Because they stood by and suffered the peace to be made, the Bill of Commerce to pass, and Dunkirk to lie undemolished longer than we expected, without raising a rebellion.

His last application is to the Tory clergy, a parcel of "blind, ignorant, dumb, sleeping, greedy, drunken dogs."[1] A pretty artful episcopal method is this, of calling his brethren as many injurious names as he pleases. It is but quoting a text of Scripture, where the characters of evil men are described, and the thing is done; and at the same time the appearances of piety and devotion preserved. I would engage, with the help of a good Concordance, and the liberty of perverting Holy Writ, to find out as many injurious appellations, as the *Englishman* throws out in any of his politic papers, and apply them to those persons "who call good evil, and evil good;" to those who cry without cause, "Every man to his tent, O Israel! and to those who curse the Queen in their hearts!"

These decent words he tells us, make up a "lively description of such pastors, as will not study controversy, nor know the depths of Satan." He means I suppose, the controversy between us and the papists; for as to the freethinkers and

---

[1] This is the bishop's reference to the Tory clergy: "But, in the last place, Those who are appointed to be the watchmen, who ought to give warning, and to lift up their voice as a trumpet, when they see those wolves ready to break in and devour the flock, have the heaviest account of all others to make, if they neglect their duty; much more if they betray their trust. If they are so set on some smaller matters, and are so sharpened upon that account, that they will not see their danger, nor awaken others to see it, and to fly from it; the guilt of those souls who have perished by their means, God will require at their hands. If they, in the view of any advantage to themselves, are silent when they ought to cry out day and night, they will fall under the character given by the prophet, of the watchmen in his time: 'They are blind, they are all dumb dogs, they cannot bark, sleeping, lying down, loving to slumber: Yea, they are greedy dogs, which can never have enough. And they are shepherds that cannot understand; they all look to their own way, every one for his gain from his quarter; that say, come, I will fetch wine, and we will fill ourselves with strong drink; to-morrow shall be as this day, and much more abundant.'"—BURNET's *History of the Reformation*, vol. iii. p. xxii. [T. S.]

dissenters of every denomination, they are some of the best friends to the cause. Now I have been told, there is a body of that kind of controversy published by the London divines, which is not to be matched in the world. I believe likewise, there is a good number of the clergy at present, thoroughly versed in that study; after which I cannot but give my judgment, that it would be a very idle thing for pastors in general to busy themselves much in disputes against Popery. It being a dry heavy employment of the mind at best, especially when, God be thanked, there is so little occasion for it, in the generality of parishes throughout the kingdom, and must be daily less and less by the just severity of the laws, and the utter aversion of our people from that idolatrous superstition.

If I might be so bold as to name those who have the honour to be of his Lordship's party, I would venture to tell him, that pastors have much more occasion to study controversies against the several classes of freethinkers and dissenters; the former (I beg his Lordship's pardon for saying so) being a little worse than papists, and both of them more dangerous at present to our constitution both in church and state. Not that I think Presbytery so corrupt a system of Christian religion as Popery; I believe it is not above onethird as bad: but I think the Presbyterians, and their clans of other fanatics of freethinkers and atheists that dangle after them, are as well inclined to pull down the present establishment of monarchy and religion, as any set of Papists in Christendom, and therefore that our danger as things now stand, is infinitely greater from our Protestant enemies; because they are much more able to ruin us, and full as willing. There is no doubt, but Presbytery, and a commonwealth, are less formidable evils than Popery, slavery, and the Pretender; for if the fanatics were in power, I should be in more apprehension of being starved than burned. But there are probably in England forty dissenters of all kinds, including their brethren the freethinkers, for one papist; and, allowing one papist to be as terrible as three dissenters, it will appear by arithmetic, that we are thirteen times and onethird more in danger of being ruined by the latter than the former.

The other qualification necessary for all pastors, if they

will not be "blind, ignorant, greedy, drunken dogs," &c., is, "to know the depths of Satan." This is harder than the former; that a poor gentleman ought not to be parson, vicar, or curate of a parish, except he be cunninger than the devil. I am afraid it will be difficult to remedy this defect for one manifest reason, because whoever had only half the cunning of the devil, would never take up with a vicarage of £10 a-year, "to live on at his ease," as my Lord expresseth it; but seek out for some better livelihood. His Lordship is of a nation very much distinguished for that quality of cunning (though they have a great many better) and I think he was never accused for wanting his share. However upon a trial of skill I would venture to lay six to four on the devil's side, who must be allowed to be at least the older practitioner. Telling truth shames him, and resistance makes him fly: But to attempt outwitting him, is to fight him at his own weapon, and consequently no cunning at all. Another thing I would observe is, that a man may be "in the depths of Satan," without knowing them all, and such a man may be so far in Satan's depths as to be out of his own. One of the depths of Satan, is to counterfeit an angel of light. Another, I believe, is, to stir up the people against their governors, by false suggestions of danger. A third is to be a prompter to false brethren, and to send wolves about in sheep's clothing. Sometimes he sends Jesuits about England in the habit and cant of fanatics, at other times he has fanatic missionaries in the habits of ———. I shall mention but one more of Satan's depths, for I confess I know not the hundredth part of them; and that is, to employ his emissaries in crying out against remote imaginary dangers, by which we may be taken off from defending ourselves against those which are real and just at our elbows.

But his Lordship draws towards a conclusion, and bids us "look about, to consider the danger we are in, before it is too late;" for he assures us, we are already "going into some of the worst parts of popery;"[1] like the man who was so much in haste for his new coat, that he put it on the wrong side out. "Auricular confession, priestly absolution, and the sacrifice of the mass," have made great progress in

---

[1] Page 70.

England, and nobody has observed it: several other popish points "are carried higher with us than by the papists themselves."¹ And somebody, it seems, "had the impudence to propose a union with the Gallican church."² I have indeed heard that Mr Lesley³ published a discourse to that purpose, which I have never seen; nor do I perceive the evil in proposing an union between any two churches in Christendom. Without doubt Mr Lesley is most unhappily misled in his politics; but if he be the author of the late tract against Popery,⁴ he has given the world such a proof of his soundness in religion, as many a bishop ought to be proud of. I never saw the gentleman in my life: I know he is the son of a great and excellent prelate, who upon several accounts was one of the most extraordinary men of his age. Mr Lesley has written many useful discourses upon several subjects, and hath so well deserved of the Christian religion, and the Church of England in particular, that to accuse him of "impudence for proposing an union" in two very different faiths, is a style which I hope few will imitate. I detest Mr Lesley's political principles as much as his Lordship can do for his heart; but I verily believe he acts from a mistaken conscience, and therefore I distinguish between the principles and the person. However, it is some mortification to me, when I see an avowed nonjuror contribute more to the

---

¹ Page 70.
² Swift here disowns a charge loudly urged by the Whigs of the time against the high churchmen. There were, however, strong symptoms of a nearer approach on their part to the church of Rome. Hickes, the head of the Jacobite writers, had insinuated, that there was a proper sacrifice in the Eucharist; Brett had published a Sermon on the "Doctrine of Priestly Absolution as essential to Salvation;" Dodwell had written against Lay-Baptism, and his doctrine at once excluded all the dissenters (whose teachers are held as lay-men) from the pale of Christianity; and, upon the whole, there was a general disposition among the clergy to censure, if not the Reformation itself, at least the mode in which it was carried on. [S.]
³ Charles Lesley, or Leslie, the celebrated nonjuror. He published a Jacobite paper, called the "Rehearsal," and was a strenuous assertor of divine right; but he was also so steady a Protestant, that he went to Bar-le-Duc to convert the Chevalier de St George from the errors of Rome. [S.] See note on p. 63. [T. S.]
⁴ "The Case stated between the Church of Rome and the Church of England," 1713.

confounding of Popery, than could ever be done by a hundred thousand such Introductions as this.

His Lordship ends with discovering a small ray of comfort. "God be thanked there are many among us that stand upon the watch-tower, and that give faithful warning; that stand in the breach, and make themselves a wall for their church and country; that cry to God day and night, and lie in the dust mourning before him, to avert those judgments that seem to hasten towards us. They search into the mystery of iniquity that is working among us, and acquaint themselves with that mass of corruption that is in popery."[1] He prays "that the number of these may increase, and that he may be of that number, ready either to die in peace, or to seal that doctrine he has been preaching above fifty years, with his blood."[2] This being his last paragraph, I have made bold to transcribe the most important parts of it. His design is to end after the manner of orators, with leaving the strongest impression possible upon the minds of his hearers. A great breach is made; "the mystery of popish iniquity is working among us;" may God avert those "judgments that are hastening towards us!" I am an old man, "a preacher above fifty years," and I now expect and am ready to die a martyr for the doctrines I have preached. What an amiable idea does he here leave upon our minds, of Her Majesty and her government! He has been poring so long upon Fox's Book of Martyrs, that he imagines himself living in the reign of Queen Mary, and is resolved to set up for a knight-errant against Popery. Upon the supposition of his being in earnest, (which I am sure he is not) it would require but a very little more heat of imagination, to make a history of such a knight's adventures. What would he say, to behold the "fires kindled in Smithfield, and all over the town," on the 17th of November; to behold the Pope borne in triumph on the shoulders of the people, with a cardinal on the one side, and the Pretender on the other? He would never believe it was Queen Elizabeth's day, but that of her persecuting sister: In short, how easily might a windmill be taken for the whore of Babylon, and a puppet-show for a popish procession?

[1] Page 71.   [2] Page 72.

But enthusiasm is none of his Lordship's faculty: I am inclined to believe he might be melancholy enough when he writ this Introduction: The despair at his age of seeing a faction restored, to which he hath sacrificed so great a part of his life: The little success he can hope for in case he should resume those High-Church Principles, in defence of which he first employed his pen: No visible expectation of removing to Farnham or Lambeth: And lastly, the misfortune of being hated by every one, who either wears the habit, or values the profession of a clergyman: No wonder such a spirit, in such a situation, is provoked beyond the regards of truth, decency, religion, or self-conviction. To do him justice, he seems to have nothing else left, but to cry out, halters, gibbets, faggots, inquisition, Popery, slavery, and the Pretender. But in the meantime, he little considers what a world of mischief he does to his cause. It is very convenient, for the present designs of that faction, to spread the opinion of our immediate danger from Popery and the Pretender. His directors therefore ought, in my humble opinion, to have employed his Lordship in publishing a book, wherein he should have asserted, by the most solemn asseverations, that all things were safe and well; for the world has contracted so strong a habit of believing him backwards, that I am confident, nine parts in ten of those who have read or heard of his Introduction, have slept in greater security ever since. It is like the melancholy tone of a watchman at midnight, who thumps with his pole, as if some thief were breaking in, but you know by the noise, that the door is fast.

However, he "thanks God there are many among us who stand in the breach:" I believe they may; 'tis a breach of their own making, and they design to come forward, and storm and plunder, if they be not driven back. "They make themselves a wall for their church and country." A south wall, I suppose, for all the best fruit of the church and country to be nailed on. Let us examine this metaphor: The wall of our church and country is built of those who love the constitution in both: Our domestic enemies undermine some parts of the wall, and place themselves in the breach; and then they cry, "We are the wall!" We do not like such patchwork, they build with untempered mortar; nor can they ever cement with us, till they get better materials and better workmen: God keep us from having our breaches made up with such rubbish! "They stand upon the watch-tower;" they are indeed pragmatical enough to do so; but who assigned them that post, to give us false intelligence, to alarm us with false dangers, and send us to defend one gate, while their accomplices are breaking in at another? "They cry to God, day and night to avert the judgment of Popery which seems to hasten towards us." Then I affirm, they are hypocrites by day, and filthy dreamers by night. When they cry unto him, he will not hear them: For they cry against the plainest dictates of their own conscience, reason, and belief.

But lastly, "They lie in the dust, mourning before him." Hang me if I believe that, unless it be figuratively spoken. But suppose it to be true; why do "they lie in the dust?" Because they love to raise it: For what do "they mourn?" Why, for power, wealth, and places. There let the enemies of the Queen, and monarchy, and the church, lie, and mourn, and lick the dust, like serpents, till they are truly sensible of their ingratitude, falsehood, disobedience, slander, blasphemy, sedition, and every evil work!

I cannot find in my heart to conclude without offering his Lordship a little humble advice upon some certain points.

First, I would advise him, if it be not too late in his life, to endeavour a little at mending his style, which is mighty defective in the circumstances of grammar, propriety, politeness, and smoothness;[1] I fancied at first, it might be owing to the prevalence of his passion, as people sputter out nonsense for haste when they are in a rage. And indeed I believe this piece before me has received some additional imperfections from that occasion. But whoever has heard his sermons, or read his other tracts, will find him very unhappy in his choice and disposition of his words, and, for want of variety, repeating them, especially the particles, in a manner very grating to an English ear. But I confine myself to this Introduction, as his last work, where endeavouring at rhetorical flowers, he gives us only bunches of

[1] In Swift's notes on Burnet's "History of his Own Times," he points out many instances of the deficiency here stated. [S.]

THISTLES; of which I could present the reader with a plentiful crop; but I refer him to every page and line of the pamphlet itself.

Secondly, I would most humbly advise his Lordship to examine a little into the nature of truth, and sometimes to hear what she says. I shall produce two instances among a hundred. When he asserts that we are "now in more danger of Popery than toward the end of King Charles II.'s reign," and gives the broadest hints, that the Queen, the ministry, the parliament, and the clergy, are just going to introduce it; I desire to know, whether he really thinks truth is of his side, or whether he be not sure she is against him? If the latter, then truth and he will be found in two different stories; and which are we to believe? Again, when he gravely advises the clergy and laity of the Tory side, not to "light the fires in Smithfield," and goes on in twenty places already quoted, as if the bargain was made for Popery and slavery to enter: I ask again, whether he has rightly considered the nature of truth? I desire to put a parallel case. Suppose his Lordship should take it into his fancy to write and publish a letter to any gentleman of no infamous character for his religion or morals; and there advise him with great earnestness, not to rob or fire churches, ravish his daughter, or murder his father; show him the sin and the danger of these enormities, that if he flattered himself, he could escape in disguise, or bribe his jury, he was grievously mistaken: That he must in all probability forfeit his goods and chattels, die an ignominious death, and be cursed by posterity; Would not such a gentleman justly think himself highly injured, though his Lordship did not affirm that the said gentleman had his picklocks or combustibles ready, that he had attempted his daughter, and drawn his sword against his father in order to stab him? Whereas, in the other case, this writer affirms over and over, that all attempts for introducing Popery and slavery are already made, the whole business concerted, and that little less than a miracle can prevent our ruin.

Thirdly, I could heartily wish his Lordship would not undertake to charge the opinions of one or two, and those probably nonjurors, upon the whole body of the nation that differs from him. Mr Lesley writ a "Proposal for a Union with the Gallican Church;" somebody else has "carried the necessity of priesthood in the point of baptism farther than popery;" a third has " asserted the independency of the church on the state, and in many things arraigned the supremacy of the crown." Then he speaks in a dubious insinuating way, as if some other popish tenets had been already advanced: And at last concludes in this affected strain of despondency, "What will all these things end in? and on what design are they driven? Alas, it is too visible!" 'Tis as clear as the sun, that these authors are encouraged by the ministry with a design to bring in Popery; and in Popery all these things will end.

I never was so uncharitable as to believe, that the whole party of which his Lordship professeth himself a member, had a real formed design of establishing atheism among us. The reason why the Whigs have taken the atheists, or free-thinkers, into their body, is because they wholly agree in their political schemes, and differ very little in church power and discipline. However, I could turn the argument against his Lordship with very great advantage, by quoting passages from fifty pamphlets wholly made up of Whiggism and atheism, and then conclude; "What will all these things end in? And on what design are they driven? Alas, it is too visible!"

Lastly, I would beg his Lordship not to be so exceedingly outrageous upon the memory of the dead; because it is highly probable, that, in a very short time he will be one of the number. He has in plain words given Mr Wharton the character of a "most malicious, revengeful, treacherous, lying, mercenary villain." To which I shall only say, that the direct reverse of this amiable description is what appears from the works of that most learned divine, and from the accounts given me by those who knew him much better than the Bishop seems to have done. I meddle not with the moral part of his treatment. God Almighty forgive his Lordship this manner of revenging himself; and then there will be but little consequence from an accusation which the dead cannot feel, and which none of the living will believe.

# MR COLLINS'S DISCOURSE

OF

# FREETHINKING;

PUT INTO PLAIN ENGLISH,

BY WAY OF ABSTRACT,

## FOR THE USE OF THE POOR.

BY A FRIEND OF THE AUTHOR.

FIRST PRINTED IN 1713.

# NOTE.

OF the deistical writers of the early eighteenth century, Anthony Collins (1676-1729) is, perhaps, the most celebrated. He was born near Hounslow and educated at Eton and Cambridge. His writings were mainly attacks on Christianity, and, in addition to the "Discourse on Freethinking," he published: "Discourse of the Grounds and Reasons of the Christian Religion;" "Scheme of Literal Prophecy Considered;" "Priestcraft in Perfection;" "Historical and Critical Essay on the Thirty-Nine Articles;" and "A Philosophical Enquiry concerning Human Liberty." Most of these writings engaged him in many and violent controversies with some of the ablest divines of his time. Among these, beside Swift, may be named, Whiston, Hare, Hoadly, Bentley, and Samuel Clarke. Steele, also, had his fling at Collins, and thought that "if ever man deserved to be denied the common benefits of air and water, it is the author of 'A Discourse upon Freethinking'" ("Guardian," No. 3). But then Steele's opinion on such a matter was of no great moment. What was of more, was the fact that the school to which Collins belonged found a decided opponent in Locke, from the writings of whom the members of the school professed to draw their strongest arguments. For a philosophical appreciation of Toland, Collins, and the rest, see Mr. Leslie Stephen's "English Thought in the Eighteenth Century" (chaps. iii. and iv. of vol. i. 1881).

Swift took an entirely different attitude towards Collins from that assumed by the professional controversialists. He refused to take him seriously, and no doubt he felt that ridicule would as effectually serve his purpose as another method. Moreover, he sought to use the opportunity for scoring a point against the Whigs, by insisting on the political side of the matter, and, in the person of an assumed defender of Collins, betrayed undoubted Whig leanings. Swift, at this time, was deep in work, pamphleteering for Harley and St. John. He had already written "The Conduct of the Allies," and "Some Remarks on the Barrier Treaty," and was soon to write "The Public Spirit of the Whigs." The assumed and sarcastic defence of Collins must be taken as a Swiftian dodge to bring odium and suspicion on the opponents of the Tory ministry, by showing that the propounders of the hateful and ridiculous atheism were themselves Whigs.

Sir Henry Craik, in a note to his reprint of this tract ("Selections from Swift," Oxford, 1893, vol. ii. p. 42), agrees with Scott as to the motive which urged Swift in writing it. "In this later tract," he says, "Swift makes no attempt to cloak his enmity; and he boldly assumes the character of a Whig as the propounder of those atheistical absurdities, which he wished, as a useful political move, but without any scrupulous regard to fairness, to represent as part and parcel of the tenets of that party." "What gave colour," says Scott, "though only a colour, to his charge was, that Toland, Tindal, Collins, and most of those who carried to licence their abhorrence of Church-government, were naturally enough enrolled among that party in politics who professed most attachment to freedom of sentiment." It must not, however, be forgotten, that Swift's attachment to his Church, as it influenced him against the Whigs, would naturally influence him against the deistical writers also, and that he must be credited, to that extent, with honesty of purpose. That these writers were Whigs was, if one may so put it, an accident, of which it would have been more than a human act for Swift not to take advantage, for party purposes.

Curiously enough, none of Swift's more modern biographers have thought this imitation of Collins's "Discourse" worthy of a mention; yet it is, in its way, as fine a performance as his castigation of Bishop Burnet and his "Introduction." The fooling is admirably carried on, and the intention, as explained in the introduction, is excellently well realized. It frightened Collins into Holland. To appreciate the cleverness with which it has been done, one should read Swift's "Abstract" side by side with Collins's "Discourse."

The pamphlet was advertised for sale in "The Examiner" for Tuesday, January 26th, 1712-13. In his "Letters to Stella" (January 16th and 21st, 1712-13), Swift makes the following references to it: "I came home at seven, and began a little whim which just came into my head, and will make a three-penny pamphlet. It shall be finished in a week; and, if it succeeds, you shall know what it is; otherwise not. . . . I was to-day with my printer, to give him a little pamphlet I have written; but not politics. It will be out by Monday."

The present text is based on that of the first edition, collated with those given by Nichols, Hawkesworth and Scott. None of the "Miscellanies" prints this tract, nor is it given in Faulkner's edition of 1735-38 (6 vols.). It is fully annotated and edited by Nichols in the first volume of his "Supplement to Swift's Works" (1779).

[T. S.]

# Mr. C——ns's
# DISCOURSE
# OF
# 𝔉ree-𝔗hinking,

Put into plain *English*, by way of

# ABSTRACT,

FOR THE

# Use of the Poor.

---

*By a Friend of the* AUTHOR.

---

*LONDON*,
Printed for *John Morphew*, near *Stationers-Hall*, 1713.   Price 4 *d*.

# MR. COLLINS'S DISCOURSE OF FREE-THINKING; PUT INTO PLAIN ENGLISH, BY WAY OF ABSTRACT, FOR THE USE OF THE POOR.

## INTRODUCTION.

*OUR party having failed, by all their political arguments, to re-establish their power; the wise leaders have determined, that the last and principal remedy should be made use of, for opening the eyes of this blinded nation; and that a short, but perfect, system of their divinity, should be published, to which we are all of us ready to subscribe, and which we lay down as a model, bearing a close analogy to our schemes in religion. Crafty, designing men, that they might keep the world in awe, have, in their several forms of government, placed a* Supreme Power *on earth, to keep human-kind in fear of being hanged; and a supreme power in heaven, for fear of being damned. In order to cure men's apprehensions of the former, several of our learned members have writ many profound treatises on Anarchy; but a brief complete body of Atheology seemed yet wanting, till this irrefragable Discourse appeared. However, it so happens, that our ablest brethren, in their elaborate disquisitions upon this subject, have written with so much caution, that ignorant unbelievers have edified very little by them. I grant that those daring spirits, who first adventured to write against the direct rules of the gospel, the current of antiquity, the religion of the magistrate, and the laws of the land, had some measures to keep; and particularly when they railed at religion, were in the right to use little artful disguises, by which a jury could only find them guilty of abusing heathenism or popery. But the mystery is now revealed, that there is no such thing as mystery or revelation; and though our friends are out of place and power, yet we may have so much confidence in the present ministry, to be secure, that those who suffer so many free speeches against their sovereign and themselves, to pass unpunished, will never resent our expressing the freest thoughts against their religion; but think with Tiberius, that if there be a God, he is able enough to revenge any injuries done to himself, without expecting the civil power to interpose.*[1]

*By these reflections I was brought to think, that the most ingenious author of the Discourse upon Freethinking, in a letter to Somebody, Esq.; although he hath used less reserve than any of his predecessors, might yet have been more free and open. I considered, that several well-willers to infidelity, might be discouraged by a show of logic, and a multiplicity of quotations, scattered through his book, which to understandings of that size, might carry an appearance of something like booklearning, and consequently fright them from reading for their improvement: I could see no reason why these great discoveries should be hid from our youth of quality, who frequent White's and Tom's; why they should not be adapted to the capacities of the Kit-Cat and Hanover Clubs,*[2] *who might then be able to read lectures on them to their several toasts: and it will be allowed on all hands, that nothing can sooner help to restore our abdicated cause, than a firm universal belief of the principles laid down by this sublime author.*

*For I am sensible that nothing would more contribute to "the continuance of the war," and the restoration of the late ministry, than to have the doctrines delivered in this treatise well infused into the people. I have therefore compiled them into the following Abstract, wherein I have adhered to the very words of our author, only adding some few explanations of my own, where the terms happen to be too learned, and consequently a little beyond the comprehension of those for whom the work was principally intended, I mean the nobility and gentry of our*

---

[1] Swift was evidently very fond of this reference, since he uses it several times in his writings. [T. S.]

[2] These were chocolate houses of the time, supported mainly by the aristocracy and the gamblers. White's is still in existence, and has had the honour of having had a special history written about it. Tom's was in Russell Street, and so-called after its landlord, Tom West. The Kit-Cat Club was the resort of the Whig wits of the day, and the Hanover Club of those who favoured the Hanover succession. [T. S.]

*party. After which I hope it will be impossible for the malice of a Jacobite, highflying, priestridden faction, to misrepresent us. The few additions I have made are for no other use than to help the transition, which could not otherwise be kept in an abstract; but I have not presumed to advance anything of my own; which besides would be needless to an author who hath so fully handled and demonstrated every particular. I shall only add, that though this writer, when he speaks of priests, desires chiefly to be understood to mean the English clergy, yet he includes all priests whatsoever, except the ancient and modern heathens, the Turks, Quakers, and Socinians.*

## THE LETTER.

SIR,

I SEND you this apology for Freethinking,[1] without the least hopes of doing good, but purely to comply with your request; for those truths which nobody can deny, will do no good to those who deny them. The clergy, who are so impudent to teach the people the doctrines of faith, are all either cunning knaves or mad fools; for none but artificial, designing men, and crack-brained enthusiasts, presume to be guides to others in matters of speculation, which all the doctrines of Christianity are; and whoever has a mind to learn the Christian religion, naturally chooses such knaves and fools to teach them. Now the Bible, which contains the precepts of the priests' religion, is the most difficult book in the world to be understood; it requires a thorough knowledge in natural, civil, ecclesiastical history, law, husbandry, sailing, physic, pharmacy, mathematics, metaphysics, ethics, and everything else that can be named: And everybody who believes it ought to understand it, and must do so by force of his own freethinking, without any guide or instructor.

How can a man think at all, if he does not think freely? A man who does not eat and drink freely, does not eat and drink at all. Why may not I be denied the liberty of free-

---

[1] The chief strain of Collins's "Discourse" is an eulogium upon the necessity and advantage of Freethinking; in which it is more than insinuated that the advocates of revealed religion are enemies to the progress of enlightened inquiry. This insidious position is ridiculed in the following parody. [S.]

seeing, as well as freethinking? Yet nobody pretends that the first is unlawful, for a cat may look on a king; though you be near-sighted, or have weak or sore eyes, or are blind, you may be a free-seer; you ought to see for yourself, and not trust to a guide to choose the colour of your stockings, or save you from falling into a ditch.

In like manner, there ought to be no restraint at all on thinking freely upon any proposition, however impious or absurd. There is not the least hurt in the wickedest thoughts, provided they be free; nor in telling those thoughts to everybody, and endeavouring to convince the world of them; for all this is included in the doctrine of freethinking, as I shall plainly show you in what follows; and therefore you are all along to understand the word freethinking in this sense.

If you are apt to be afraid of the devil, think freely of him, and you destroy him and his kingdom. Freethinking has done him more mischief than all the clergy in the world ever could do; they believe in the devil, they have an interest in him, and therefore are the great supports of his kingdom. The devil was in the States-General before they began to be freethinkers. For England and Holland[1] were formerly the Christian territories of the devil; I told you how he left Holland; and freethinking and the revolution banished him from England; I defy all the clergy to shew me when they ever had such success against him. My meaning is, that to think freely of the devil, is to think there is no devil at all; and he that thinks so, the devil's in him if he be afraid of the devil.

But, within these two or three years, the devil has come into England again, and Dr Sacheverell[2] has given him commission to appear in the shape of a cat, and carry old women about upon broomsticks: And the devil has now so many "ministers ordained to his service," that they have rendered freethinking odious, and nothing but the second coming of Christ can restore it.

The priests tell me, I am to believe the Bible, but freethinking tells me otherwise in many particulars: The Bible says, the Jews were a nation favoured by God; but I who

[1] Collins is supposed to have imbibed his freethinking philosophy during his repeated visits to Holland. [S.]
[2] See note on p. 147.

am a freethinker say, that cannot be, because the Jews lived in a corner of the earth, and freethinking makes it clear, that those who live in corners cannot be favourites of God. The New Testament all along asserts the truth of Christianity, but freethinking denies it; because Christianity was communicated but to a few; and whatever is communicated but to a few, cannot be true; for that is like whispering, and the proverb says, that there is no whispering without lying.

Here is a society in London for propagating freethinking throughout the world, encouraged and supported by the Queen and many others. You say, perhaps, it is for propagating the Gospel. Do you think the missionaries we send will tell the heathens that they must not think freely? No, surely; why then, it is manifest, those missionaries must be freethinkers, and make the heathens so too. But why should not the king of Siam, whose religion is heathenism and idolatry, send over a parcel of his priests to convert us to his church, as well as we send missionaries there? Both projects are exactly of a piece, and equally reasonable; and if those heathen priests were here, it would be our duty to hearken to them, and think freely whether they may not be in the right rather than we. I heartily wish a detachment of such divines as Dr Atterbury, Dr Smallridge,[1] Dr Swift, Dr Sacheverell, and some others, were sent every year to the farthest part of the heathen world, and that we had a cargo of their priests in return, who would spread freethinking among us; then the war would go on, the late ministry be restored, and faction cease, which our priests inflame by haranguing upon texts, and falsely call that preaching the Gospel.

I have another project in my head, which ought to be put in execution, in order to make us freethinkers: It is a great hardship and injustice, that our priests must not be disturbed while they are prating in the pulpit. For example: Why should not William Penn the Quaker, or any Anabaptist, Papist, Muggletonian, Jew, or Sweet-Singer,[2] have liberty to

---

[1] Dr. Smallridge, it will be remembered, was the gentleman who indignantly denied the authorship of "A Tale of a Tub" (see vol. i. of this edition). He became Bishop of Bristol in 1714, and died in 1719. His style was well thought of at the time. [T. S.]

[2] The Sweet-Singers were a fanatical sect of wailers, founded in Scotland, but which had no long life. [T. S.]

come into St Paul's Church, in the midst of divine service, and endeavour to convert first the aldermen, then the preacher, and singing-men? Or pray, why might not poor Mr Whiston,[1] who denies the divinity of Christ, be allowed to come into the Lower House of Convocation, and convert the clergy? But, alas! we are overrun with such false notions, that, if Penn or Whiston should do their duty, they would be reckoned fanatics, and disturbers of the holy synod, although they have as good a title to it as St Paul had to go into the synagogues of the Jews; and their authority is full as divine as his.

Christ himself commands us to be freethinkers; for he bids us search the scriptures, and take heed what and whom we hear; by which he plainly warns us, not to believe our bishops and clergy; for Jesus Christ, when he considered that all the Jewish and heathen priests, whose religion he came to abolish, were his enemies, rightly concluded that those appointed by him to preach his own gospel, would probably be so too; and could not be secure, that any set of priests, of the faith he delivered, would ever be otherwise; therefore it is fully demonstrated that the clergy of the Church of England are mortal enemies to Christ, and ought not to be believed.

But, without the privilege of freethinking, how is it possible to know which is the right Scripture? Here are perhaps twenty sorts of Scriptures in the several parts of the world, and every set of priests contend that their Scripture is the true one. The Indian Brahmins have a book of scripture called the Shaster; the Persees their Zundivastaw;[2] the Bonzes in China have theirs, written by the disciples of Fo-he, whom they call *God and Saviour of the world, who was born to teach the way of salvation, and to give satisfaction for all men's sins:* which, you see, is directly the same with what our priests pretend of Christ. And must we not think

---

[1] Yet Whiston, who receives this side-cut, was himself an anxious combatant of Collins, in his "Reflections on an Anonymous Pamphlet, entitled, 'A Defence of Freethinking.'" 1713. [S.]

[2] Swift means here, of course, the Zendavesta, the commentaries on the sacred books of the Parsees. Not that Swift could have known much of these Oriental religions; but the names were good enough for his purpose. [T. S]

freely, to find out which are in the right, whether the Bishops or the Bonzes? But the Talapoins, or heathen clergy of Siam, approach yet nearer to the system of our priests; they have a Book of Scripture written by Sommonocodam, who, the Siamese say, was "born of a virgin," and was "the God expected by the Universe;" just as our priests tell us, that Jesus Christ was born of the Virgin Mary, and was the Messiah so long expected. The Turkish priests, or dervises, have their Scripture which they call the Alcoran. The Jews have the Old Testament for their Scripture, and the Christians have both the Old and the New. Now among all these Scriptures, there cannot above one be right; and how is it possible to know which is that, without reading them all, and then thinking freely, every one of us for ourselves, without following the advice or instruction of any guide, before we venture to choose? The parliament ought to be at the charge of finding a sufficient number of these Scriptures, for every one of Her Majesty's subjects, for there are twenty to one against us, that we may be in the wrong: But a great deal of freethinking will at last set us all right, and every one will adhere to the Scripture he likes best; by which means, religion, peace, and wealth, will be for ever secured in Her Majesty's realms.

And it is the more necessary that the good people of England should have liberty to choose some other Scripture, because all Christian priests differ so much about the copies of theirs, and about the various readings of the several manuscripts, which quite destroys the authority of the Bible: for what authority can a book pretend to, where there are various readings?[1] And for this reason, it is manifest that no man can know the opinions of Aristotle or Plato, or believe the facts related by Thucydides or Livy, or be pleased with the poetry of Homer and Virgil, all which books are utterly useless, upon account of their various readings. Some books of Scripture are said to be lost, and this utterly destroys the credit of those that are left: some we reject, which the Africans and Copticks receive; and why may we not think freely, and reject the rest? Some think

---

[1] In the discourse on "Freethinking," p. 80, Collins insists much on a passage in Victor of Tunis, from which he infers, that the Gospels were corrected and altered in the fourth century. [S.]

the scriptures wholly inspired, some partly; and some not at all. Now this is just the very case of the Bramins, Persees, Bonzes, Talapoins, Dervises, Rabbis, and all other priests, who build their religion upon books, as our priests do upon their Bibles; they all equally differ about the copies, various readings and inspirations, of their several Scriptures, and God knows which are in the right: Freethinking alone can determine it.

It would be endless to show in how many particulars the priests of the Heathen and Christian churches, differ about the meaning even of those Scriptures which they universally receive as sacred. But, to avoid prolixity, I shall confine myself to the different opinions among the priests of the Church of England, and here only give you a specimen, because even these are too many to be enumerated.

I have found out a bishop, (though indeed his opinions are condemned by all his brethren,) who allows the Scriptures to be so difficult, that God has left them rather as a trial of our industry than a repository of our faith, and furniture of creeds and articles of belief; with several other admirable schemes of freethinking, which you may consult at your leisure.

The doctrine of the Trinity is the most fundamental point of the whole Christian religion. Nothing is more easy to a freethinker, yet what different notions of it do the English priests pretend to deduce from Scripture, explaining it by "specific unities, eternal modes of subsistence," and the like unintelligible jargon? Nay, it is a question whether this doctrine be fundamental or no; for though Dr South and Bishop Bull affirm it, yet Bishop Taylor and Dr Wallis deny it.[1] And that excellent freethinking prelate, Bishop Taylor,

---

[1] Dr. Robert South (1633-1716), rector of Islip. The reference by Swift is to his controversy with Sherlock on the doctrine of the Trinity. The two disputants got into such depths that both were charged with heresy.

Dr. George Bull (1634-1710), Bishop of St. David's, wrote the "Defensio Fidei Nicenæ." For his exposition of the necessity for the belief in the divinity of the Son of God he received the thanks of Bossuet.

Dr. Jeremy Taylor, Bishop of Down and Connor (1613-1667), and author of "Holy Living" and "Holy Dying," wrote also "Unum Necessarium, or the Doctrine and Practice of Repentance." His treatment, in this work, of the doctrine of original sin was considered

observes, that Athanasius's example was followed with too much greediness; by which means it has happened, that the greater number of our priests are in that sentiment, and think it necessary to believe the Trinity, and incarnation of Christ.[1]

Our priests likewise dispute several circumstances about the resurrection of the dead, the nature of our bodies after the resurrection, and in what manner they shall be united to our souls. They also attack one another "very weakly with great vigour," about predestination. And it is certainly true, (for Bishop Taylor and Mr Whiston the Socinian say so,) that all churches in prosperity alter their doctrines every age, and are neither satisfied with themselves, nor their own confessions; neither does any clergyman of sense believe the Thirty-nine Articles.

Our priests differ about the eternity of hell torments. The famous Dr Henry More,[2] and the most pious and rational of all priests, Dr Tillotson,[3] (both freethinkers,) believe them to be not eternal. They differ about keeping the sabbath, the divine right of episcopacy, and the doctrine of original sin; which is the foundation of the whole Christian religion; for if men are not liable to be damned for Adam's sin, the Christian religion is an imposture: Yet this is now disputed among them; so is lay baptism; so was formerly the lawfulness of usury, but now the priests are common stock-jobbers, attorneys, and scriveners. In short there is no end of

heterodox by Bishop Warner and Dr. Sanderson, and a controversy ensued, in the course of which Taylor was imprisoned in Chepstow Castle on a charge of being concerned in a Royalist insurrection.
Dr. John Wallis (1616-1703), here referred to, is the famous mathematician and divine, and one of the original members of the Royal Society. He is mentioned in the text by Swift because of a work he published on the Trinity, which brought him into collision with the Arians. But the Doctor seems to have been addicted to views of a controversial nature, for his opinions on infant baptism and the keeping of the Sabbath found many objectors. He was Savilian Professor of Geometry at Oxford in 1648. [T. S.]

[1] See Swift's opinion of controversies on this subject in his "Sermon upon the Trinity." [S.]

[2] Dr. Henry More (1614-1687), the Platonist theologian, wrote a philosophical poem entitled, "Psycho-Zoia, or the Life of the Soul" (1640). [T.S.]

[3] Dr. John Tillotson (1630-1694) succeeded Sancroft as Archbishop of Canterbury. He published some eloquent sermons and several controversial tracts against Catholicism. [T. S.]

disputing among priests, and therefore I conclude, that there ought to be no such thing in the world as priests, teachers, or guides, for instructing ignorant people in religion; but that every man ought to think freely for himself.

I will tell you the meaning in all this; the priests dispute every point in the Christian religion, as well as almost every text in the Bible; and the force of my argument lies here, that whatever point is disputed by one or two divines, however condemned by the Church, not only that particular point, but the whole article to which it relates, may lawfully be received or rejected by any freethinker. For instance, suppose More and Tillotson deny the eternity of hell torments, a freethinker may deny all future punishments whatsoever. The priests dispute about explaining the Trinity; therefore a freethinker may reject one or two, or the whole three persons; at least he may reject Christianity, because the Trinity is the most fundamental doctrine of that religion. So I affirm original sin, and that men are now liable to be damned for Adam's sin, to be the foundation of the whole Christian religion; but this point was formerly, and is now disputed, therefore, a freethinker may deny the whole. And I cannot help giving you one farther direction, how I insinuate all along, that the wisest freethinking priests, whom you may distinguish by the epithets I bestow them, were those who differed most from the generality of their brethren.

But besides, the conduct of our priests in many other points, makes freethinking unavoidable; for some of them own, that the doctrines of the Church are contradictory to one another, as well as to reason; which I thus prove: Dr Sacheverell says in his speech at his trial, That by abandoning passive obedience we must render ourselves the most inconsistent Church in the world: Now 'tis plain, that one inconsistency could not make the most inconsistent Church in the world; *ergo*, there must have been a great many inconsistencies and contradictory doctrines in the Church before. Dr South describes the incarnation of Christ, as an astonishing mystery, impossible to be conceived by man's reason; *ergo*, it is contradictory to itself, and to reason, and ought to be exploded by all freethinkers.

Another instance of the priests' conduct, which multiplies freethinkers, is their acknowledgment of abuses, defects, and false doctrines, in the Church; particularly that of eating black pudding,[1] which is so plainly forbid in the Old and New Testament, that I wonder those who pretend to believe a syllable in either will presume to taste it. Why should I mention the want of discipline, and of a sideboard at the altar, with complaints of other great abuses and defects made by some of the priests, which no man can think on without freethinking, and consequently rejecting Christianity?

When I see an honest freethinking bishop endeavour to destroy the power and privileges of the Church, and Dr Atterbury angry with him for it, and calling it "dirty work," what can I conclude, by virtue of being a freethinker, but that Christianity is all a cheat?

Mr Whiston has published several tracts, wherein he absolutely denies the divinity of Christ: A bishop tells him, "Sir, in any matter where you have the Church's judgment against you, you should be careful not to break the peace of the Church, by writing against it, though you are sure you are in the right."[2] Now my opinion is directly contrary; and I affirm, that if ten thousand freethinkers thought differently from the received doctrine, and from each other, they would be all in duty bound to publish their thoughts (provided they were all sure of being in the right) though it broke the peace of the Church and state ten thousand times.

And here I must take leave to tell you, although you cannot but have perceived it from what I have already said, and shall be still more amply convinced by what is to follow; that freethinking signifies nothing, without freespeaking and freewriting. It is the indispensable duty of a freethinker, to endeavour forcing all the world to think as he does, and by that means make them freethinkers too. You are also to understand, that I allow no man to be a freethinker, any further than as he differs from the received doctrines of religion. Where a man falls in, though by perfect chance,

---

[1] Collins in his pamphlet quotes a Dr. Grabe, who, following the Jewish code of rules as regards food, considered the eating of blood one of the points on which the Church did not insist against. In the text Swift ridicules this in the reference to "black pudding." [T. S.]

[2] Swift's "Sermon on the Trinity," as well as a passage in his "Thoughts upon Religion," shews the weight which he attached to this important argument. [S.]

with what is generally believed, he is in that point a confined and limited thinker; and you shall see by and by, that I celebrate those for the noblest freethinkers in every age, who differed from the religion of their countries in the most fundamental points, and especially in those which bear any analogy to the chief fundamentals of religion among us.

Another trick of the priests is, to charge all men with atheism, who have more wit than themselves; which therefore I expect will be my case for writing this discourse: This is what makes them so implacable against Mr Gildon, Dr Tindal, Mr Toland,[1] and myself, and when they call us wits, atheists, it provokes us to be freethinkers.

Again; the priests cannot agree when their Scripture was written. They differ about the number of canonical books, and the various readings. Now those few among us who understand Latin, are careful to tell this to our disciples, who presently fall a-freethinking, that the Bible is a book not to be depended upon in anything at all.

There is another thing, that mightily spreads freethinking, which I believe you would hardly guess. The priests have got a way of late of writing books against freethinking; I mean treatises in dialogue, where they introduce atheists, deists, sceptics, and Socinians offering their several arguments. Now these freethinkers are too hard for the priests themselves in their own books; and how can it be otherwise? For if the arguments usually offered by atheists, are fairly represented in these books, they must needs convert everybody that reads them; because atheists, deists, sceptics, and Socinians, have certainly better arguments to maintain their opinions, than any the priests can produce to maintain the contrary.

Mr Creech,[2] a priest, translated Lucretius into English, which is a complete system of atheism; and several young students, who were afterwards priests, wrote verses in praise of this translation. The arguments against Providence in that book are so strong, that they have added mightily to the number of freethinkers.

Why should I mention the pious cheats of the priests,

---

[1] See notes on pp. 9, 79, 80, 82.
[2] This is Thomas Creech, the translator of Horace, to whom Swift refers in "The Battle of the Books" (see vol. i. p. 180). The translation of Lucretius was published in English verse in 1682. [T. S.]

who in the New Testament translate the word *ecclesia* sometimes the *church*, and sometimes the *congregation ;* and *episcopus*, sometimes a *bishop*, and sometimes an *overseer ?* A priest,[1] translating a book, left out a whole passage that reflected on the king, by which he was an enemy to political freethinking, a most considerable branch of our system. Another priest, translating a book of travels,[2] left out a lying miracle, out of mere malice, to conceal an argument for freethinking. In short, these frauds are very common in all books which are published by priests: But however, I love to excuse them whenever I can: And as to this accusation, they may plead the authority of the ancient fathers of the Church, for forgery, corruption, and mangling of authors, with more reason than for any of their articles of faith. St Jerom, St Hilary, Eusebius Vercellensis, Victorinus,[3] and several others, were all guilty of arrant forgery and corruption: For when they translated the works of several freethinkers, whom they called heretics, they omitted all their heresies or freethinkings, and had the impudence to own it to the world.

From these many notorious instances of the priests' conduct, I conclude they are not to be relied on in any one

---

[1] Collins refers to the Rev. Mr. Brown, who translated Father Paul's "Letters," and omitted the words, "If the King of England [James I.] were not more a doctor than a king."

[2] Baumgarten's "Travels." [T. S.]

[3] Jerome, or St. Hieronymus (*circa* 340-420), wrote the Latin vulgate translation of the Scriptures. Is accepted as one of the Fathers of the Church.

St. Hilary, another accepted Father, was bishop of Poictiers. He died 367 or 368.

The Eusebius here named was Bishop of Vercelli, a city of Liguria. He flourished about A.D. 360, and distinguished himself at the Council of Milan in A.D. 355, for his attacks against Arianism. He was exiled to Upper Thebais, with several other bishops who refused to subscribe to the condemnation of Athanasius; but was recalled with Lucifer, bishop of Cagliari, Sardinia. In conjunction with Athanasius he attended an Alexandrian synod which declared the Trinity consubstantial. He travelled much in the Eastern provinces and Italy, engaging in missionary work. He died about A.D. 373.

Fabius Marius Victorinus was born in Africa, and died at Rome in 370. He was a distinguished orator, grammarian, and rhetorician. His chief work was a treatise entitled "De Orthographia." He also wrote many theological books. [T.S.]

thing relating to religion; but that every man must think freely for himself.

But to this it may be objected, that the bulk of mankind is as well qualified for flying as thinking, and if every man thought it his duty to think freely, and trouble his neighbour with his thoughts (which is an essential part of freethinking,) it would make wild work in the world. I answer; whoever cannot think freely, may let it alone if he pleases, by virtue of his right to think freely; that is to say, if such a man freely thinks that he cannot think freely, of which every man is a sufficient judge, why, then, he need not think freely, unless he thinks fit.

Besides, if the bulk of mankind cannot think freely in matters of speculation, as the being of a God, the immortality of the soul, &c. why then, freethinking is indeed no duty: But then the priests must allow, that men are not concerned to believe whether there is a God or no. But still those who are disposed to think freely, may think freely if they please.

It is again objected, that freethinking will produce endless divisions in opinion, and by consequence disorder society. To which I answer;

When every single man comes to have a different opinion every day from the whole world, and from himself, by virtue of freethinking, and thinks it his duty to convert every man to his own freethinking (as all we freethinkers do) how can that possibly create so great a diversity of opinions, as to have a set of priests agree among themselves to teach the same opinions in their several parishes to all who will come to hear them? Besides, if all people were of the same opinion, the remedy would be worse than the disease; I will tell you the reason some other time.

Besides, difference in opinion, especially in matters of great moment, breeds no confusion at all. Witness Papist and Protestant, Roundhead and Cavalier, Whig and Tory, now among us. I observe, the Turkish empire is more at peace within itself, than Christian princes are with one another. Those noble Turkish virtues of charity and toleration, are what contribute chiefly to the flourishing state of that happy monarchy. There Christians and Jews are tolerated, and live at ease, if they can hold their tongues and think freely, provided they never set foot within the mosques, nor write against Mahomet: A few plunderings now and then by the janissaries are all they have to fear.

It is objected, that by freethinking, men will think themselves into atheism; and indeed I have allowed all along, that atheistical books convert men to freethinking. But suppose that to be true; I can bring you two divines who affirm superstition and enthusiasm to be worse than atheism, and more mischievous to society, and in short it is necessary that the bulk of the people should be atheists or superstitious.

It is objected, that priests ought to be relied on by the people, as lawyers and physicians, because it is their faculty.

I answer, 'Tis true, a man who is no lawyer is not suffered to plead for himself; but every man may be his own quack if he pleases, and he only ventures his life; but in the other case the priest tells him he must be damned: Therefore do not trust the priest, but think freely for yourself, and if you happen to think there is no hell, there certainly is none, and consequently you cannot be damned; I answer further, that wherever there is no lawyer, physician, or priest, the country is paradise. Besides, all priests, (except the orthodox, and those are not ours, nor any that I know,) are hired by the public to lead men into mischief; but lawyers and physicians are not, you hire them yourself.

It is objected, (by priests no doubt, but I have forgot their names,) that false speculations are necessary to be imposed upon men, in order to assist the magistrate in keeping the peace, and that men ought therefore to be deceived, like children, for their own good. I answer, that zeal for imposing speculations, whether true or false (under which name of speculations I include all opinions of religion, as the belief of a God, Providence, immortality of the soul, future rewards and punishments, &c.) has done more hurt than it is possible for religion to do good. It puts us to the charge of maintaining ten thousand priests in England, which is a burden upon society never felt upon any other occasion; and a greater evil to the public than if these ecclesiastics were only employed in the most innocent offices of life, which I take to be eating and drinking. Now if you offer to impose anything on mankind besides what relates to moral duties, as to pay your debts, not pick pockets, nor commit murder, and the like; that is to say, if, besides this, you oblige them to believe in God and Jesus Christ, what you add to their faith will take just so much off from their morality. By this argument it is manifest, that a perfect moral man must be a perfect atheist; every inch of religion he gets loses him an inch of morality: For there is a certain *quantum* belongs to every man, of which there is nothing to spare. This is clear from the common practice of all our priests, they never once preach to you to love your neighbour, to be just in your dealings, or to be sober and temperate. The streets of London are full of common whores, publicly tolerated in their wickedness; yet the priests make no complaints against this enormity, either from the pulpit or the press: I can affirm, that neither you nor I, sir, have ever heard one sermon against whoring since we were boys. No, the priests allow all these vices, and love us the better for them, provided we will promise not "to harangue upon a text," nor to sprinkle a little water in a child's face, which they call baptizing, and would engross it all to themselves.

Besides, the priests engage all the rogues, villains, and fools in their party, in order to make it as large as they can: By this means they seduced Constantine the Great[1] over to their religion, who was the first Christian emperor, and so horrible a villain, that the heathen priests told him they could not expiate his crimes in their church; so he was at a loss to know what to do, till an Ægyptian bishop assured him, that there was no villainy so great, but was to be expiated by the sacraments of the Christian religion; upon which he became a Christian, and to him that religion owes its first settlement.

It is objected, that freethinkers themselves are the most infamous, wicked, and senseless of all mankind.

I answer, first, we say the same of priests, and other believers. But the truth is, men of all sects are equally good and bad; for no religion whatsoever contributes in the least to mend men's lives.

I answer, secondly, that freethinkers use their understanding, but those who have religion do not; therefore the first

[1] The reference here is to the luminous cross which Constantine said he saw in the heavens, and which influenced him to embrace Christianity. [T. S.]

have more understanding than the others; witness Toland, Tindal, Gildon, Clendon,[1] Coward, and myself. For, use legs and have legs.

I answer, thirdly, that freethinkers are the most virtuous persons in the world; for all freethinkers must certainly differ from the priests, and from nine hundred ninety-nine of a thousand of those among whom they live; and are therefore virtuous of course, because everybody hates them.

I answer, fourthly, that the most virtuous people in all ages have been freethinkers; of which I shall produce several instances.[2]

Socrates was a freethinker; for he disbelieved the gods of his country, and the common creeds about them, and declared his dislike when he heard men attribute "repentance, anger, and other passions to the gods, and talk of wars and battles in heaven, and of the gods getting women with child," and such like fabulous and blasphemous stories. I pick out these particulars, because they are the very same with what the priests have in their Bibles, where repentance and anger are attributed to God; where it is said, there was "war in heaven;" and that "the Virgin Mary was with child by the Holy Ghost," whom the priests call God; all fabulous and blasphemous stories. Now, I affirm Socrates to have been a true Christian. You will ask, perhaps, how that can be, since he lived three or four hundred years before Christ? I answer, with Justin Martyr, that Christ is nothing else but reason, and I hope you do not think Socrates lived before reason. Now, this true Christian Socrates never made notions, speculations, or mysteries, any part of his religion, but demonstrated all men to be fools who troubled themselves with enquiries into heavenly things. Lastly, 'tis plain

[1] John Clendon, of the Middle Temple, published in 1709-1710, "Tractatus Philosophico-Theologicus de Persona; or, a Treatise of the Word Person." This singular book appears to have been written principally to prove that the doctrine of the Trinity was very well explained by an Act of Parliament, 9 and 10 Will. III. It was complained of in the House of Commons, March 25th, 1710, and was judged to be a scandalous, seditious, and blasphemous libel . . . . and was burnt by the common hangman at the same time with Tindal's "Rights." [N.]

[2] What follows is in ridicule of a long list of freethinkers, as he calls them, with which Collins has graced his discourse; in which he includes not only the ancient philosophers, but the inspired prophets, and even "King Solomon the wise." [S.]

that Socrates was a freethinker, because he was calumniated for an atheist, as freethinkers generally are, only because he was an enemy to all speculations and inquiries into heavenly things. For I argue thus, that if I never trouble myself to think whether there be a God or no, and forbid others to do it, I am a freethinker, but not an atheist.

Plato was a freethinker, and his notions are so like some in the Gospel, that a heathen charged Christ with borrowing his doctrine from Plato. But Origen[1] defends Christ very well against this charge, by saying he did not understand Greek, and therefore could not borrow his doctrine from Plato. However their two religions agreed so well, that it was common for Christians to turn Platonists, and Platonists Christians. When the Christians found out this, one of their zealous priests (worse than any atheist) forged several things under Plato's name, but conformable to Christianity, by which the heathens were fraudulently converted.

Epicurus was the greatest of all freethinkers, and consequently the most virtuous man in the world. His opinions in religion were the most complete system of atheism that ever appeared. Christians ought to have the greatest veneration for him, because he taught a higher point of virtue than Christ; I mean the virtue of friendship, which in the sense we usually understand it, is not so much as named in the New Testament.

Plutarch was a freethinker, notwithstanding his being a priest; but indeed he was a heathen priest. His freethinking appears by showing the innocence of atheism, (which at worst is only false reasoning,) and the mischiefs of superstition; and explains what superstition is, by calling it a conceit of immortal ills after death, the opinion of hell torments, dreadful aspects, doleful groans, and the like. He is likewise very satirical upon the public forms of devotion in his own country (a qualification absolutely necessary to a freethinker) yet those forms which he ridicules, are the very same that now pass for true worship in almost all countries: I am sure

---

[1] Origen, a Father of the Church, was born about 185. He carried to extremes the celibate life taught in the Gospel; and his "Treatise against Celsus" contains, according to St. Jerome and Eusebius, the refutation of "all the objections which have been made, and all which ever will be made against Christianity." [T. S.]

some of them do so in ours; such as abject looks, distortions, wry faces, beggarly tones, humiliation, and contrition.

Varro,[1] the most learned among the Romans, was a freethinker; for he said, the heathen divinity contained many fables below the dignity of immortal beings; such, for instance, as Gods BEGOTTEN and PROCEEDING from other Gods. These two words I desire you will particularly remark, because they are the very terms made use of by our priests in their doctrine of the Trinity: He says likewise, that there are many things false in religion, and so say all freethinkers; but then he adds; "which the vulgar ought not to know, but it is expedient they should believe." In this last he indeed discovers the whole secret of a statesman and politician, by denying the vulgar the privilege of freethinking, and here I differ from him. However, it is manifest from hence, that the Trinity was an invention of statesmen and politicians.

The grave and wise Cato the censor will for ever live in that noble freethinking saying—"I wonder," said he, "how one of our priests can forbear laughing when he sees another!" (For contempt of priests is another grand characteristic of a freethinker). This shews that Cato understood the whole mystery of the Roman religion "as by law established." I beg you, sir, not to overlook these last words, "religion as by law established." I translate *haruspex*, into the general word, *priest*. Thus I apply the sentence to our priests in England, and, when Dr. Smallridge sees Dr Atterbury, I wonder how either of them can forbear laughing at the cheat they put upon the people, by making them believe their "religion as by law established."

Cicero, that consummate philosopher, and noble patriot, though he was a priest, and consequently more likely to be a knave; gave the greatest proofs of his freethinking. First, he professed the sceptic philosophy, which doubts of everything. Then, he wrote two treatises;[2] in the first, he shews the weakness of the Stoics' arguments for the being of the

---

[1] Marcus Terentius Varro (born B.C. 117) was the friend of Cicero. He was a profound grammarian, historian, and philosopher. The expression Swift applies to him as "the most learned among the Romans" is one by which he is generally called. [T. S.]

[2] "De Natura Deorum." [T. S.]

Gods: In the latter, he has destroyed the whole revealed religion of the Greeks and Romans (for why should not theirs be a revealed religion as well as that of Christ?) Cicero likewise tells us, as his own opinion, that they who study philosophy, do not believe there are any Gods: He denies the immortality of the soul, and says, there can be nothing after death.

And because the priests have the impudence to quote Cicero in their pulpits and pamphlets, against freethinking; I am resolved to disarm them of his authority. You must know, his philosophical works are generally in dialogues, where people are brought in disputing against one another: Now the priests when they see an argument to prove a God, offered perhaps by a Stoic, are such knaves or blockheads, to quote it as if it were Cicero's own; whereas Cicero was so noble a freethinker, that he believed nothing at all of the matter, nor ever shews the least inclination to favour superstition, or the belief of a God, and the immortality of the soul; unless what he throws out sometimes to save himself from danger, in his speeches to the Roman mob; whose religion was, however, much more innocent and less absurd, than that of popery at least: And I could say more--but you understand me.

Seneca was a great freethinker, and had a noble notion of the worship of the gods, for which our priests would call any man an atheist: He laughs at morning devotions, or worshipping upon Sabbath-days; he says God has no need of ministers and servants, because he himself serves mankind. This religious man, like his religious brethren the Stoics, denies the immortality of the soul, and says, all that is feigned to be so terrible in hell, is but a fable: Death puts an end to all our misery, &c. Yet the priests were anciently so fond of Seneca, that they forged a correspondence of letters between him and St. Paul.

Solomon himself, whose writings are called "the word of God," was such a freethinker, that if he were now alive, nothing but his building of churches could have kept our priests from calling him an atheist. He affirms the eternity of the world almost in the same manner with Manilius,[1] the

[1] Marcus Manilius, who probably flourished under Theodosius the Great, was a Latin poet, who wrote a poem entitled "Astronomica." [T.S.]

heathen philosophical poet, (which opinion entirely overthrows the history of the creation by Moses, and all the New Testament): He denies the immortality of the soul, assures us that men die like beasts, and that both go to one place.

The prophets of the Old Testament were generally freethinkers: you must understand, that their way of learning to prophesy was by music and drinking.[1] These prophets writ against the established religion of the Jews, (which those people looked upon as the institution of God himself,) as if they believed it was all a cheat: that is to say, with as great liberty against the priests and prophets of Israel, as Dr. Tindal did lately against the priests and prophets of our Israel, who has clearly shewn them and their religion to be cheats. To prove this, you may read several passages in Isaiah, Ezekiel, Amos, Jeremiah, &c., wherein you will find such instances of freethinking, that, if any Englishman had talked so in our days, their opinions would have been registered in Dr. Sacheverell's trial, and in the representation of the Lower House of Convocation, and produced as so many proofs of the profaneness, blasphemy, and atheism of the nation; there being nothing more profane, blasphemous, or atheistical in those representations, than what these prophets have spoke, whose writings are yet called by our priests, "the word of God." And therefore these prophets are as much atheists as myself, or as any of my freethinking brethren whom I lately named to you.

Josephus was a great freethinker: I wish he had chosen a better subject to write on, than those ignorant, barbarous, ridiculous scoundrels, the Jews, whom God (if we may believe the priests) thought fit to choose for his own people. I will give you some instances of his freethinking. He says, Cain travelled through several countries, and kept company with rakes and profligate fellows; he corrupted the simplicities

---

[1] Collins, after making the charge, which has been repeated by all freethinkers down to Thomas Paine, that the prophets acquired their fervour of spirit by the aid of music and wine, allows, nevertheless, that they were great freethinkers, and "writ with as great liberty against the established religion of the Jews, which the people looked on as the institution of God himself, as if they looked upon it all to be imposture."—*Discourse*, p. 153, *et sequen.* [S.]

of former times, &c., which plainly supposes men before Adam, and consequently that the priests' history of the creation by Moses, is an imposture. He says, the Israelites' passing through the Red Sea, was no more than Alexander's passing at the Pamphilian sea; that as for the appearance of God at Mount Sinai, the reader may believe it as he pleases; that Moses persuaded the Jews he had God for his guide, just as the Greeks pretended they had their laws from Apollo. These are noble strains of freethinking, which the priests knew not how to solve, but by thinking as freely: For one of them says, that Josephus writ this to make his work acceptable to the heathens, by striking out everything that was incredible.

Origen, who was the first Christian that had any learning, has left a noble testimony of his freethinking; for a general council has determined him to be damned; which plainly shews he was a freethinker, and was no saint; for people were only sainted because of their want of learning and excess of zeal; so that all the fathers, who are called saints by the priests, were worse than atheists.

Minutius Felix[1] seems to be a true modern latitudinarian, freethinking Christian; for he is against altars, churches, public preaching, and public assemblies; and likewise against priests; for, he says, there were several great flourishing empires before there were any orders of priests in the world.

Synesius,[2] who had too much learning and too little zeal for a saint, was for some time a great freethinker; he could not believe the resurrection till he was made a bishop, and then pretended to be convinced by a lying miracle.

To come to our own country: My Lord Bacon was a great freethinker, when he tells us, that whatever has the least relation to religion, is particularly liable to suspicion; by which he seems to suspect all the facts whereon most of the superstitions (that is to say, what the priests call the

---

[1] Marcus Minutius Felix is said to have been born in Africa. He flourished in the third century, and wrote a defence of Christianity, in dialogue form, entitled, "Octavius." The work has been translated into English by Lord Hailes. [T. S.]

[2] Synesius of Cyrene, born 379, is the Platonic philosopher who became Bishop of Ptolemais. [T. S.]

religions) of the world are grounded. He also prefers atheism before superstition.

Mr. Hobbes was a person of great learning, virtue, and freethinking, except in the high church politics.

But Archbishop Tillotson is the person whom all English freethinkers own as their head; and his virtue is indisputable for this manifest reason; that Dr Hickes, a priest, calls him an atheist; says, he caused several to turn atheists, and to ridicule the priesthood and religion. These must be allowed to be noble effects of freethinking. This great prelate assures us, that all the duties of the Christian religion, with respect to God, are no other but what natural light prompts men to, except the two sacraments, and praying to God in the name and mediation of Christ. As a priest and prelate, he was obliged to say something of Christianity; but pray observe, sir, how he brings himself off. He justly affirms that even these things are of less moment than natural duties; and because mothers' nursing their children is a natural duty, it is of more moment than the two sacraments, or than praying to God in the name and by the mediation of Christ. This freethinking archbishop could not allow a miracle sufficient to give credit to a prophet who taught anything contrary to our natural notions: By which it is plain, he rejected at once all the mysteries of Christianity.

I could name one-and-twenty more great men, who were all freethinkers; but that I fear to be tedious: For, 'tis certain that all men of sense depart from the opinions commonly received; and are consequently more or less men of sense, according as they depart more or less from the opinions commonly received; neither can you name an enemy to freethinking, however he be dignified or distinguished, whether archbishop, bishop, priest, or deacon, who has not been either "a crack-brained enthusiast, a diabolical villain, or a most profound ignorant brute."

Thus, sir, I have endeavoured to execute your commands, and you may print this Letter, if you please; but I would have you conceal my name. For my opinion of virtue is, that we ought not to venture doing ourselves harm, by endeavouring to do good.

I am yours, &c.

*I have here given the public a brief, but faithful abstract of this most excellent Essay; wherein I have all along religiously adhered to our author's notions, and generally to his words, without any other addition than that of explaining a few necessary consequences, for the sake of ignorant readers; for, to those who have the least degree of learning, I own they will be wholly useless. I hope I have not, in any single instance, misrepresented the thoughts of this admirable writer. If I have happened to mistake through inadvertency, I entreat he will condescend to inform me, and point out the place, upon which I will immediately beg pardon both of him and the world. The design of his piece is to recommend freethinking, and one chief motive is the example of many excellent men who were of that sect. He produces as the principal points of their freethinking; that they denied the Being of a God, the Torments of Hell, the Immortality of the Soul, the Trinity, Incarnation, the history of the creation by Moses, with many other such "fabulous and blasphemous stories," as he judiciously calls them: And he asserts, that whoever denies the most of these, is the completest freethinker, and consequently the wisest and most virtuous man. The author, sensible of the prejudices of the age, does not directly affirm himself an atheist; he goes no further than to pronounce that atheism is the most perfect degree of freethinking; and leaves the reader to form the conclusion. However, he seems to allow, that a man may be a tolerable freethinker, though he does believe a God; provided he utterly rejects " Providence, Revelation, the Old and New Testament, Future Rewards and Punishments, the Immortality of the Soul," and other the like impossible absurdities. Which mark of superabundant caution, sacrificing truth to the superstition of priests, may perhaps be forgiven, but ought not to be imitated by any who would arrive (even in this author's judgment) at the true perfection of freethinking.*

# SOME THOUGHTS

ON

# FREETHINKING.

WRITTEN IN ENGLAND, BUT LEFT UNFINISHED.

DISCOURSING one day with a prelate of the kingdom of Ireland, who is a person of excellent wit and learning, he offered a notion applicable to the subject we were then upon, which I took to be altogether new and right. He said, that the difference betwixt a madman and one in his wits, in what related to speech, consisted in this; that the former spoke out whatever came into his mind, and just in the confused manner as his imagination presented the ideas: The latter only expressed such thoughts as his judgment directed him to choose, leaving the rest to die away in his memory; and that, if the wisest man would, at any time, utter his thoughts in the crude indigested manner as they come into his head, he would be looked upon as raving mad. And, indeed, when we consider our thoughts, as they are the seeds of words and actions, we cannot but agree that they ought to be kept under the strictest regulation; and that in the great multiplicity of ideas which one's mind is apt to form, there is nothing more difficult than to select those which are most proper for the conduct of life. So that I cannot imagine what is meant by the mighty zeal in some people for asserting the freedom of thinking; because, if such thinkers keep their thoughts within their own breasts, they can be of no consequence, farther than to themselves. If they publish them to the world, they ought to be answerable for the effects their thoughts produce upon others. There are thousands in this kingdom, who, in their thoughts, prefer a republic, or absolute power of a prince, before a limited monarchy; yet, if any of these should publish their opinions, and go about, by writing or discourse, to persuade the people to innovations in government, they would be liable to the severest punishments the law can inflict; and therefore they are usually so wise as to keep their sentiments to themselves. But, with respect to religion, the matter is quite otherwise: and the public, at least here in England, seems to be of opinion with *Tiberius*, that *Deorum injuriæ diis curæ*. They leave it to God Almighty to vindicate the injuries done to himself, who is no doubt sufficiently able, by perpetual miracles, to revenge the affronts of impious men. And, it should seem, that is what princes expect from him, though I cannot readily conceive the grounds they go upon; nor why, since they are God's vicegerents, they do not think themselves at least equally obliged to preserve their master's honour as their own; since this is what they expect from those they depute, and since they never fail to represent the disobedience of their subjects, as offences against God. It is true, the visible reason of this neglect is obvious enough: The consequences of atheistical opinions, published to the world, are not so immediate, or so sensible, as doctrines of rebellion and sedition, spread in a proper season. However, I cannot but think the same consequences are as natural and probable from the former, though more remote: And whether these have not been in view among our great planters of infidelity in England, I shall hereafter examine.

# A LETTER
### TO
# A YOUNG CLERGYMAN,
#### LATELY ENTERED INTO
## HOLY ORDERS.
#### 1719-20.

## NOTE.

No stronger proof could be adduced of Swift's genuine and earnest belief in the dignity of a clergyman of the Church than this letter. In spite of the sarcasms which here and there are levelled against the mediocre members of the class, it is evident Swift felt that these might be made worthy teachers and preachers of the doctrines of an institution founded, in his opinion, for the best regulation of mankind. The letter serves also to present us with an outline of a picture of the clergyman of his day; and if this picture be not flattering, it seems faithfully to reflect the social conditions which we know to have prevailed at the time.

The letter was written in the years of quiet which Swift enjoyed between the pamphleteering crusade against the Whigs, when Harley and St. John were in power, and the famous social and political troubles which began with Wood's halfpence.

The text of this letter is practically that of the first edition; but I have collated this with the texts given by Hawkesworth, Scott, the first volume of the "Miscellanies" of 1728, and the second volume of the "Miscellanies" of 1745. In the original edition, and in the reprints published to the time of Faulkner's collected edition, the title reads "A Letter to a Young Gentleman," etc.

[T. S.]

# A LETTER TO A Young Gentleman,

Lately enter'd into

# HOLY ORDERS.

By a Person of QUALITY.

☞ *It is certainly known, that the following Treatise was writ in* Ireland *by the Reverend Dr.* SWIFT, *Dean of* St. Patrick's *in that Kingdom.*

LONDON:

Printed for J. ROBERTS at the *Oxford Arms* in *Warwick-Lane.* MDCCXXI.  Price 6 d.

# A LETTER TO A YOUNG CLERGYMAN, LATELY ENTERED INTO HOLY ORDERS

Dublin, *January the 9th*, 1719-20.

SIR,

ALTHOUGH it was against my knowledge or advice, that you entered into holy orders, under the present dispositions of mankind toward the Church, yet since it is now supposed too late to recede, (at least according to the general practice and opinion,) I cannot forbear offering my thoughts to you upon this new condition of life you are engaged in.

I could heartily wish that the circumstances of your fortune, had enabled you to have continued some years longer in the university; at least till you were ten years standing; to have laid in a competent stock of human learning, and some knowledge in divinity, before you attempted to appear in the world: For I cannot but lament the common course, which at least nine in ten of those who enter into the ministry are obliged to run. When they have taken a degree, and are consequently grown a burden to their friends, who now think themselves fully discharged, they get into orders as soon as they can; (upon which I shall make no remarks,) first solicit a readership, and if they be very fortunate, arrive in time to a curacy here in town, or else are sent to be assistants in the country, where they probably continue several years, (many of them their whole lives,) with thirty or forty pounds a-year for their support, till some bishop, who happens to be not overstocked with relations, or attached to favourites, or is content to supply his diocese without colonies from England, bestows upon them some inconsiderable benefice, when it is odds they are already encumbered with a numerous family. I should be glad to know what intervals of life such persons can possibly set apart for the improvement of their minds; or which way they could be furnished with books, the library they brought with them from their college being usually not the most numerous, or judiciously chosen. If such gentlemen arrive to be great scholars, it must, I think, be either by means supernatural, or by a method altogether out of any road yet known to the learned. But I conceive the fact directly otherwise, and that many of them lose the greatest part of the small pittance they receive at the university.

I take it for granted, that you intend to pursue the beaten track, and are already desirous to be seen in a pulpit, only I hope you will think it proper to pass your quarantine among some of the desolate churches five miles round this town, where you may at least learn to read and to speak before you venture to expose your parts in a city congregation; not that these are better judges, but because, if a man must needs expose his folly, it is more safe and discreet to do so before few witnesses, and in a scattered neighbourhood. And you will do well if you can prevail upon some intimate and judicious friend to be your constant hearer, and allow him with the utmost freedom to give you notice of whatever he shall find amiss either in your voice or gesture; for want of which early warning, many clergymen continue defective, and sometimes ridiculous, to the end of their lives; neither is it rare to observe among excellent and learned divines, a certain ungracious manner, or an unhappy tone of voice, which they never have been able to shake off.

I should likewise have been glad, if you had applied yourself a little more to the study of the English language, than I fear you have done; the neglect whereof is one of the most general defects among the scholars of this kingdom, who seem not to have the least conception of a style, but run on in a flat kind of phraseology, often mingled with barbarous terms and expressions, peculiar to the nation: Neither do I perceive that any person, either finds or acknowledges his wants upon this head, or in the least desires to have them supplied. Proper words in proper places, make the true definition of a style. But this would require too ample a disquisition to be now dwelt on: however, I shall venture to name one or two faults, which are easy to be remedied, with a very small portion of abilities.

The first is the frequent use of obscure terms, which by the women are called hard words, and by the better sort of vulgar, fine language; than which I do not know a more universal, inexcusable, and unnecessary mistake, among the clergy of all distinctions, but especially the younger practitioners. I have been curious enough to take a list of several hundred words in a sermon of a new beginner, which not one of his hearers among a hundred could possibly understand, neither can I easily call to mind any clergyman of my own acquaintance who is wholly exempt from this error, although many of them agree with me in the dislike of the thing. But I am apt to put myself in the place of the vulgar, and think many words difficult or obscure, which they will not allow to be so, because those words are obvious to scholars. I believe the method observed by the famous Lord Falkland[1] in some of his writings, would not be an ill one for young divines: I was assured by an old person of quality who knew him well, that when he doubted whether a word was perfectly intelligible or no, he used to consult one of his lady's chambermaids, (not the waiting-woman, because it was possible she might be conversant in romances,) and by her judgment was guided whether to receive or reject it. And if that great person thought such a caution necessary in treatises offered to the learned world, it will be sure at least as proper in sermons, where the meanest hearer is supposed to be concerned, and where very often a lady's chambermaid may be allowed to

[1] Lucius Cary, second Viscount Falkland (1610-1643), who was killed at the battle of Newbury in the great Civil War, was a generous patron of learning and of the literary men of his day. He was himself a fine scholar and able writer. Clarendon has recorded his character in the seventh book of his "History of the Great Rebellion": "A person of such prodigious parts of learning and knowledge, of that inimitable sweetness and delight in conversation, of so flowing and obliging an humanity and goodness to mankind, that, if there were no other brand upon this odious and accursed Civil War than that single loss, it must be infamous and execrable to all posterity." Falkland has been made the hero of a romance by Lord Lytton. [T. S.]

equal half the congregation, both as to quality and understanding. But I know not how it comes to pass, that professors in most arts and sciences are generally the worst qualified to explain their meanings to those who are not of their tribe: a common farmer shall make you understand in three words, that his foot is out of joint, or his collar-bone broken, wherein a surgeon, after a hundred terms of art, if you are not a scholar, shall leave you to seek. It is frequently the same case in law, physic, and even many of the meaner arts.

And upon this account it is, that among hard words, I number likewise those which are peculiar to divinity as it is a science, because I have observed several clergymen, otherwise little fond of obscure terms, yet in their sermons very liberal of those which they find in ecclesiastical writers, as if it were our duty to understand them; which I am sure it is not. And I defy the greatest divine to produce any law either of God or man, which obliges me to comprehend the meaning of *omniscience, omnipresence, ubiquity, attribute, beatific vision*, with a thousand others so frequent in pulpits, any more than that of *eccentric, idiosyncracy, entity*, and the like. I believe I may venture to insist farther, that many terms used in Holy Writ, particularly by St Paul, might with more discretion be changed into plainer speech, except when they are introduced as part of a quotation.[1]

I am the more earnest in this matter, because it is a general complaint, and the justest in the world. For a divine has nothing to say to the wisest congregation of any parish in this kingdom, which he may not express in a manner to be understood by the meanest among them. And this assertion must be true, or else God requires from us more than we are able to perform. However, not to contend whether a logician might possibly put a case that would serve for an exception, I will appeal to any man of letters, whether at least nineteen in twenty of those perplexing words might not be changed into easy ones, such as naturally first occur to ordinary men, and probably did so

---

[1] Swift refers to this point in his "Thoughts on Religion," and regrets that the explanation of matters of doctrine, which St. Paul expressed in the current eastern vocabulary, should have been perpetuated in terms founded on the same terminology. [T. S.]

at first to those very gentlemen who are so fond of the former.

We are often reproved by divines from the pulpits, on account of our ignorance in things sacred, and perhaps with justice enough. However, it is not very reasonable for them to expect, that common men should understand expressions which are never made use of in common life. No gentleman thinks it safe or prudent to send a servant with a message, without repeating it more than once, and endeavouring to put it into terms brought down to the capacity of the bearer: yet after all this care, it is frequent for servants to mistake, and sometimes to occasion misunderstandings among friends. Although the common domestics in some gentlemen's families have more opportunities of improving their minds than the ordinary sort of tradesmen.

It is usual for clergymen who are taxed with this learned defect, to quote Dr Tillotson, and other famous divines, in their defence; without considering the difference between elaborate discourses upon important occasions, delivered to princes or parliaments, written with a view of being made public, and a plain sermon intended for the middle or lower size of people. Neither do they seem to remember the many alterations, additions, and expungings, made by great authors in those treatises which they prepare for the public. Besides, that excellent prelate above-mentioned, was known to preach after a much more popular manner in the city congregations: and if in those parts of his works he be any where too obscure for the understandings of many who may be supposed to have been his hearers, it ought to be numbered among his omissions.

The fear of being thought pedants hath been of pernicious consequence to young divines. This hath wholly taken many of them off from their severer studies in the university, which they have exchanged for plays, poems, and pamphlets, in order to qualify them for tea-tables and coffee-houses. This they usually call "polite coversation; knowing the world; and reading men instead of books." These accomplishments, when applied to the pulpit, appear by a quaint, terse, florid style, rounded into periods and cadences, commonly without either propriety or meaning. I have listen'd with my utmost attention for half an hour to an orator of this species, without being able to understand, much less to carry away one single sentence out of a whole sermon. Others, to shew that their studies have not been confined to sciences, or ancient authors, will talk in the style of a gaming ordinary, and White Friars,[1] when I suppose the hearers can be little edified by the terms of *palming, shuffling, biting, bamboozling*, and the like, if they have not been sometimes conversant among pick-pockets and sharpers. And truly, as they say, a man is known by his company, so it should seem that a man's company may be known by his manner of expressing himself, either in public assemblies, or private conversation.

It would be endless to run over the several defects of style among us; I shall therefore say nothing of the mean and paltry (which are usually attended by the fustian), much less of the slovenly or indecent. Two things I will just warn you against; the first is the frequency of flat unnecessary epithets, and the other is the folly of using old threadbare phrases, which will often make you go out of your way to find and apply them, are nauseous to rational hearers, and will seldom express your meaning as well as your own natural words.

Although, as I have already observed, our English tongue is too little cultivated in this kingdom; yet the faults are nine in ten owing to affectation, and not to the want of understanding. When a man's thoughts are clear, the properest words will generally offer themselves first, and his own judgment will direct him in what order to place them, so as they may be best understood. Where men err against this method, it is usually on purpose, and to shew their learning, their oratory, their politeness, or their knowledge of the world. In short, that simplicity without which no human performance can arrive to any great perfection, is nowhere more eminently useful than in this.

I have been considering that part of oratory which relates to the moving of the passions; this I observe is in esteem and practice among some church divines, as well as among all the preachers and hearers of the fanatic or enthusiastic

---

[1] See note on "Alsatia," p. 100. [T. S.]

strain. I will here deliver to you (perhaps with more freedom than prudence) my opinion upon the point.

The two great orators of Greece and Rome, Demosthenes and Cicero, though each of them a leader (or as the Greeks call it a demagogue) in a popular state, yet seem to differ in their practice upon this branch of their art; the former who had to deal with a people of much more politeness, learning, and wit, laid the greatest weight of his oratory upon the strength of his arguments, offered to their understanding and reason: whereas Tully considered the dispositions of a sincere, more ignorant, and less mercurial nation, by dwelling almost entirely on the pathetic part.

But the principal thing to be remembered is, that the constant design of both these orators in all their speeches, was to drive some one particular point, either the condemnation or acquittal of an accused person, a persuasive to war, the enforcing of a law, and the like; which was determined upon the spot, according as the orators on either side prevailed. And here it was often found of absolute necessity to inflame or cool the passions of the audience, especially at Rome where Tully spoke, and with whose writings young divines (I mean those among them who read old authors) are more conversant than with those of Demosthenes, who by many degrees excelled the other at least as an orator. But I do not see how this talent of moving the passions can be of any great use toward directing Christian men in the conduct of their lives, at least in these northern climates, where I am confident the strongest eloquence of that kind will leave few impressions upon any of our spirits deep enough to last till the next morning, or rather to the next meal.[1]

But what hath chiefly put me out of conceit with this moving manner of preaching, is the frequent disappointment it meets with. I know a gentleman, who made it a rule in reading, to skip over all sentences where he spied a note of admiration at the end. I believe those preachers who abound in *epiphonemas*,[2] if they look about them, would find

---

[1] Swift's own sermons rarely appealed to the emotions; they were, in his own phrase, political pamphlets, and aimed at convincing the reason. [T. S.]

[2] *Epiphonema* is a figure in rhetoric, signifying a sententious kind of exclamation. [S.]

one part of their congregation out of countenance, and the other asleep, except perhaps an old female beggar or two in the aisles, who (if they be sincere) may probably groan at the sound.

Nor is it a wonder, that this expedient should so often miscarry, which requires so much art and genius to arrive at any perfection in it, as any man will find, much sooner than learn by consulting Cicero himself.

I therefore entreat you to make use of this faculty (if you ever be so unfortunate as to think you have it) as seldom, and with as much caution as you can, else I may probably have occasion to say of you as a great person said of another upon this very subject. A lady asked him coming out of church, whether it were not a very moving discourse? "Yes," said he, "I was extremely sorry, for the man is my friend."

If in company you offer something for a jest, and nobody second you in your own laughter, nor seems to relish what you said, you may condemn their taste, if you please, and appeal to better judgments; but in the meantime, it must be agreed you make a very indifferent figure; and it is at least equally ridiculous to be disappointed in endeavouring to make other folks grieve, as to make them laugh.

A plain convincing reason may possibly operate upon the mind both of a learned and ignorant hearer as long as they live, and will edify a thousand times more than the art of wetting the handkerchiefs of a whole congregation, if you were sure to attain it.

If your arguments be strong, in God's name offer them in as moving a manner as the nature of the subject will properly admit, wherein reason and good advice will be your safest guides; but beware of letting the pathetic part swallow up the rational: For I suppose, philosophers have long agreed, that passion should never prevail over reason.

As I take it, the two principal branches of preaching are first to tell the people what is their duty, and then to convince them that it is so. The topics for both these, we know, are brought from Scripture and reason. Upon this first, I wish it were often practised to instruct the hearers in the limits, extent, and compass of every duty, which requires a good deal of skill and judgment: the other branch is, I think, not so difficult. But what I would offer them both, is this; that it seems to be in the power of a reasonable clergyman, if he will be at the pains, to make the most ignorant man comprehend what is his duty, and to convince him by argument drawn to the level of his understanding, that he ought to perform it.

But I must remember that my design in this paper was not so much to instruct you in your business either as a clergyman or a preacher, as to warn you against some mistakes which are obvious to the generality of mankind as well as to me; and we who are hearers, may be allowed to have some opportunities in the quality of being standers-by. Only perhaps I may now again transgress by desiring you to express the heads of your divisions in as few and clear words as you possibly can, otherwise, I and many thousand others will never be able to retain them, nor consequently to carry away a syllable of the sermon.

I shall now mention a particular wherein your whole body will be certainly against me, and the laity almost to a man on my side. However it came about, I cannot get over the prejudice of taking some little offence at the clergy for perpetually reading their sermons;[1] perhaps my frequent hearing of foreigners, who never made use of notes, may have added to my disgust. And I cannot but think, that whatever is read, differs as much from what is repeated without book, as a copy does from an original. At the same time, I am highly sensible what an extreme difficulty it would be upon you to alter this method, and that, in such a case, your sermons would be much less valuable than they are, for want of time to improve and correct them. I would therefore gladly come to a compromise with you in this matter. I knew a clergyman of some distinction, who appeared to deliver his sermon without looking into his notes, which when I complimented him upon, he assured me he could not repeat six lines; but his method was to write the whole sermon in a large plain hand, with all the forms of margin, paragraph, marked page, and the like;

---

[1] "The custom of reading sermons," notes Scott, "seems originally to have arisen in opposition to the practice of Dissenters, many of whom affected to trust to their inspiration in their *extempore* harangues." [T. S.]

then on Sunday morning he took care to run it over five or six times, which he could do in an hour; and when he deliver'd it, by pretending to turn his face from one side to the other, he would (in his own expression) pick up the lines, and cheat his people by making them believe he had it all by heart. He farther added, that whenever he happened by neglect to omit any of these circumstances, the vogue of the parish was, "Our doctor gave us but an indifferent sermon to-day." Now among us, many clergymen act too directly contrary to this method, that from a habit of saving time and paper, which they acquired at the University, they write is so diminutive a manner, with such frequent blots and interlineations, that they are hardly able to go on without perpetual hesitations or extemporary expletives: And I desire to know what can be more inexcusable, than to see a divine and a scholar, at a loss in reading his own compositions, which it is supposed he has been preparing with much pains and thought for the instruction of his people? The want of a little more care in this article, is the cause of much ungraceful behaviour. You will observe some clergymen with their heads held down from the beginning to the end, within an inch of the cushion, to read what is hardly legible; which, besides the untoward manner, hinders them from making the best advantage of their voice: others again have a trick of popping up and down every moment from their paper to the audience, like an idle school-boy on a repetition day.

Let me entreat you, therefore, to add one half-crown a year to the article of paper; to transcribe your sermons in as large and plain a manner as you can, and either make no interlineations, or change the whole leaf; for we your hearers would rather you should be less correct than perpetually stammering, which I take to be one of the worst solecisms in rhetoric: And lastly, read your sermon once or twice for a few days before you preach it: to which you will probably answer some years hence, "that it was but just finished when the last bell rang to church:" and I shall readily believe, but not excuse you.

I cannot forbear warning you in the most earnest manner against endeavouring at wit in your sermons, because by the strictest computation, it is very near a million to one that you have none; and because too many of your calling have consequently made themselves everlastingly ridiculous by attempting it. I remember several young men in this town, who could never leave the pulpit under half a dozen conceits; and this faculty adhered to those gentlemen a longer or shorter time exactly in proportion to their several degrees of dulness: accordingly, I am told that some of them retain it to this day. I heartily wish the brood were at an end.

Before you enter into the common insufferable cant of taking all occasions to disparage the heathen philosophers, I hope you will differ from some of your brethren, by first enquiring what those philosophers can say for themselves. The system of morality to be gathered out of the writings or sayings of those ancient sages, falls undoubtedly very short of that delivered in the Gospel, and wants besides, the divine sanction which our Saviour gave to His. Whatever is further related by the evangelists, contains chiefly, matters of fact, and consequently of faith, such as the birth of Christ, His being the Messiah, His Miracles, His death, resurrection, and ascension. None of which can properly come under the appellation of human wisdom, being intended only to make us wise unto salvation. And therefore in this point nothing can justly be laid to the charge of the philosophers further than that they were ignorant of certain facts that happened long after their death. But I am deceived, if a better comment could be anywhere collected, upon the moral part of the Gospel, than from the writings of those excellent men; even that divine precept of loving our enemies, is at large insisted on by Plato, who puts it, as I remember, into the mouth of Socrates.[1] And as to the reproach of heathenism, I doubt they had less of it than the corrupted Jews in whose time they lived. For it is a gross piece of ignorance among us to conceive that in those polite and learned ages, even persons of any tolerable education, much less the wisest philosophers did acknowledge or worship any more than one almighty power, under several denominations, to whom they allowed all those attributes we ascribe to the Divinity: and as I take it, human comprehension reacheth no further: neither did our Saviour think it necessary to explain to us the nature of

---

[1] This is in the "Crito" of Plato, where Socrates says it is wrong to do harm to our enemies. [T. S.]

God, because I suppose it would be impossible without bestowing on us other faculties than we possess at present. But the true misery of the heathen world appears to be what I before mentioned, the want of a Divine Sanction, without which the dictates of the philosophers failed in the point of authority, and consequently the bulk of mankind lay indeed under a great load of ignorance even in the article of morality, but the philosophers themselves did not. Take the matter in this light, it will afford field enough for a divine to enlarge on, by shewing the advantages which the Christian world has over the heathen, and the absolute necessity of Divine Revelation, to make the knowledge of the true God, and the practice of virtue more universal in the world.

I am not ignorant how much I differ in this opinion from some ancient fathers in the Church, who arguing against the heathens, made it a principal topic to decry their philosophy as much as they could: which, I hope, is not altogether our present case. Besides, it is to be considered, that those fathers lived in the decline of literature; and in my judgment (who should be unwilling to give the least offence) appear to be rather most excellent, holy persons, than of transcendent genius and learning. Their genuine writings (for many of them have extremely suffered by spurious editions) are of admirable use for confirming the truth of ancient doctrines and discipline, by shewing the state and practice of the primitive church. But among such of them as have fallen in my way, I do not remember any whose manner of arguing or exhorting I could heartily recommend to the imitation of a young divine when he is to speak from the pulpit. Perhaps I judge too hastily; there being several of them in whose writings I have made very little progress, and in others none at all. For I perused only such as were recommended to me, at a time when I had more leisure and a better disposition to read, than have since fallen to my share.[1]

To return then to the heathen philosophers, I hope you

---

[1] Swift must refer here to the years he spent at Moor Park, in the house of Sir William Temple. The "Tale of a Tub," however, shows that he had not idled his time, and that his acquaintance with the writings of the fathers was fairly intimate. [T. S.]

will not only give them quarter, but make their works a considerable part of your study: To these I will venture to add the principal orators and historians, and perhaps a few of the poets: by the reading of which, you will soon discover your mind and thoughts to be enlarged, your imagination extended and refined, your judgment directed, your admiration lessened, and your fortitude increased; all which advantages must needs be of excellent use to a divine, whose duty it is to preach and practise the contempt of human things.

I would say something concerning quotations, wherein I think you cannot be too sparing, except from Scripture, and the primitive writers of the Church. As to the former, when you offer a text as a proof of an illustration, we your hearers expect to be fairly used, and sometimes think we have reason to complain, especially of you younger divines, which makes us fear that some of you conceive you have no more to do than to turn over a concordance, and there having found the principal word, introduce as much of the verse as will serve your turn, though in reality it makes nothing for you. I do not altogether disapprove the manner of interweaving texts of scripture through the style of your sermons, wherein however, I have sometimes observed great instances of indiscretion and impropriety, against which I therefore venture to give you a caution.

As to quotations from ancient fathers, I think they are best brought in to confirm some opinion controverted by those who differ from us: in other cases we give you full power to adopt the sentence for your own, rather than tell us, "as St. Austin excellently observes." But to mention modern writers by name, or use the phrase of "a late excellent prelate of our Church," and the like, is altogether intolerable, and for what reason I know not, makes every rational hearer ashamed. Of no better a stamp is your "heathen philosopher" and "famous poet," and "Roman historian," at least in common congregations, who will rather believe you on your own word, than on that of Plato or Homer.

I have lived to see Greek and Latin almost entirely driven out of the pulpit, for which I am heartily glad. The frequent use of the latter was certainly a remnant of Popery which never admitted Scripture in the vulgar language; and I wonder, that practice was never accordingly objected to us by the fanatics.

The mention of quotations puts me in mind of commonplace books, which have been long in use by industrious young divines, and I hear do still continue so. I know they are very beneficial to lawyers and physicians, because they are collections of facts or cases, whereupon a great part of their several faculties depend; of these I have seen several, but never yet any written by a clergyman; only from what I am informed, they generally are extracts of theological and moral sentences drawn from ecclesiastical and other authors, reduced under proper heads, usually begun, and perhaps finished, while the collectors were young in the church, as being intended for materials or nurseries to stock future sermons. You will observe the wise editors of ancient authors, when they meet a sentence worthy of being distinguished, take special care to have the first word printed in capital letters, that you may not overlook it: Such, for example, as the INCONSTANCY of FORTUNE, the GOODNESS of PEACE, the EXCELLENCY of WISDOM, the CERTAINTY of DEATH: that PROSPERITY makes men INSOLENT, and ADVERSITY HUMBLE; and the like eternal truths, which every ploughman knows well enough before Aristotle or Plato were born.[1] If theological commonplace books be no better filled, I think they had better be laid aside, and I could wish that men of tolerable intellectuals would rather trust their own natural reason, improved by a general conversation with books, to enlarge on points which they are supposed already to understand. If a rational man reads an excellent author with just application, he shall find himself extremely improved, and perhaps insensibly led to imitate that author's perfections, although in a little time he should not remember one word in the book, nor even the subject it handled: for books give the same turn to our thoughts and way of reasoning, that good and ill company do to our behaviour and conversation; without either loading our memories, or making us even sensible of the change. And particularly I have observed in preaching, that no men succeed better than

[1] Thus in first edition. Scott and Hawkesworth have: "though he never heard of Aristotle or Plato." [T. S.]

those who trust entirely to the stock or fund of their own reason, advanced indeed, but not overlaid by commerce with books: Whoever only reads in order to transcribe wise and shining remarks, without entering into the genius and spirit of the author, as it is probable he will make no very judicious extract, so he will be apt to trust to that collection in all his compositions, and be misled out of the regular way of thinking, in order to introduce those materials, which he has been at the pains to gather: and the product of all this will be found a manifest incoherent piece of patchwork.

Some gentlemen abounding in their university erudition, are apt to fill their sermons with philosophical terms and notions of the metaphysical or abstracted kind, which generally have one advantage, to be equally understood by the wise, the vulgar, and the preacher himself. I have been better entertained, and more informed by a chapter[1] in the "Pilgrim's Progress," than by a long discourse upon the will and the intellect, and simple or complex ideas. Others again, are fond of dilating on matter and motion, talk of the fortuitous concourse of atoms, of theories, and phenomena; directly against the advice of St Paul, who yet appears to have been conversant enough in those kinds of studies.

I do not find that you are anywhere directed in the canons or articles, to attempt explaining the mysteries of the Christian religion. And indeed since Providence intended there should be mysteries, I do not see how it can be agreeable to piety, orthodoxy or good sense, to go about such a work. For, to me there seems to be a manifest dilemma in the case: if you explain them, they are mysteries no longer; if you fail, you have laboured to no purpose. What I should think most reasonable and safe for you to do upon this occasion is, upon solemn days to deliver the doctrine as the Church holds it, and confirm it by Scripture. For my part, having considered the matter impartially, I can see no great reason which those gentlemen you call the freethinkers can have for their clamour against religious mysteries; since it is plain, they were not invented by the clergy, to whom they bring no profit, nor acquire any honour. For every clergy-

---

[1] Thus in first edition. Scott and Hawkesworth have "a few pages" instead of "a chapter." [T. S.]

man is ready either to tell us the utmost he knows, or to confess that he does not understand them; neither is it strange that there should be mysteries in divinity as well as in the commonest operations of nature.

And here I am at a loss what to say upon the frequent custom of preaching against atheism, deism, freethinking, and the like, as young divines are particularly fond of doing especially when they exercise their talent in churches frequented by persons of quality, which as it is but an ill compliment to the audience; so I am under some doubt whether it answers the end.

Because persons under those imputations are generally no great frequenters of churches, and so the congregation is but little edified for the sake of three or four fools who are past grace. Neither do I think it any part of prudence to perplex the minds of well-disposed people with doubts, which probably would never have otherwise come into their heads. But I am of opinion, and dare be positive in it, that not one in an hundred of those who pretend to be freethinkers, are really so in their hearts. For there is one observation which I never knew to fail, and I desire you will examine it in the course of your life, that no gentleman of a liberal education, and regular in his morals, did ever profess himself a freethinker: where then are these kind of people to be found? Among the worst part of the soldiery made up of pages, younger brothers of obscure families, and others of desperate fortunes; or else among idle town fops, and now and then a drunken 'squire of the country. Therefore nothing can be plainer, than that ignorance and vice are two ingredients absolutely necessary in the composition of those you generally call freethinkers, who in propriety of speech, are no thinkers at all. And since I am in the way of it, pray consider one thing farther: as young as you are, you cannot but have already observed, what a violent run there is among too many weak people against university education. Be firmly assured, that the whole cry is made up by those who were either never sent to a college; or through their irregularities and stupidity never made the least improvement while they were there. I have at least[1] forty of the latter sort now in my

---

[1] Scott and Hawkesworth print "above forty." [T. S.]

eye; several of them in this town, whose learning, manners, temperance, probity, good-nature, and politics, are all of a piece. Others of them in the country, oppressing their tenants, tyrannizing over the neighbourhood, cheating the vicar, talking nonsense, and getting drunk at the sessions. It is from such seminaries as these, that the world is provided with the several tribes and denominations of freethinkers, who, in my judgment, are not to be reformed by arguments offered to prove the truth of the Christian religion, because reasoning will never make a man correct an ill opinion, which by reasoning he never acquired: for in the course of things, men always grow vicious before they become unbelievers; but if you would once convince the town or country profligate, by topics drawn from the view of their own quiet, reputation, health, and advantage, their infidelity would soon drop off: This I confess is no easy task, because it is almost in a literal sense, to fight with beasts. Now, to make it clear, that we are to look for no other original of this infidelity, whereof divines so much complain, it is allowed on all hands, that the people of England are more corrupt in their morals than any other nation at this day under the sun: and this corruption is manifestly owing to other causes, both numerous and obvious, much more than to the publication of irreligious books, which indeed are but the consequence of the former. For all the writers against Christianity since the Revolution have been of the lowest rank among men in regard to literature, wit, and good sense, and upon that account wholly unqualified to propagate heresies, unless among a people already abandoned.

In an age where everything disliked by those who think with the majority is called disaffection, it may perhaps be ill interpreted, when I venture to tell you that this universal depravation of manners is owing to the perpetual bandying of factions among us for thirty years past; when without weighing the motives of justice, law, conscience, or honour, every man adjusts his principles to those of the party he hath chosen, and among whom he may best find his own account: But by reason of our frequent vicissitudes, men who were impatient of being out of play, have been forced to recant, or at least to reconcile their former tenets with every new system of administration. Add to this, that the old fundamental custom of annual parliaments being wholly laid aside, and elections growing chargeable, since gentlemen found that their country seats brought them in less than a seat in the House, the voters, that is to say, the bulk of the common people have been universally seduced into bribery, perjury, drunkenness, malice, and slanders.

Not to be further tedious, or rather invidious, these are a few among other causes which have contributed to the ruin of our morals, and consequently to the contempt of religion: For imagine to yourself, if you please, a landed youth, whom his mother would never suffer to look into a book for fear of spoiling his eyes, got into parliament, and observing all enemies to the clergy heard with the utmost applause, what notions he must imbibe; how readily he will join in the cry; what an esteem he will conceive of himself; and what a contempt he must entertain, not only for his vicar at home, but for the whole order.

I therefore again conclude, that the trade of infidelity hath been taken up only for an expedient to keep in countenance that universal corruption of morals, which many other causes first contributed to introduce and to cultivate. And thus, Mr Hobbes' saying upon reason may be much more properly applied to religion: that, "if religion will be against a man, a man will be against religion." Though after all, I have heard a profligate offer much stronger arguments against paying his debts, than ever he was known to do against Christianity; indeed the reason was, because in that juncture he happened to be closer pressed by the bailiff than the parson.

Ignorance may perhaps be the mother of superstition; but experience hath not proved it to be so of devotion: for Christianity always made the most easy and quickest progress in civilized countries. I mention this because it is affirmed that the clergy are in most credit where ignorance prevails (and surely this kingdom would be called the paradise of clergymen if that opinion were true) for which they instance England in the times of Popery. But whoever knows anything of three or four centuries before the Reformation, will find the little learning then stirring was more equally divided between the English clergy and laity than it is at present. There were several famous lawyers in that period, whose writings are still in the highest repute, and some historians and poets who were not of the Church.¹ Whereas now-a-days our education is so corrupted, that you will hardly find a young person of quality with the least tincture of knowledge, at the same time that many of the clergy were never more learned, or so scurvily treated. Here among us, at least, a man of letters out of the three professions, is almost a prodigy. And those few who have preserved any rudiments of learning are (except perhaps one or two smatterers) the clergy's friends to a man: and I dare appeal to any clergyman in this kingdom, whether the greatest dunce in the parish be not always the most proud, wicked, fraudulent, and intractable of his flock.

I think the clergy have almost given over perplexing themselves and their hearers with abstruse points of Predestination, Election, and the like; at least it is time they should; and therefore I shall not trouble you further upon this head.

I have now said all I could think convenient with relation to your conduct in the pulpit: your behaviour in life² is another scene, upon which I shall readily offer you my thoughts, if you appear to desire them from me by your approbation of what I have here written; if not, I have already troubled you too much.

I am, Sir,<br>Your Affectionate<br>Friend and Servant<br>A. B.

January 9th.
1719-20.

---

[1] What Swift calls learning was, in his day, the property, so to speak, of professional men, such as divines, lawyers, and university teachers. The common man was too poor or too much taxed to acquire it; the aristocrat often too lazy or too fond of pleasure-seeking to bother about it. The Pre-Reformation days, to which Swift refers, could boast such men as Fabyan, Hall, Chaucer, Gower, and Caxton, as well as Lord Berners, Sir Thomas More, and Lydgate, who were not, in any sense, professional men. [T. S.]

[2] Scott and Hawkesworth print "your behaviour in the world." The above is the reading of the first edition. [T. S.]

# SOME ARGUMENTS AGAINST ENLARGING THE POWER OF BISHOPS IN LETTING OF LEASES.

### NOTE.

THE years between that which saw the publication of the "Drapier Letters," and that which rang with the fame of "Gulliver's Travels," were busy fighting years for Swift. Apart from his vigorous championship of the Test, and his war against the Dissenters, he espoused the cause of the inferior clergy of his own Church, as against the bishops. The business of filling the vacant sees of Ireland had degenerated into what we should now call "jobbery"; and during the period of Sir Robert Walpole's administration it was rarely that an Irishman was selected. On any question, therefore, which affected the welfare of the lower clergy, it will at once be seen, that the Lords Spiritual, sitting in the Irish Upper House, would find little difficulty in coming to a solution. That the solution should also be one which only increased the clergy's difficulties, might be expected from a body which aimed chiefly at acquiring wealth and power for itself.

In the reign of Charles I. an act was passed, "prohibiting all bishops, and other ecclesiastical corporations, from setting their lands for above the term of twenty-one years: the rent reserved to be half the real value of such lands at the time they were set." As Swift points out, about the time of the Reformation, a trade was carried on by the popish bishops, who felt that their terms of office would be short, and who, consequently, to get what benefit they could while in office, "made long leases and fee-farms of great part of their lands, reserving very inconsiderable rents, sometimes only a chiefry." It was owing to a continuance in this traffic by the bishops when they became Protestants, and to a recognition of the injustice of such alienation, that the legislature passed the act. In 1723, however, an attempt was made for its repeal. Swift was not the man to permit the bishops to have their way, if he could help it. His opinion of Irish bishops is well known. "No blame," he said, "rested with the court for these appointments. Excellent and moral men had been selected upon every occasion of vacancy; but it unfortunately happened, that as these worthy divines crossed Hounslow Heath, on their way to Ireland, to take possession of their bishoprics, they have been regularly robbed and murdered by the highwaymen frequenting that common, who seize upon their robes and patents, come over to Ireland, and are consecrated bishops in their stead." To prevent, therefore, the encroachments of such individuals he wrote this tract, in which he clearly demonstrates the justice and salutariness of Charles's act. His contention, as Monck Mason points out ("History of St. Patrick's Cathedral," p. 392, note l.) "is confirmed by all writers upon the subject," and quotes from Carte's "Life of James, Duke of Ormond," where it is stated that the bishoprics in Ireland had, "the greatest part of them, been depauperated in the change of religion by absolute grants and long leases (made generally by the popish bishops that conformed) —some of them not able to maintain a bishop; several were, by these means, reduced to £50 a year, as Waterford, Kilfenora, and others; and some to five marks, as Cloyne and Kilmacduagh." To Swift is largely due the fact that the House of Commons, when they received the bill from the Lords, threw it out.

Scott, in his note on this pamphlet (amended from one by Lord Orrery), takes his usual course when considering Swift's attitude of opposition—he implies a motive of prejudice. In his opinion, Swift considered the bill for the repeal of Charles's act, "an indirect mode of gratifying the existing bishops, whom he did not regard with peculiar respect or complacency, at the expense of the Church establishment," and that, therefore, "the spirit of his opposition is, in this instance, peculiarly caustic." As a matter of fact, the spirit of Swift's opposition was always peculiarly caustic, in this case no more so than in any other. But to imply that his motive was a self-gratifying one only, is to treat Swift unfairly. If the bishops required an example as to how they should deal with their lands, they could easily have found one in Swift himself. In all the renewals of the leases of the Deanery lands, Swift never sought his own immediate advantage: his terms were based on the consideration that the lands were his only in trust for a successor. To take one instance only, the instance of the parish of Kilberry in county Kildare, cited by Monck Mason (p. 27, note h). In 1695 the rent of this parish was reserved at £100 English sterling; in 1717, Swift raised this rent to £150; in 1731 to £170, and in 1741 to £200 per annum, with a proportionable loss of fine upon each occasion.

The tract is dated October 21st, 1723, but as I have not come across a copy of the original separate issue, I have based the text on that given by Faulkner (vol. iv., 1735), and the title-page here reproduced is from that edition. The fifth volume of "Miscellanies," also issued in 1735, contains this tract, and I have compared the texts of the two. The notes given in Scott's edition are, in the main, altered from Faulkner's edition.

[T. S.]

SOME
# ARGUMENTS
Againſt ENLARGING the
*Power of BISHOPS,*
In LETTING of
# LEASES.
WITH
REMARKS on ſome *Queries*
lately publiſhed.

---

*Mihi credite, major hæreditas venit unicuique ve-
ſtrûm in iiſdem bonis à jure & à legibus, quam ab
iis à quibus illa ipſa bona relicta ſunt.*

Cicero pro A. Cæcina.

---

Written in the Year 1723.

---

---

Printed in the Year MDCCXXXIII.

# SOME ARGUMENTS

AGAINST

## ENLARGING THE POWER OF BISHOPS IN LETTING OF LEASES.

IN handling this subject, I shall proceed wholly upon the supposition, that those of our party, who profess themselves members of the church established, and under the apostolical government of bishops, do desire the continuance and transmission of it to posterity, at least, in as good a condition as it is at present. Because, as this discourse is not calculated for dissenters of any kind; so neither will it suit the talk or sentiments of those persons, who, with the denomination of churchmen, are oppressors of the inferior clergy, and perpetually quarrelling at the great incomes of the bishops; which is a traditional cant delivered down from former times, and continued with great reason, although it be now near 200 years since almost three parts in four of the church revenues have been taken from the clergy: Besides the spoils that have been gradually made ever since, of glebes and other lands, by the confusion of times, the fraud of encroaching neighbours, or the power of oppressors, too great to be encountered.

About the time of the Reformation, many popish bishops of this kingdom, knowing they must have been soon ejected, if they would not change their religion, made long leases and fee-farms of great part of their lands, reserving very inconsiderable rents, sometimes only a chiefry; by a power they assumed, directly contrary to many ancient canons, yet consistent enough with the common law. This trade held on for many years after the bishops became Protestants;

and some of their names are still remembered with infamy, on account of enriching their families by such sacrilegious alienations. By these means, episcopal revenues were so low reduced, that three or four sees were often united to make a tolerable competency. For some remedy to this evil, King James the First, by a bounty that became a good Christian prince, bestowed several forfeited lands on the northern bishoprics: But in all other parts of the kingdom, the Church continued still in the same distress and poverty; some of the sees hardly possessing enough to maintain a country vicar. About the middle of King Charles the First's reign, the legislature here thought fit to put a stop, at least, to any farther alienations; and so a law was enacted, prohibiting all bishops, and other ecclesiastical corporations, from setting their lands for above the term of twenty-one years; the rent reserved to be one half of the real value or such lands at the time they were set, without which condition the lease to be void.

Soon after the restoration of King Charles the Second, the parliament taking into consideration the miserable estate of the Church, certain lands, by way of augmentation, were granted to eight bishops in the act of settlement, and confirmed in the act of explanation; of which bounty, as I remember, three sees were, in a great measure, defeated; but by what accidents, it is not here of any importance to relate.

This, at present, is the condition of the Church in Ireland, with regard to Episcopal revenues: Which I have thus briefly (and, perhaps, imperfectly) deduced for some information to those, whose thoughts do not lead them to such considerations.

By virtue of the statute, already mentioned, under King Charles the First, limiting ecclesiastical bodies to the term of twenty-one years, under the reserved rent of half real value, the bishops have had some share in the gradual rise of lands, without which they could not have been supported, with any common decency that might become their station. It is above eighty years since the passing of that act: The see of Meath, one of the best in the kingdom, was then worth about £400 *per annum;* the poorer ones in the same proportion. If this were their present condition, I cannot conceive how they would have been able to pay for their patents, or buy their robes: But this will certainly be the condition of their successors, if such a bill should pass, as they say is now intended, which I will suppose, and believe, many persons, who may give a vote for it, are not aware of.

However, this is the act which is now attempted to be repealed, or, at least, eluded; some are for giving bishops leave to let fee-farms; others would allow them to let leases for lives; and the most moderate would repeal that clause, by which the bishops are bound to let their lands at half value.

The reasons for the rise of value in lands, are of two kinds. Of the first kind, are long peace and settlement after the devastations of war; plantations, improvements of bad soil, recovery of bogs and marshes, advancement of trade and manufactures, increase of inhabitants, encouragement of agriculture, and the like.

But there is another reason for the rise of land, more gradual, constant and certain; which will have its effects in countries that are very far from flourishing in any of the advantages I have just mentioned: I mean *the perpetual decrease in the value of gold and silver*. I shall discourse upon these two different kinds, with a view towards the bill now attempted.

As to the first: I cannot see how this kingdom is at any height of improvement, while four parts in five of the plantations for 30 years past, have been real disimprovements; nine in ten of the quick-set hedges being ruined for want of care or skill. And as to forest trees, they being often taken out of woods, and planted in single rows on the tops of ditches, it is impossible they should grow to be of use, beauty, or shelter. Neither can it be said, that the soil of Ireland is improved to its full height, while so much lies all winter under water, and the bogs made almost desperate by the ill cutting of the turf. There hath, indeed, been some little improvement in the manufactures of linen and woollen, although very short of perfection: But our trade was never in so low a condition: And as to agriculture, of which all wise nations have been so tender, the desolation made in the country by engrossing graziers, and the great yearly importation of corn from England, are lamentable instances under what discouragement it lies.

But, notwithstanding all these mortifications, I suppose there is no well-wisher to his country, without a little hope, that in time the kingdom may be on a better foot in some of the articles above mentioned. But it would be hard, if ecclesiastical bodies should be the only persons excluded from any share in public advantages; which yet can never happen, without a greater share of profit to their tenants: If God "sends rain equally upon the just and the unjust;" why should those who wait at His altars, and are instructors of the people, be cut off from partaking in the general benefits of law, or of nature?

But, as this way of reasoning may seem to to bear a more favourable eye to the clergy, than perhaps will suit with the present disposition, or fashion of the age; I shall, therefore, dwell more largely upon the second reason for the rise of land, which is the perpetual decrease of the value of gold and silver.

This may be observed from the course of the Roman history, above two thousand years before those inexhaustible silver mines of Potosi were known. The value of an obolus, and of every other coin between the time of Romulus and that of Augustus, gradually sunk about five parts in six, as appears by several passages out of the best authors. And yet, the prodigious wealth of that state did not arise from the increase of bullion in the world, by the discovery of new mines, but from a much more accidental cause, which was, the spreading of their conquests, and thereby importing into Rome and Italy, the riches of the east and west.

When the seat of empire was removed to Constantinople, the tide of money flowed that way, without ever returning; and was scattered in Asia. But when that mighty empire was overthrown by the northern people, such a stop was put to all trade and commerce, that vast sums of money were buried, to escape the plundering of the conquerors; and what remained was carried off by those ravagers.

It were no difficult matter to compute the value of money in England, during the Saxon reigns; but the monkish and other writers since the Conquest, have put that matter in a clearer light, by the several accounts they have given us of the value of corn and cattle, in years of dearth and plenty. Every one knows, that King John's whole portion, before he came to the crown, was but five thousand pounds, without a foot of land.

I have likewise seen the steward's accounts, of an ancient noble family in England, written in Latin, between three and four hundred years ago, with the several prices of wine and victuals, to confirm my observations.

I have been at the trouble of computing (as others have done) the different values of money for about four hundred years past. Henry Duke of Lancaster, who lived about that period, founded an hospital in Leicester, for a certain number of old men; charging his lands with a groat a week to each for their maintenance, which is to this day duly paid them. In those times, a penny was equal to ten-pence half-penny, and somewhat more than half a farthing in ours; which makes about eight ninths' difference.

This is plain also, from the old custom upon many estates in England, to let for leases of lives, (renewable at pleasure) where the reserved rent is usually about twelve-pence a pound, which then was near the half real value: And although the fines be not fixed, yet the landlord gets altogether not above three shillings in the pound of the worth of his land: And the tenants are so wedded to this custom, that if the owner suffer three lives to expire, none of them will take a lease on other conditions; or, if he brings in a foreigner who will agree to pay a reasonable rent, the other tenants, by all manner of injuries, will make that foreigner so uneasy, that he must be forced to quit the farm; as the late Earl of Bath felt, by the experience of above ten thousand pounds loss.

The gradual decrease for about two hundred years after, was not considerable, and therefore I do not rely on the account given by some historians, that Harry the Seventh left behind him eighteen hundred thousand pounds; for although the West Indies were discovered before his death, and although he had the best talents and instruments for exacting of money, ever possessed by any prince since the time of Vespasian, (whom he resembled in many particulars); yet I conceive, that in his days the whole coin of England could hardly amount to such a sum. For in the reign of

Philip and Mary, Sir Thomas Cokayne of Derbyshire,[1] the best housekeeper of his quality in the county, allowed his lady fifty pounds a year for maintaining the family, one pound a year wages to each servant, and two pounds to the steward; as I was told by a person of quality who had seen the original account of his economy. Now this sum of fifty pound, added to the advantages of a large domain, might be equal to about five hundred pounds a year at present, or somewhat more than four-fifths.

The great plenty of silver in England began in Queen Elizabeth's reign, when Drake, and others, took vast quantities of coin and bullion from the Spaniards, either upon their own American coasts, or in their return to Spain. However, so much hath been imported annually from that time to this, that the value of money in England, and most parts of Europe, is sunk above one half within the space of an hundred years, notwithstanding the great export of silver for about eighty years past, to the East Indies, from whence it never returns. But gold being not liable to the same accident, and by new discoveries growing every day more plentiful, seems in danger of becoming a drug.

This hath been the progress of the value of money in former ages, and must of necessity continue so for the future, without some new invasion of Goths and Vandals to destroy law, property and religion, alter the very face of nature; and turn the world upside down.

I must repeat, that what I am to say upon this subject, is intended only for the conviction of those among our own party, who are true lovers of the Church, and would be glad it should continue in a tolerable degree of prosperity to the end of the world.

The Church is supposed to last for ever, both in its discipline and doctrine; which is a privilege common to every petty corporation, who must likewise observe the laws of their foundation. If a gentleman's estate which now yields

---

[1] Sir Thomas Cokayne (1519?-1592), known as "a professed hunter and not a scholler." He was the eldest son of Francis Cokayne, or Cockaine, of Ashbourne, Derbyshire. One of his sons, Edward, was the father of Thomas Cokayne, the lexicographer. Sir Thomas, in 1591, published "A Short Treatise of Hunting, compyled for the Delight of Noblemen and Gentlemen." [T. S.]

him a thousand pounds a year, had been set for ever at the highest value, even in the flourishing days of King Charles the Second, would it now amount to above four or five hundred at most? What if this had happened two or three hundred years ago; would the reserved rent at this day be any more than a small chiefry? Suppose the revenues of a bishop to have been under the same circumstances; could he now be able to perform works of hospitality and charity? Thus, if the revenues of a bishop be limited to a thousand pounds a year; how will his successor be in a condition to support his station with decency, when the same denomination of money shall not answer an half, a quarter, or an eighth part of that sum? Which must unavoidably be the consequence of any bill to elude the limiting act, whereby the Church was preserved from utter ruin.

The same reason holds good in all corporations whatsoever, who cannot follow a more pernicious practice than that of granting perpetuities, for which many of them smart to this day; although the leaders among them are often so stupid as not to perceive it, or sometimes so knavish as to find their private account in cheating the community.

Several colleges in Oxford, were aware of this growing evil about an hundred years ago; and, instead of limiting their rents to a certain sum of money, prevailed with their tenants to pay the price of so many barrels of corn, to be valued as the market went, at two seasons (as I remember) in the year. For a barrel of corn is of a real intrinsic value, which gold and silver are not: And by this invention, these colleges have preserved a tolerable subsistence, for their fellows and students, to this day.

The present bishops will, indeed be no sufferers by such a bill; because, their ages considered, they cannot expect to see any great decrease in the value of money; or, at worst, they can make it up in the fines, which will probably be greater than usual, upon the change of leases into fee-farms, or lives; or without the power of obliging their tenants to a real half value. And, as I cannot well blame them for taking such advantages, (considering the nature of human kind) when the question is only, whether the money shall be put into their own or another man's pocket: So they will be never excusable before God or man, if they do not to the death oppose, declare, and protest against any such bill, as must in its consequences complete the ruin of the Church, and of their own order in this kingdom.

If the fortune of a private person be diminished by the weakness, or inadvertency of his ancestors, in letting leases for ever at low rents, the world lies open to his industry for purchasing of more; but the Church is barred by a *dead hand;* or if it were otherwise, yet the custom of making bequests to it, hath been out of practice for almost two hundred years, and a great deal directly contrary hath been its fortune.

I have been assured by a person of some consequence, to whom I am likewise obliged for the account of some other facts already related, that the late Bishop of Salisbury,[1] (the greatest Whig of that bench in his days) confessed to him, that the liberty which bishops in England have of letting leases for lives, would, in his opinion, be one day the ruin of Episcopacy there; and thought the Church in this kingdom happy by the limitation act.

And have we not already found the effect of this different proceeding in both kingdoms? Have not two English prelates quitted their peerage and seats in Parliament, in a nation of freedom, for the sake of a more ample revenue, even in this unhappy kingdom, rather thon lie under the mortification of living below their dignity at home? For which, however, they cannot be justly censured. I know indeed, some persons, who offer, as an argument for repealing the limiting bill, that it may in future ages prevent the practice of providing this kingdom with bishops from England, when the only temptation will be removed. And they allege, that, as things have gone for some years past, gentlemen will grow discouraged from sending their sons to the university, and from suffering them to enter into holy orders, when they are likely to languish under a curacy, or small vicarage, to the end of their lives: But this is all a vain imagination; for the decrease in the value of money will equally affect both kingdoms. And besides, when bishoprics here grow too small to invite over men of credit and consequence, they will he left more fully to the disposal of a chief governor, who can never fail of some worthless illiterate

---

[1] Dr. Burnet.

chaplain, fond of a title and precedence. Thus will that whole bench, in an age or two, be composed of mean, ignorant, fawning gownmen, humble suppliants and dependants upon the court for a morsel of bread, and ready to serve every turn that shall be demanded from them, in hopes of getting some *commendam* tacked to their sees; which must then be the trade, as it is now too much in England, to the great discouragement of the inferior clergy. Neither is that practice without example among us.

It is now about eighty-five years since the passing of that limiting act, and there is but one instance, in the memory of man, of a bishop's lease broken upon the plea of not being statutable; which, in everybody's opinion, could have been lost by no other person than he who was then tenant, and happened to be very ungracious in his county. In the present Bishop of Meath's[1] case, that plea did not avail, although the lease were notoriously unstatutable; the rent reserved, being, as I have been told, not a seventh part of the real value; yet the jury, upon their oaths, very gravely found it to be according to the statute; and one of them was heard to say, That he would *eat his shoes* before he would give a verdict for the bishop. A very few more have made the same attempt with as little success. Every bishop, and other ecclesiastical body, reckon forty pounds in an hundred to be a reasonable half value; or if it be only a third part, it seldom, or never, breeds any difference between landlord and tenant. But when the rent is from five to nine or ten parts less than the worth; the bishop, if he consults the good of his see, will be apt to expostulate; and the tenant, if he be an honest man, will have some regard to the reasonableness and justice of the demand, so as to yield to a moderate advancement, rather than engage in a suit, where law and equity are directly against him. By these means, the bishops have been so true to their trusts, as to procure some small share in the advancement of rents; although it be notorious that they do not receive the third penny (fines included) of the real value of their lands throughout the kingdom.

I was never able to imagine what inconvenience could

[1] Dr. Evans, a Welchman. [Faulkner, 1735.]

accrue to the public, by one or two thousand pounds a year, in the hands of a Protestant bishop, any more than of a lay person.[1] The former, generally speaking, liveth as piously and hospitably as the other; pays his debts as honestly, and spends as much of his revenue among his tenants: Besides, if they be his immediate tenants, you may distinguish them, at first sight, by their habits and horses; or if you go to their houses, by their comfortable way of living. But the misfortune is, that such immediate tenants, generally speaking, have others under them, and so a third and fourth in subordination, till it comes to the welder (as they call him) who sits at a rack-rent, and lives as miserably as an Irish farmer upon a new lease from a lay landlord. But suppose a bishop happens to be avaricious, (as being composed of the same stuff with other men) the consequence to the public is no worse than if he were a squire; for he leaves his fortune to his son, or near relation, who, if he be rich enough, will never think of entering into the Church.

And, as there can be no disadvantage to the public, in a Protestant country, that a man should hold lands as a bishop, any more than if he were a temporal person; so it is of great advantage to the community, where a bishop lives as he ought to do. He is bound, in conscience, to reside in his diocese, and, by a solemn promise, to keep hospitality; his estate is spent in the kingdom, not remitted to England; he keeps the clergy to their duty, and is an example of virtue both to them and the people. Suppose him an ill man; yet his very character will withhold him from any great or open exorbitancies. But, in fact, it must be allowed, that some bishops of this kingdom, within twenty years past, have done very signal and lasting acts of public charity; great instances whereof, are the late[2] and present[3] Primate, the Lord Archbishop of Dublin[4] that now is, who hath left memorials of his bounty in many parts of his province. I might add, the Bishop of Raphoe,[5] and several others: Not

---

[1] This part of the paragraph is to be applied to the period when the whole was written, which was in 1723, when several of Queen Anne's bishops were living. [Note in edition of 1761, as amended from the edition of 1735. T. S.]

[2] Dr. Marsh.   [3] Dr. Lindsay.
[4] Dr. King.   [5] Dr. Forster.

forgetting the late Dean of Down, Dr. Pratt, who bestowed one thousand pounds upon the university: Which foundation, (that I may observe by the way) if the bill proposed should pass, would be in the same circumstances with the bishops, nor ever able again to advance the stipends of the fellows and students, as lately they found it necessary to do; the determinate sum appointed by the statute for commons, being not half sufficient, by the fall of money, to afford necessary sustenance. But the passing of such a bill must put an end to all ecclesiastical beneficence for the time to come; and whether this will be supplied by those who are to reap the benefit, better than it hath been done by the grantees of impropriate tithes, who received them upon the old church conditions of keeping hospitality; it will be easy to conjecture.

To allege, that passing such a bill would be a good encouragement to improve bishops' lands, is a great error. Is it not the general method of landlords, to wait the expiration of a lease, and then cant[1] their lands to the highest bidder? And what should hinder the same course to be taken in church leases, when the limitation is removed of paying half the real value to the bishop? In riding through the country, how few improvements do we see upon the estates of laymen, farther than about their own domains? To say the truth, it is a great misfortune as well to the public as to the bishops themselves, that their lands are generally let to lords and great squires, who, in reason, were never designed to be tenants; and therefore may naturally murmur at the payment of rent, as a subserviency they were not born to. If the tenants to the Church were honest farmers, they would pay their fines and rents with cheerfulness, improve their lands, and thank God they were to give but a moderate half value for what they held. I have heard a man of a thousand pounds a year, talk with great contempt of bishops' leases, as being on a worse foot than the rest of his estate; and he had certainly reason: My answer was, that such leases were originally intended only for the benefit of industrious husbandmen, who would think it a great blessing to be so provided for, instead of having his farm screwed up to the

[1] To cant means to call for bidders at an auction sale. Probably derived from the O. French *cant* = *quantum* = how much. [T. S.]

height, not eating one comfortable meal in a year, nor able to find shoes for his children.

I know not any advantage that can accrue by such a bill, except the preventing of perjury in jurymen, and false dealing in tenants; which is a remedy like that of giving my money to an highwayman, before he attempts to take it by force; and so I shall be sure to prevent the sin of robbery.

I had wrote thus far, and thought to have put an end; when a bookseller sent me a small pamphlet, entitled, "The Case of the Laity, with some Queries;" full of the strongest malice against the clergy, that I have anywhere met with since the reign of Toland, and others of that tribe. These kinds of advocates do infinite mischief to OUR GOOD CAUSE, by giving grounds to the unjust reproaches of TORIES and JACOBITES, who charge us with being enemies to the Church. If I bear an hearty unfeigned loyalty to his Majesty King George, and the House of Hanover, not shaken in the least by the hardships we lie under, which never can be imputable to so gracious a prince: If I sincerely abjure the Pretender, and all Popish successors; if I bear a due veneration to the glorious memory of the late King William, who preserved these kingdoms from Popery and slavery, with the expense of his blood, and hazard of his life: And lastly, if I am for a proper indulgence to all dissenters; I think nothing more can be reasonably demanded of me as a WHIG, and that my political catechism is full and complete. But whoever, under the shelter of that party denomination, and of many great professions of loyalty, would destroy, or undermine, or injure the Church established; I utterly disown him, and think he ought to choose another name of distinction for himself, and his adherents. I came into the cause upon other principles, which, by the grace of God, I mean to preserve as long as I live. Shall we justify the accusations of our adversaries? *Hoc Ithacus velit.*—The Tories and Jacobites will behold us with a malicious pleasure, determined upon the ruin of our friends: For is not the present set of bishops almost entirely of that number, as well as a great majority of the principal clergy? And a short time will reduce the whole, by vacancies upon death.

An impartial reader, if he pleases to examine what I have already said, will easily answer the bold "Queries" in the pamphlet I mentioned: He will be convinced, that "the reason still strongly exists, for which" that limiting law was enacted. A reasonable man will wonder, where can be the insufferable grievance, that an ecclesiastical landlord should expect a moderate, or third part value in rent for his lands, when his title is, *at least*, as ancient and as legal as that of a layman; who is yet but seldom guilty of giving such beneficial bargains. Has "the nation been thrown into confusion"? And have "many poor families been ruined" by rack-rents paid for the lands of the church? Does "the nation cry out" to have a law that must, in time, send their bishops a-begging? But, God be thanked, the clamour of enemies to the Church is not yet the cry, and, I hope, will never prove the voice of the nation. The clergy, I conceive, will hardly allow that "the people maintain them," any more than in the sense, that all landlords whatsoever are maintained by the people. Such assertions as these, and the insinuations they carry along with them, proceed from principles which cannot be avowed by those who are for preserving the happy constitution in Church and State. Whoever were the proposers of such "queries," it might have provoked a bold writer to retaliate, perhaps with more justice than prudence, by shewing at whose door the grievance lies, and that the bishops, *at least*, are not to answer for the poverty of tenants.

To gratify this great reformer, who enlarges the episcopal rent-roll almost one half; let me suppose that all the Church lands in the kingdom were thrown up to the laity; would the tenants, in such a case, sit easier in their rents than they do now? Or, would the money be equally spent in the kingdom? No: The farmer would be screwed up to the utmost penny, by the agents and stewards of absentees, and the revenues employed in making a figure at London; to which city a full third part of the whole income of Ireland is annually returned, to answer that single article of maintenance for Irish landlords.

Another of his quarrels is against pluralities and non-residence: As to the former, it is a word of ill name, but not well understood. The clergy having been stripped of the greatest part of their revenues, the glebes being generally lost, the tithes in the hands of laymen, the churches demolished, and the country depopulated; in order to preserve a face of Christianity, it was necessary to unite small vicarages, sufficient to make a tolerable maintenance for a minister. The profit of ten or a dozen of these unions, do seldom amount to above eighty or an hundred pounds a year: If there be a very few dignitaries, whose preferments are, perhaps, more liable to this accusation, it is to be supposed, they may be favourites of the time, or persons of superior merit, for whom there hath ever been some indulgence in all governments.

As to non-residence, I believe there is no Christian country upon earth, where the clergy have less to answer for upon that article. I am confident there are not ten clergymen in the kingdom, who, properly speaking, can be termed non-residents: For surely, we are not to reckon in that number, those who, for want of glebes, are forced to retire to the nearest neighbouring village for a cabin to put their heads in; the leading man of the parish, when he makes the greatest clamour, being least disposed to accommodate the minister with an acre of ground. And, indeed, considering the difficulties the clergy lie under upon this head, it hath been frequent matter of wonder to me, how they are able to perform that part of their duty as well as they do.

There is a noble author,[1] who hath lately addressed to the House of Commons, an excellent discourse for the "Encouragement of Agriculture"; full of most useful hints, which, I hope, that honourable assembly will consider as they deserve. I am not a stranger to his lordship; and, excepting in what relates to the Church, there are few persons with whose opinions I am better pleased to agree; and am, therefore, grieved when I find him charging the inconveniencies in the payment of tithes upon the clergy and their proctors. His lordship is above considering a very known and vulgar truth, that the meanest farmer hath all manner of advantages against the most powerful clergyman, by whom it is impossible he can be wronged, although the minister were ever so evil disposed; the whole system of teasing, perplexing, and defrauding the proctor, or his master, being as well known to every ploughman, as the reaping or sowing of his

---

[1] The late Lord Molesworth.

corn, and much more artfully practised. Besides, the leading man in the parish must have his tithes at his own rate, which is hardly ever above one quarter of the value. And I have heard it computed by many skilful observers, whose interest was not concerned, that the clergy did not receive, throughout the kingdom, one half of what the laws have made their due.

As to his lordship's discontent against the Bishops' Courts, I shall not interpose further than in venturing my private opinion, that the clergy would be very glad to recover their just dues by a more short, decisive, and compulsive method, than such a cramped and limited juirsdiction will allow.

His lordship is not the only person disposed to give the clergy the honour of being the *sole* encouragers of all new improvements. If hops, hemp, flax, and twenty things more are to be planted, the clergy, *alone*, must reward the industrious farmer, by abatement of the tithe. What if the owner of nine parts in ten would please to abate proportionably in his rent, for every acre thus improved? Would not a man just dropped from the clouds, upon a full hearing, judge the demand to be, at least, as reasonable?

I believe no man will dispute his lordship's title to his estate; nor will I the *jus divinum* of tithes, which he mentions with some emotion. I suppose the affirmative would be of little advantage to the clergy, for the same reason that a maxim in law hath more weight in the world than an article of faith. And yet, I think there may be such a thing as sacrilege; because it is frequently mentioned by Greek and Roman authors, as well as described in Holy Writ. This I am sure of; that his lordship would, at any time, excuse a parliament for not concerning itself in his properties, without his own consent.

The observations I have made upon his lordship's discourse, have not, I confess, been altogether proper to my subject: However, since he hath been pleased therein to offer some proposals to the House of Commons, with relation to the clergy, I hope he will excuse me for differing from him; which proceeds from his own principle, the desire of defending liberty and property, that he hath so strenuously and constantly maintained.

But the other writer openly declares for a law, empowering the bishops to set fee-farms; and says, "Whoever intimates that they will deny their consent to such a reasonable law, which the whole nation cries for, are enemies to them and the Church." Whether this be his real opinion, or only a strain of mirth and irony, the matter is not much. However, my sentiments are so directly contrary to his; that I think, whoever impartially reads and considers what I have written upon this argument, hath either no regard for the Church established under the hierarchy of bishops, or will never consent to any law that shall repeal, or elude the limiting clause, relating to the real half value, contained in the act of parliament *decimo Caroli*, "For the preservation of the inheritance, rights and profits of lands belonging to the Church, and persons ecclesiastical"; which was grounded upon reasons that do still, and must for ever subsist.

October 21,
1723.

[REASONS HUMBLY OFFERED]
TO HIS GRACE
## WILLIAM, LORD ARCHBISHOP OF DUBLIN, &c.

THE HUMBLE REPRESENTATION OF THE CLERGY
OF THE CITY OF DUBLIN.

## NOTE.

SCOTT's text has been collated with that given in volume eight of the quarto edition of Swift's Works (1765). In that edition the title is given as: "The Representation of the Clergy of Dublin," &c.

[T. S.]

# [REASONS HUMBLY OFFERED] TO HIS GRACE WILLIAM, LORD ARCHBISHOP OF DUBLIN, &c.[1]

### THE HUMBLE REPRESENTATION OF THE CLERGY OF THE CITY OF DUBLIN.

*Jan.* 1724.

MY LORD,

YOUR Grace having been pleased to communicate to us a certain brief, by letters patents, for the relief of one Charles M'Carthy, whose house in College-Green, Dublin, was burnt by an accidental fire; and having desired us to consider of the said brief, and give our opinions thereof to your Grace;

---

[1] William King, D.D. (1650-1729), Archbishop of Dublin, was born in Antrim, and educated at a school at Dungannon and Trinity College, Dublin. He was installed Dean of St. Patrick's in 1688-9 (February 1st). For his open espousal of the Prince of Orange, he was confined to the Castle, and suffered many indignities. In 1690-1 (January 9th) he was promoted to the see of Derry. His conduct through life was that of an ardent Irish Protestant patriot. He fought against Sectarianism, Roman Catholicism, and the interference of the English Parliament in Irish affairs. He opposed the Toleration Bill, and protested against the act confirming the Articles of Limerick. His relationship with Swift became close when he sent the vicar of Laracor to London, to obtain for the Irish clergy the restoration of the first-fruits and twentieth parts; but it was a relationship never cemented by feelings warmer than those of esteem. King acknowledged the ability of Swift, but found him ambitious and overbearingly proud. Throughout life he remained a consistent High Churchman, and a strenuous supporter of the rights of the Church in Ireland, but his attempt, in 1727, to interfere with the affairs of the Deanery of St. Patrick's, brought down upon him Swift's wrath,

We the Clergy of the city of Dublin, in compliance with your Grace's desire, and with great acknowledgments for your paternal tenderness towards us, having maturely considered the said brief by letters patents, compared the several parts of it with what is enjoined us by the rubric, (which is confirmed by act of parliament) and consulted persons skilled in the laws of the Church; do, in the names of ourselves and of the rest of our brethren, the Clergy of the diocese of Dublin, most humbly represent to your Grace:

First, That, by this brief, your Grace is required and commanded, to recommend and command all the parsons, vicars, &c., to advance so great an act of charity.

We shall not presume to determine how far your Grace may be commanded by the said brief; but we humbly conceive that the Clergy of your diocese cannot, by any law now in being, be commanded by your Grace to advance the said act of charity, any other ways than by reading the said brief in our several churches, as prescribed by the rubric.

Secondly, Whereas it is said in the said brief, "That the parsons, vicars, &c. upon the first Lord's day, or opportunity after the receipt of the copy of the said brief, shall, deliberately and affectionately, publish and declare the tenor thereof to His Majesty's subjects, and earnestly persuade, exhort, and stir them up to contribute freely and cheerfully towards the relief of the said sufferer;"

We do not comprehend what is meant by the word *opportunity*. We never do preach upon any day except the Lord's day, or some solemn days legally appointed; neither is it possible for the strongest constitution among us to obey this command (which includes no less than a whole sermon) upon any other opportunity than when our people are met together in the church; and to perform this work in every

and an open quarrel ensued which was partly softened by the Archbishop retiring from the matter and tacitly acknowledging Swift's right.

King's chief published work is his treatise "De Origine Mali," published in 1702, and received with respectful consideration by the eminent thinkers of the day. He wrote other minor works, but none of any distinguished merit. He succeeded Narcissus Marsh as Archbishop of Dublin in 1702-3 (March 11th). Swift's letters to King during the former's embassy on the matter of first-fruits, make a most interesting chapter in the six volumes which Scott devotes to Swift's correspondence. [T. S.]

house where the parishes are very populous, consisting sometimes here in town of 900 or 1,000 houses, would take up the space of a year, although we should preach in two families every day; and almost as much time in the country, where the parishes are of large extent, the roads bad, and the people too poor to receive us, and give charity at once.

But, if it be meant that these exhortations are commanded to be made in the church, upon the Lord's day, we are humbly of opinion, that it is left to the discretion of the clergy, to choose what subjects they think most proper to preach on, and at what times; and, if they preach either false doctrine or seditious principles, they are liable to be punished.

It may possibly happen that the sufferer recommended may be a person not deserving the favour intended by the brief; in which case no minister, who knows the sufferer to be an undeserving person, can with a safe conscience, deliberately and affectionately publish the brief, much less earnestly persuade, exhort, and stir up the people to contribute freely and cheerfully towards the relief of such a sufferer.[1]

Thirdly, Whereas in the said brief the ministers and curates are required, "on the week-days next after the Lord's day when the brief was read, to go from house to house, with their church-wardens, to ask and receive from all persons the said charity:" We cannot but observe here, that the said ministers are directly made collectors of the said charity in conjunction with the church-wardens; which however, we presume, was not intended, as being against all law and precedent: And therefore, we apprehend, there may be some inconsistency, which leaves us at a loss how to proceed. For, in the next paragraph, the ministers and curates are only required, where they conveniently can, to accompany the church-wardens, or procure some other of the chief inhabitants, to do the same. And, in a following paragraph, the whole work seems left entirely to the church-wardens,

---

[1] This M'Carthy's house was burnt in the month of August 1723, and the universal opinion of mankind was, that M'Carthy himself was the person who had set fire to the house. [Note in edition of Swift's Works, vol. viii., 1765, 4to.]

who are required to use their utmost diligence to gather and collect the said charity, and to pay the same, in ten days after, to the parson, vicar, &c.

In answer to this, we do represent to your Grace our humble opinion, that neither we nor our church-wardens can be legally commanded or required to go from house to house to receive the said charity; because your Grace hath informed us in your order, at your visitation An. Dom. 1712, that neither we nor our church-wardens are bound to make any collections for the poor, save in the church; which also appears plainly by the rubric, that appoints both time and place, as your Grace hath observed in your said order.

We do likewise assure your Grace, that it is not in our power to procure some of the chief inhabitants of our parishes to accompany the church-wardens from house to house in these collections: And we have reason to believe, that such a proposal, made to our chief inhabitants (particularly in this city, where our chief inhabitants are often peers of the land) would be received in a manner very little to our own satisfaction, or to the advantage of the said collections.

Fourthly, The brief doth will, require, and command the bishops, and all other dignitaries of the Church, that they make their contributions distinctly, to be returned in the several provinces to the several archbishops of the same.

Upon which we take leave to observe that the terms of expression here are of the strongest kind, and in a point that may subject the said dignitaries (for we shall say nothing of the bishops) to great inconveniencies.

The said dignitaries are here willed, required, and commanded to make their contributions distinctly; by which it should seem that they are absolutely commanded to make contributions (for the word *distinctly* is but a circumstance), and may be understood not very agreeable to a voluntary, cheerful contribution. And therefore, if any bishop or dignitary should refuse to make his contribution, (perhaps for very good reasons) he may be thought to incur the crime of disobedience to His Majesty, which all good subjects abhor, when such a command is according to law.

Most dignities of this kingdom consist only of parochial tithes, and the dignitaries are ministers of parishes. A doubt may therefore arise, whether the said dignitaries are willed, required, and commanded, to make their contributions in both capacities, distinctly as dignitaries, and jointly as parsons or vicars.

Many dignities in this kingdom are the poorest kind of benefices; and it should seem hard to put poor dignitaries under the necessity either of making greater contributions than they can afford, or of exposing themselves to the censure of wanting charity, by making their contributions public.

Our Saviour commands us, in works of charity, to "let not our left hand know what our right hand doeth;" which cannot well consist with our being willed, required, and commanded by any earthly power, where no law is prescribed, to publish our charity to the world, if we have a mind to conceal it.

Fifthly, Whereas it is said in the said brief, "That the parson, vicar, &c. of every parish, shall, in six days after the receipt of the said charity, return it to his respective chancellor, &c." This may be a great grievance, hazard, and expense to the said parson, in remote and desolate parts of the country, where often an honest messenger (if such a one can be got) must be hired to travel forty or fifty miles going and coming; which will probably cost more than the value of the contribution he carries with him. And this charge, if briefs should happen to be frequent, would be enough to undo many a poor clergyman in the kingdom.

Sixthly, We observe in the said brief, that the provost and fellows of the University, judges, officers of the courts, and professors of laws common and civil, are neither willed, required, nor commanded to make their contributions; but that so good a work is only recommended to them. Whereas we conceive, that all His Majesty's subjects are equally obliged, with or without His Majesty's commands, to promote works of charity according to their power; and that the clergy, in their ecclesiastical capacity, are only liable to such commands as the rubric, or any other law shall enjoin, being born to the same privileges of freedom with the rest of His Majesty's subjects.

We cannot but observe to your Grace, that, in the English act of the fourth year of Queen Anne, for the better collecting charity money on briefs by letters-patent, &c. the ministers are obliged only to read the briefs in their churches, without any particular exhortations; neither are they commanded to go from house to house with the church-wardens, nor to send the money collected to their respective chancellors, but pay it to the undertaker or agent of the sufferer. So that, we humbly hope, the clergy of this kingdom shall not, without any law in being, be put to greater hardships in this case than their brethren in England, where the legislature, intending to prevent the abuses in collecting charity money on briefs, did not think fit to put the clergy under any of those difficulties we now complain of, in the present brief by letters patent, for the relief of Charles M'Carthy aforesaid.

The collections upon the Lord's day are the principal support of our own numerous poor in our several parishes; and therefore every single brief, with the benefit of a full collection over the whole kingdom, must deprive several thousands of poor of their weekly maintenance, for the sake only of one person, who often becomes a sufferer by his own folly or negligence, and is sure to overvalue his losses double or treble: So that, if this precedent be followed, as it certainly will if the present brief should succeed, we may probably have a new brief every week; and thus, for the advantage of fifty-two persons, whereof not one in ten is deserving, and for the interest of a dozen dexterous clerks and secretaries, the whole poor in the kingdom will be likely to starve.

We are credibly informed, that neither the officers of the Lord Primate, in preparing the report of his Grace's opinion, nor those of the great-seal, in passing the patent for briefs, will remit any of their fees, both which do amount to a considerable sum : And thus the good intentions of well-disposed people are in a great measure disappointed, a large part of their charity being anticipated, and alienated by fees and gratuities.

Lastly, We cannnot but represent to your Grace our great concern and grief, to see the pains and labour of our church-wardens so much increased, by the injunctions and commands put upon them in this brief, to the great disadvantage of the clergy and the people, as well as to their own trouble, damage, and loss of time, to which great additions have been already made, by laws appointing them to collect the taxes for the watch and the poor-house, which they bear with great unwillingness; and, if they shall find themselves further laden with such briefs as this of M'Carthy, it will prove so great a discouragement, that we shall never be able to provide honest and sufficient persons for that weighty office of church-warden, so necessary to the laity as well as the clergy, in all things that relate to the order and regulation of parishes.

Upon all these considerations, we humbly hope that your Grace, of whose fatherly care, vigilance, and tenderness, we have had so many and great instances, will represent our case to his Most Excellent Majesty, or to the chief governor in this kingdom, in such a manner, that we may be neither under the necessity of declining His Majesty's commands in his letters patent, or of taking new and grievous burthens upon ourselves and our church-wardens, to which neither the rubric nor any other law in force oblige us to submit.

ON

# THE BILL

FOR

## THE CLERGY'S RESIDING ON THEIR LIVINGS.

### NOTE.

IN the note to the tract, "Some Arguments against enlarging the Power of Bishops in letting Leases" (p. 219), it was pointed out that the Bill against which this tract was written was an attempt on the part of the bishops to get back a power which they once had abused. Failing in this attempt, in 1723, they renewed the attack in 1731 by promoting two bills, one called a Bill of Residence, the other a Bill of Division.

The ostensible object of the Bill of Residence was to compel the clergy to reside on their livings. By this bill, any person taking a benefice, with cure of souls, of the annual value of £100, was forced, if the land attached to that benefice had no house fit for residence, to build one thereon, in any situation the bishop might think suitable, this house to cost one year and a half's income, and to be completed within a time fixed by the bishop. It will at once be seen that the power over the inferior clergy which this bill placed in the bishops' hands was by no means insignificant; and Swift felt that to make such a bill law would not only tend to impoverish the inferior clergy, but would place them in a position of subjection at once degrading and dispiriting. He opposed the bill, with the consequence that the House of Commons rejected it.

By the Bill of Division "it was intended to be enacted that whenever a church should become vacant, although the incumbent should refuse his consent, it might be lawful for the chief governor, with the assent of the major part of the Privy Council, six at least consenting, by and with the consent of the ordinary and the patron, to subdivide any parish into as many portions as they might think fit, provided that, after such division, the church of the old parish should continue worth, at the least, £300 per annum." This bill, which passed the House of Lords two days after the Bill of Residence, Swift opposed in a spirited and somewhat bitter manner. His opposition largely influenced the Lower House in rejecting it. The two tracts which state the grounds of his opposition to both bills are the present one, and the following tract, "Considerations upon two Bills, sent down from the House of Lords to the House of Commons in Ireland, relating to the Clergy."

Scott notes that the "tone of *aigreur*," which is more distinctly felt in the second of these tracts, intimates a "deep dissatisfaction with late ecclesiastical preferments, which may perhaps be traced as much to personal disappointment as to any better cause;" a statement which it was hardly worth making; since, however deep may have been Swift's personal feelings, he never allowed them to be the impelling motive to his work. It should suffice us to know that the cause which Swift espoused was a disinterested one. As Vicar of Laracor he knew what it was to make a shift of living on an insufficient income; and it may have been this experience as much as "personal disappointment" which gave pungency to his criticism. It is easy enough to find questionable motives for a satirist, especially when that satirist is Swift; let us not, however, forget that in his case the personal element was never permitted to overweight the impersonal purpose. Other men when they reach prosperity often forget or ignore the hard conditions of their previous state; to Swift these conditions were always existing factors in his considerations for the amelioration of his fellow-men. This it is which gives to his writings so much of the "tone of *aigreur*."

In his letter to John Stearne, Bishop of Clogher, dated July, 1733, which is one of Swift's most characteristic epistles—characteristic, because the embodiment of truthful candour—he gives no equivocal expression of opinion on these two bills. He calls them, "abominable bills, for enslaving and beggaring the clergy, (which took their birth from hell)." "I call God to witness," he adds, "that I did then, and do now, and shall for ever, firmly believe, that every Bishop who gave his vote for either of these bills, did it with no other view (bating further promotion), than a premeditated design, from the spirit of ambition, and love of arbitrary power, to make the whole body of the clergy their slaves and vassals until the day of judgment, under the load of poverty and contempt."

About the same time, 1732, appeared another pamphlet entitled, "The Reconciler . . . shewing how all the good ends proposed by either of those bills, may, by a more gentle and easy method, be attained, without injury to the rights of my lords the bishops; or rigour and violence to the inferior clergy." In the main, the writer agrees with Swift; but the tract is valuable as showing that the controversy was no small one, and it furnishes also what is, apparently, an impartial history of the whole affair. Three Irish prelates voted against the bills on a division—Theophilus Bolton, Archbishop of Cashel, Charles Carr, Bishop of Killaloe, and Robert Howard, Bishop of Elphin.

The text of this tract is based on that which appeared in a volume of "Miscellanies in Prose and Verse" in the year 1789. It has been collated with those given by Scott, Hawkesworth, and other editors.

[T. S.]

# ON THE BILL FOR THE CLERGY'S RESIDING ON THEIR LIVINGS.

THOSE gentlemen who have been promoted to bishoprics in this kingdom for several years past, are of two sorts: first, certain private clergymen from England, who, by the force of friends, industry, solicitation, or other means and merits to me unknown, have been raised to that character by the *mero motu* of the crown.

Of the other sort, are some clergymen born in this kingdom, who have most distinguished themselves by their warmth against Popery, their great indulgence to Dissenters, and all true loyal Protestants; by their zeal for the House of Hanover, abhorrence of the Pretender, and an implicit readiness to fall into any measures that will make the government easy to those who represent His Majesty's person.

Some of the former kind are such as are said to have enjoyed tolerable preferments in England; and it is therefore much to their commendation that they have condescended to leave their native country, and come over hither to be bishops, merely to promote Christianity among us; and therefore in my opinion, both their lordships, and the many defenders they bring over, may justly claim the merit of missionaries sent to convert a nation from heresy and heathenism.

Before I proceed farther, it may be proper to relate some particulars wherein the circumstances of the English clergy differ from those of Ireland.

The districts of parishes throughout England continue much the same as they were before the Reformation; and most of the churches are of the gothic architecture, built some hundred years ago; but the tithes of great numbers of churches having been applied by the Pope's pretended authority to several abbeys, and even before the Reformation bestowed by that sacrilegious tyrant Henry VIII., on his ravenous favourites, the maintenance of an incumbent in most parts of the kingdom is contemptibly small; and yet a vicar there of forty pounds a year, can live with more comfort, than one of three times the nominal value with us. For his forty pounds are duly paid him, because there is not one farmer in a hundred, who is not worth five times the rent he pays to his landlord, and fifty times the sum demanded for the tithes; which, by the small compass of his parish, he can easily collect or compound for; and if his behaviour and understanding be supportable, he will probably receive presents now and then from his parishioners, and perhaps from the squire; who, although he may sometimes be apt to treat his parson a little superciliously, will probably be softened by a little humble demeanour. The vicar is likewise generally sure to find upon his admittance to his living, a convenient house and barn in repair, with a garden, and a field or two to graze a few cows, and one horse for himself and his wife. He hath probably a market very near him, perhaps in his own village. No entertainment is expected from his visitor beyond a pot of ale, and a piece of cheese. He hath every Sunday the comfort of a full congregation, of plain, cleanly people of both sexes, well to pass, and who speak his own language. The scene about him is fully cultivated (I mean for the general) and well inhabited. He dreads no thieves for anything but his apples, for the trade of universal stealing is not so epidemic there as with us. His wife is little better than Goody, in her birth, education, or dress; and as to himself, we must let his parentage alone. If he be the son of a farmer it is very sufficient, and his sister may very decently be chambermaid to the squire's wife. He goes about on working days in a grazier's coat, and will not scruple to assist his workmen in harvest time. He is usually wary and thrifty, and often more able to provide for a numerous family than some of ours can do with a rectory called 300*l.* a year. His daughters shall go to service, or be sent 'prentice to the sempstress of the next town; and his sons are put to honest trades. This is the usual course of an English country vicar from twenty to sixty pounds a year.

As to the clergy of our own kingdom, their livings are generally larger. Not originally, or by the bounty of princes, parliaments, or charitable endowments, for the same degradations (and as to glebes, a much greater) have been made here, but, by the destruction and desolation in the long wars between the invaders and the natives; during which time a great part of the bishops' lands, and almost all the glebes, were lost in the confusion. The first invaders had almost the whole kingdom divided amongst them. New invaders succeeded, and drove out their predecessors as native Irish. These were expelled by others who came after, and upon the same pretensions. Thus it went on for several hundred years, and in some degree even to our own memories. And thus it will probably go on, although not in a martial way, to the end of the world. For not only the purchasers of debentures forfeited in 1641, were all of English birth, but those after the Restoration, and many who came hither even since the Revolution, are looked upon as perfect Irish; directly contrary to the practice of all wise nations, and particularly of the Greeks and Romans, in establishing their colonies, by which name Ireland is very absurdly called.

Under these distractions the conquerors always seized what lands they could with little ceremony, whether they belonged to the Church or not: Thus the glebes were almost universally exposed to the first seizers, and could never be recovered, although the grants, with the particular denominations, are manifest, and still in being. The whole lands of the see of Waterford were wholly taken by one family; the like is reported of other bishoprics.

King James the First, who deserves more of the Church of Ireland than all other princes put together, having the forfeitures of vast tracts of land in the northern parts (I think commonly called the escheated counties), having granted some hundred thousand acres of these lands to certain Scotch and English favourites, was prevailed on by some great prelates to grant to some sees in the north, and to many parishes there, certain parcels of land for the augmentation of poor bishoprics, did likewise endow many parishes with glebes for the incumbents, whereof a good number escaped the depredations of 1641 and 1688. These lands, when they were granted by King James, consisted mostly of woody ground, wherewith those parts of this island were then overrun. This is well known, universally allowed, and by some in part remembered; the rest being, in some places, not stubbed out to this day. And the value of the lands was consequently very inconsiderable, till Scotch colonies came over in swarms upon great encouragement to make them habitable; at least for such a race of strong-bodied people, who came hither from their own bleak barren highlands, as it were into a paradise; who soon were able to get straw for their bedding, instead of a bundle of heath spread on the ground, and sprinkled with water. Here, by degrees, they acquired some degree of politeness and civility, from such neighbouring Irish as were still left after Tyrone's last rebellion, and are since grown almost entirely possessors of the north. Thus, at length, the woods being rooted up, the land was brought in, and tilled, and the glebes which could not before yield two-pence an acre, are equal to the best, sometimes affording the minister a good demesne, and some land to let.

These wars and desolations in their natural consequences, were likewise the cause of another effect, I mean that of uniting several parishes under one incumbent. For, as the lands were of little value by the want of inhabitants to cultivate them, and many of the churches levelled to the ground, particularly by the fanatic zeal of those rebellious saints who murdered their king, destroyed the Church, and overthrew monarchy (for all which there is a humiliation day appointed by law, and soon approaching); so, in order to give a tolerable maintenance to a minister, and the country being too poor, as well as devotion too low, to think of building new churches, it was found necessary to repair some one church which had least suffered, and join sometimes three or more, enough for a bare support to some clergyman, who knew not where to provide himself better. This was a case of absolute necessity to prevent heathenism, as well as popery, from overrunning the nation. The consequence of these unions was very different, in different parts; for, in the north, by the Scotch settlement, their numbers daily increasing by new additions from their own country, and their prolific quality peculiar to northern people; and lastly by their universally feeding upon oats (which grain, under its several preparations and denominations, is the only natural luxury of that hardy people) the value of tithes increased so prodigiously, that at this day, I confess, several united parishes ought to be divided, taking in so great a compass, that it is almost impossible for the people to travel timely to their own parish church, or their little churches to contain half their number, though the revenue would be sufficient to maintain two, or perhaps three worthy clergymen with decency; provided the times mend, or that they were honestly dealt with, which I confess is seldom the case. I shall name only one, and it is the deanery of Derry; the revenue whereof, if the dean could get his dues, exceeding that of some bishoprics, both by the compass and fertility of the soil, the number as well as industry of the inhabitants, the conveniency of exporting their corn to Dublin and foreign parts; and, lastly, by the accidental discovery of marl in many places of the several parishes. Yet all this revenue is wholly founded upon corn, for I am told there is hardly an acre of glebe for the dean to plant and build on.

I am therefore of opinion, that a real undefalcated revenue of six hundred pounds a year, is a sufficient income for a country dean in this kingdom; and since the rents consist wholly of tithes, two parishes, to the amount of that value, should be united, and the dean reside as minister in that of Down, and the remaining parishes be divided among worthy clergymen, to about 300*l.* a year to each. The deanery of Derry, which is a large city, might be left worth 800*l.* a year, and Rapho according as it shall be thought proper. These three are the only opulent deaneries in the whole kingdom, and, as I am informed, consist all of tithes, which was an unhappy expedient in the Church, occasioned by the sacrilegious robberies during the several times of confusion and war; insomuch that at this day there is hardly any remainder left of dean and chapter lands in Ireland, that delicious morsel swallowed so greedily in England, under the fanatic usurpations.

As to the present scheme of a bill for obliging the clergy to residence, now or lately in the privy council, I know no more of the particulars than what hath been told me by several clergymen of distinction; who say, that a petition in the name of them all hath been presented to the lord lieutenant and council, that they might be heard by their counsel against the bill, and that the petition was rejected, with some reasons why it was rejected ; for the bishops know best what is proper for the clergy. It seems the bill consists of two parts : First, a power in the bishops, with consent of the archbishop, and the patron, to take off from any parish whatever, it is worth above £300 a year; and this to be done without the incumbent's consent, which before was necessary in all divisions. The other part of the bill obligeth all clergymen, from forty pounds a year and upwards, to reside, and build a house in his parish. But those of £40 are remitted till they shall receive £100 out of the revenue of first-fruits granted by Her late Majesty.

# CONSIDERATIONS
## UPON
# TWO BILLS, &c.

## NOTE.

"In the year 1731 a Bill was brought into the House of Lords by a great majority of the Right Reverend the Bishops, for enabling them to divide the livings of the inferior Clergy; which Bill was approved of in the Privy-Council of Ireland, and passed by the Lords in Parliament. It was afterwards sent to the House of Commons for their approbation; but was rejected by them with a great majority. The supposed author of the following Considerations, who hath always been the best friend to the inferior Clergy of the Church of England, as may be seen by many parts of his writings, opposed this pernicious project with great success; which, if it had passed into law, would have been of the worst consequence to this nation." [Advertisement to the reprint of this pamphlet in Swift's Works, vol. vi. Dublin: Faulkner, 1738.]

Fuller details of the circumstances which gave Swift the opportunity for writing this tract are given in the note prefixed to the previous pamphlet (see p. 250).

The text here given is that of the first edition.

[T. S.]

# CONSIDERATIONS
## UPON TWO
# BILLS

Sent-down from the R— H— the

# H——— of L———

To the H———ble

# H——— of C———

Relating to the

# CLERGY
## OF
# I *·*·*·*·*·D.

---

---

*L O N D O N.*

Printed for A. MOORE, near St. *Paul's*, and Sold by the Bookfellers of *Westminster* and *Southwark*, 1732.

# CONSIDERATIONS UPON TWO BILLS, &c.

I HAVE often, for above a month past, desired some few clergymen, who are pleased to visit me, that they would procure an extract of two bills, brought into the council by some of the bishops, and both of them since passed in the House of Lords: but I could never obtain what I desired, whether by the forgetfulness, or negligence of those whom I employed, or the difficulty of the thing itself. Therefore, if I shall happen to mistake in any fact of consequence, I desire my remarks upon it, may pass for nothing; for my information is no better than what I received in words from several divines, who seemed to agree with each other. I have not the honour to be acquainted with any one single prelate of the kingdom, and am a stranger to their characters, further than as common fame reports them, which is not to be depended on. Therefore, I cannot be supposed to act upon a principle of resentment. I esteem their functions (if I may be allowed to say so without offence) as truly apostolical, and absolutely necessary to the perfection of a Christian Church.

There are no qualities more incident to the frailty and corruption of human kind, than an indifference, or insensibility for other men's sufferings, and a sudden forgetfulness of their own former humble state, when they rise in the world. These two dispositions have not, I think, anywhere so strongly exerted themselves, as in the order of bishops with regard to the inferior clergy; for which I can find no reasons, but such as naturally should seem to operate a quite contrary way. The maintenance of the Clergy, throughout the kingdom, is precarious and uncertain, collected from a most miserable race of beggarly farmers; at whose mercy every minister lies to be defrauded: His office, as rector or vicar, if it be duly executed, is very laborious. As soon as he is promoted to a bishopric, the scene is entirely and happily changed; his revenues are large, and as surely paid as those of the king; his whole business is once a-year, to receive the attendance, the submission, and the proxy-money of all his clergy, in whatever part of the diocese he shall please to think most convenient for himself. Neither is his personal presence necessary, for the business may be done by a Vicar-General. The fatigue of ordination, is just what the bishops please to make it, and as matters have been for some time, and may probably remain, the fewer ordinations the better. The rest of their visible office, consists in the honour of attending parliaments and councils, and bestowing preferments in their own gift; in which last employment, and in their spiritual and temporal courts, the labour falls to their Vicars-General, Secretaries, Proctors, Apparitors, Seneschals, and the like. Now, I say, in so quick a change, where their brethren in a few days, are become their subjects, it would be reasonable, at least, to hope, that the labour, confinement, and subjection from which they have so lately escaped, like a bird out of the snare of the fowler, might a little incline them to remember the condition of those, who were but last week their equals, probably their companions or their friends, and possibly, as reasonable expectants. There is a known story of Colonel Tidcomb, who, while he continued a subaltern officer, was every day complaining against the pride, oppression, and hard treatment of colonels toward their officers; yet in a very few minutes after he had received his commission for a regiment, walking with a friend on the Mall, he confessed that the spirit of colonelship, was coming fast upon him, which spirit is said to have daily increased to the hour of his death.

It is true, the Clergy of this kingdom, who are promoted to bishoprics, have always some great advantages; either that of rich deaneries, opulent and multiplied rectories and dignities, strong alliances by birth or marriage, fortified by a superlative degree of zeal and loyalty; but, however, they were all at first no more than young beginners; and before their great promotion, were known by their plain Christian names, among their old companions, the middling rate of clergymen; nor could, therefore, be strangers to their condition, or with any good grace, forget it so soon as it hath sometimes happened.

I confess, I do not remember to have observed any body of men, acting with so little concert as our clergy have done, in a point where their opinions appeared to be unanimous: a point where their whole temporal support was concerned, as well as their power of serving God and his Church, in their spiritual functions. This hath been imputed to their fear of disobliging, or hopes of further favours upon compliance; because it was observed, that some who appeared at first with the greatest zeal, thought fit suddenly to absent themselves from the usual meetings; yet, we know what expert solicitors the Quakers, the Dissenters, and even the Papists have sometimes found, to drive a point of advantage, or prevent an impending evil.

I have not seen any extract from the two bills introduced into the Privy Council by the bishops; where the Clergy, upon some failure in favour, or through the timorousness of many among their brethren, were refused to be heard by the Council. It seems these bills were both returned, agreed to by the King and Council in England; and the House of Lords hath, with great expedition, passed them both, and it is said they are immediately to be sent down to the Commons for their consent.

The particulars, as they have been imperfectly reported to me, are as follow:

By one of the bills, the bishops have power to oblige the country clergy, to build a mansion-house upon whatever part of their glebes their lordships shall command; and if the living be above £50 a-year, the minister is bound to build, after three years, a house that shall cost one year and a half's rent of his income. For instance, if a clergyman with a wife and seven children gets a living of £55 per annum, he must after three years, build a house that shall cost £77 10s., and must support his family during the time the bishop shall appoint for the building of it with the remainder. But, if the living be under £50 a-year, the minister shall be allowed an £100 out of the first-fruits.

But, there is said to be one circumstance a little extraordinary; that if there be a single spot in the glebe more barren, more marshy, more expos'd to winds, more distant from the church, or skeleton of a church, or from any conveniency of building: the rector, or vicar may be obliged by the caprice, or pique of the bishop, to build, under pain of sequestration, (an office, which ever falls into the most knavish hands,) upon whatever point his lordship shall command; although the farmers have not paid one quarter of his due.

I believe, under the present distresses of the kingdom (which inevitably, without a miracle, must increase for ever) there are not ten country clergymen in Ireland, reputed to possess a parish of £100 per annum who, for some years past, have actually received £60, and that with the utmost difficulty and vexation. I am, therefore, at a loss what kind of valuators the bishops will make use of, and whether the starving vicar, shall be forced to build his house with the money he never received.

The other bill, which passed in two days after the former, is said to concern the division of parishes into as many parcels as the bishop shall think fit, only leaving £300 a-year to the Mother Church; which £300 by another act passed some years ago, they can divide likewise, and crumble as low as their will and pleasure will dispose them. So that instead of 600 clergymen, which, I think, is the usual computation, we may have, in a small compass of years, almost as many thousands to live with decency and comfort, provide for their children, &c., be charitable to the poor, and maintain hospitality.

But it is very reasonable to hope, and heartily to be wished by all those who have the least regard to our holy religion, as hitherto established, or to a learned, pious, diligent, conversible clergyman, or even to common humanity; that the honourable House of Commons will in their great wisdom, justice, and tenderness to innocent men, consider these bills in another light. It is said, they well know this kingdom not to be so overstocked with neighbouring gentry; but a discreet, learned clergyman, with a competency fit for one of his education, may be an entertaining, a useful, and sometimes a necessary companion. That although such a clergyman may not be able constantly to find BEEF and

WINE for his own family, yet he may be allowed sometimes to afford both to a neighbour, without distressing himself; and the rather, because he may expect at least as good a return. It will probably be considered, that in many desolate parts, there may not be always a sufficient number of persons considerable enough to be trusted with commissions of the peace, which several of the Clergy now supply much better, than a little, hedge, contemptible, illiterate vicar from twenty to fifty pounds a-year, the son of a weaver, pedlar, tailor, or miller, can be presumed to do.

The landlords and farmers by this scheme can find no profit, but will certainly be losers; for instance, if the large northern livings be split into a dozen parishes, or more, it will be very necessary for the little threadbare gownman, with his wife, his proctor and every child who can crawl, to watch the fields at harvest time, for fear of losing a single sheaf, which he could not afford under peril of a day's starving; for according to the Scotch proverb, a hungry louse bites sore. This would of necessity, breed an infinite number of brangles and litigious suits in the spiritual courts, and put the wretched pastor at perpetual variance with his whole parish. But, as they have hitherto stood, a clergyman established in a competent living is not under the necessity of being so sharp, vigilant, and exacting. On the contrary, it is well known and allowed, that the Clergy round the kingdom think themselves well treated, if they lose only one single third of their legal demands.

The honourable House may perhaps be inclined to conceive, that my lords the bishops enjoy as ample a power, both spiritual and temporal, as will fully suffice to answer every branch of their office; that they want no laws to regulate the conduct of those clergymen, over whom they preside; that if non-residence be a grievance, it is the patron's fault, who makes not a better choice, or caused the plurality. That if the general impartial character of persons chosen into the Church had been more regarded, and the motive of party, alliance, kindred, flatterers, ill judgment, or personal favour regarded less, there would be fewer complaints of non-residence, neglect of care, blameable behaviour, or any other part of misconduct, not to mention ignorance and stupidity.

I could name certain gentlemen of the gown, whose awkward, spruce, prim, sneering, and smirking countenances, the very tone of their voices, and an ungainly strut in their walk, without one single talent for any one office, have contrived to get good preferment by the mere force of flattery and cringing: for which two virtues (the only two virtues they pretend to) they were, however, utterly unqualified. And whom, if I were in power, although they were my nephews or had married my nieces, I could never in point of good conscience or honour, have recommended to a curacy in Connaught.

The honourable House of Commons may likewise perhaps consider, that the gentry of this kingdom differ from all others upon earth, being less capable of employments in their own country, than any others who come from abroad, and that most of them have little expectation of providing for their younger children, otherwise than by the Church, in which there might be some hopes of getting a tolerable maintenance. For after the patrons should have settled their sons, their nephews, their nieces, their dependants, and their followers, invited over from t'other side, there would still remain an overplus of smaller church preferments, to be given to such clergy of the nation, who shall have their quantum of whatever merit may be then in fashion. But by these bills, they will be all as absolutely excluded, as if they had passed under the denomination of Tories, unless they can be contented at the utmost with £50 a-year, which by the difficulties of collecting tithes in Ireland, and the daily increasing miseries of the people, will hardly rise to half the sum.

It is observed, that the divines sent over hither to govern this Church, have not seemed to consider the difference between both kingdoms, with respect to the inferior clergy. As to themselves, indeed, they find a large revenue in lands let at one quarter value, which consequently must be paid while there is a penny left among us; and, the public distress so little affects their interests, that their fines are now higher than ever, they content themselves to suppose that whatever a parish is said to be worth, comes all into the parson's pocket.

The poverty of great numbers among the Clergy of England, hath been the continual complaint of all men who wish well to the Church, and many schemes have been thought on to redress it; yet an English vicar of £40 a-year, lives much more comfortably than one of double the value in Ireland. His farmers generally speaking, are able and willing to pay him his full dues. He hath a decent church of ancient standing, filled every Lord's day with a large congregation of plain people, well clad, and behaving themselves as if they believed in God and Christ. He hath a house and barn in repair, a field or two to graze his cows, with a garden and orchard. No guest expects more from him than a pot of ale; he lives like an honest, plain farmer, as his wife is dressed but little better than Goody. He is sometimes graciously invited by the squire, where he sits at humble distance; if he gets the love of his people, they often make him little useful presents; he is happy by being born to no higher expectation, for he is usually the son of some ordinary tradesman or middling farmer. His learning is much of a size with his birth and education, no more of either than what a poor hungry servitor can be expected to bring with him from his college. It would be tedious to shew the reverse of all this in our distant poorer parishes, through most parts of Ireland, wherein every reader may make the comparison.

Lastly, the honourable House of Commons may consider, whether the scheme of multiplying beggarly clergymen through the whole kingdom who must all have votes for choosing parliament men (provided they can prove their freeholds to be worth 40s. per annum, *ultra reprisas*) may not, by their numbers, have great influence upon elections, being entirely under the dependance of their bishops. For by a moderate computation, after all the divisions and subdivisions of parishes, that, my lords, the bishops, have power to make by their new laws, there will, as soon as the present set of clergy go off, be raised an army of ecclesiastical militants, able enough for any kind of service, except that of the altar.

I am, indeed, in some concern about a fund for building a thousand or two churches, wherein these probationers may read their wall lectures, and begin to doubt they must be contented with barns; which barns will be one great advancing step towards an accommodation with our true Protestant brethren, the Dissenters.

The scheme of encouraging clergymen to build houses by dividing a living of £500 a-year into ten parts, is a contrivance, the meaning whereof hath got on the wrong side of my comprehension; unless it may be argued, that bishops build no houses, because they are so rich; and therefore, the inferior clergy will certainly build, if you reduce them to beggary. But I knew a very rich man of quality in England, who could never be persuaded to keep a servant out of livery; because such servants would be expensive, and apt, in time, to look like gentlemen; whereas the others were ready to submit to the basest offices, and at a cheaper pennyworth might increase his retinue.

I hear, it is the opinion of many wise men, that before these bills pass both Houses, they should be sent back to England with the following clauses inserted:

First, that whereas there may be about a dozen double bishoprics in Ireland, those bishoprics should be split and given to different persons; and those of a single denomination be also divided into two, three, or four parts, as occasion shall require; otherwise there may be a question started, whether twenty-two prelates can effectually extend their paternal care and unlimited power, for the protection and correction of so great a number of spiritual subjects. But this proposal will meet with such furious objections, that I shall not insist upon it, for I well remember to have read, what a terrible fright the frogs were in, upon a report that the sun was going to marry.

Another clause should be, that none of these twenty, thirty, forty, or fifty pounders may be suffered to marry, under the penalty of immediate deprivation, their marriages declared null, and their children bastards; for some desponding people, take the kingdom to be not in a condition of encouraging so numerous a breed of beggars.

A third clause will be necessary, that these humble gentry should be absolutely disqualified from giving votes in elections for parliament men.

Others add a fourth, which is a clause of indulgence, that these reduced divines may be permitted to follow any lawful ways of living, that will not call them too often or too far from their spiritual offices (for unless I misapprehend, they are supposed to have episcopal ordination). For example, they may be lappers of linen, bailiffs of the manor, they may let blood, or apply plasters, for three miles round; they may get a dispensation to hold the clerkship and sextonship of their own parish *in commendam*. Their wives and daughters may make shirts for the neighbourhood, or if a barrack be near, for the soldiers. In linen countries, they may card and spin, and keep a few looms in the house: they may let lodgings, and sell a pot of ale without doors, but not at home, unless to sober company, and at regular hours. It is by some thought a little hard, that in an affair of the last consequence, to the very being of the Clergy, in the points of liberty and property, as well as in their abilities to perform their duty; this whole reverend body, who are the established instructors of the nation in Christianity and moral virtues, and are the only persons concerned, should be the sole persons not consulted. Let any scholar shew the like precedent in Christendom for twelve hundred years past. An act of parliament for settling or selling an estate in a private family, is never passed till all parties give consent. But in the present case the whole body of the Clergy is, as themselves apprehend, determined to utter ruin, without once expecting or asking their opinion, and this by a scheme contrived only by one part of the convocation, while the other part which hath been chosen in the usual forms, wants only the regal permission to assemble, and consult about the affairs of the Church, as their predecessors have always done in former ages; where it is presumed, the Lower House hath a power of proposing canons, and a negative voice, as well as the Upper. And God forbid (say these objectors) that there should be a real separate interest between the bishops and Clergy, any more than there is between a man and his wife, a king and his people, or Christ and his Church.

It seems there is a provision in the bill, that no parish shall be cut into scraps, without the consent of several persons, who can be no sufferers in the matter; but I cannot find that the Clergy lay much weight on this caution, because they argue, that the very persons from whom these Bills took their rise, will have the greatest share in the decision.

I do not, by any means, conceive the crying sin of the Clergy in this kingdom, to be that of non-residence. I am sure, it is many degrees less so here than in England, unless the possession of pluralities may pass under that name; and if this be a fault, it is well known to whom it must be imputed: I believe, upon a fair inquiry (and I hear an inquiry is to be made) they will appear to be most pardonably few, especially considering how many parishes have not an inch of glebe, and how difficult it is upon any reasonable terms, to find a place of habitation. And, therefore, God knows, whether my lords the bishops will be soon able to convince the Clergy, or those who have any regard for that venerable body, that the chief motive in their lordships' minds, by procuring these bills, was to prevent the sin of non-residence, while the universal opinion of almost every clergyman in the kingdom, without distinction of party, taking in even those who are not likely to be sufferers, stands directly against them.

If some livings in the north may be justly thought too large a compass of land, which makes it inconvenient for the remotest inhabitant to attend the service of the Church, which in some instances may be true; no reasonable clergyman would oppose a proper remedy by particular acts of parliament.

Thus for instance, the deanery of Down, a country deanery, I think, without a cathedral, depending wholly upon an union of parishes joined together, in a time when the land lay waste and thinly inhabited; since those circumstances are so prodigiously changed for the better, may properly be lessened, leaving a decent competency to the dean, and placing rectories in the remaining churches, which are now served only by stipendiary curates.

The case may be probably the same in other parts: and such a proceeding discreetly managed would be truly for the good of the Church.

For it is to be observed, that the dean and chapter lands, which, in England were all seized under the fanatic usurpation, are things unknown in Ireland, having been long ravished from the Church, by a succession of confusions, and tithes applied in their stead, to support that ecclesiastical dignity.

The late Archbishop of Dublin[1] had a very different way of encouraging the clergy of his diocese to residence: When a lease had run out seven years or more, he stipulated with the tenant to resign up twenty or thirty acres to the minister of the parish where it lay convenient, without lessening his former rent; and with no great abatement of the fine; and this he did in the parts near Dublin, where land is at the highest rates, leaving a small chiefry for the minister to pay, hardly a sixth part of the value. I doubt not that almost every bishop in the kingdom may do the same generous act with less damage to their sees than his late Grace of Dublin; much of whose lands were out in fee-farms, or leases for lives, and I am sorry that the good example of that prelate hath not been followed.

But a great majority of the Clergy's friends cannot hitherto reconcile themselves to this project, which they call a levelling principle, that must inevitably root out the seeds of all honest emulation, the legal parent of the greatest virtues, and most generous actions among men; but which, in the general opinion (for I do not pretend to offer my own,) will never more have room to exert itself in the breast of any clergyman whom this kingdom shall produce.

But, whether the consequences of these Bills may, by the virtues and frailties of future bishops, sent over hither to rule the Church, terminate in good or evil, I shall not presume to determine, since God can work the former out of the latter. But one thing I can venture to assert, that from the earliest ages of Christianity to the minute I am now writing, there never was a precedent of SUCH a proceeding, much less to be feared, hoped, or apprehended from such hands in any Christian country, and so it may pass for more than a phœnix, because it hath risen without any assistance from the ashes of its sire.

The appearance of so many dissenters at the hearing of this cause, is what, I am told, hath not been charged to the account of their prudence or moderation; because that action hath been censured as a mark of triumph and insult before the victory is complete; since neither of these bills hath yet passed the House of Commons, and some are

---

[1] The Right Rev. Dr. William King (see p. 241). [T. S.]

pleased to think it not impossible that they may be rejected. Neither do I hear, that there is an enacting clause in either of the Bills to apply any part of the divided or subdivided tithes, towards increasing the stipends of the sectaries. So that these gentlemen seem to be gratified like him, who, after having been kicked downstairs, took comfort when he saw his friend kicked down after him.

I have heard many more objections against several particulars of both these Bills, but they are of a high nature, and carry such dreadful innuendos, that I dare not mention them, resolving to give no offence because I well know how obnoxious I have long been (although I conceive without any fault of my own) to the zeal and principles of those, who place all difference in opinion concerning public matters, to the score of disaffection, whereof I am at least as innocent as the loudest of my detractors.

DUBLIN,
*Feb.* 24, 1731-2.

# SOME
# REASONS
### AGAINST
## THE BILL FOR SETTLING THE TITHE
### OF
## HEMP, FLAX, &c., BY A MODUS.

## NOTE.

About the end of 1733 the Irish House of Commons had under consideration a bill for the encouragement of the growth of flax and the manufacture of linen. This bill contained a clause by which the tithe upon flax should be commuted by a *modus*, or money composition. The clergy, to whom this tithe was an important source of revenue, and, naturally, not wishing to lose its advantage, took steps to petition Parliament to be heard by counsel against the bill. Swift signed the petition, which set forth the injury which would be done to their order if the clause in the bill, then before the House, were allowed to become law. In addition to this he committed and arranged his arguments to writing, and issued them in the following pamphlet. The activity against the bill proved so efficacious that the House of Commons dropped it. It may be remarked that Swift's interference was purely disinterested, since no part of the revenue of St. Patrick's, as Monck Mason points out, comes from the "district appropriated to the culture of flax;" nor did Swift, "or any of his predecessors or successors, ever receive one shilling upon account of that tithe."

This attempt on the part of the House of Commons to regulate the affairs of the clergy of Ireland seems to have been one of a series which divided laity and clergy into two strongly opposing parties. On the one side were the House of Commons and its supporters, on the other the general body of the Irish clergy, with, for a time, at any rate, Swift at the head. The tithe of pasturage, or, as it was called, the tithe of agistment, was being strongly resisted at the time, and many of the clergy were forced to sue in court before they could obtain it. The matter of this tithe had been already before an Irish court in 1707, and had been settled in favour of the suing clergyman, one Archdeacon Neal; and although the cause was removed to King's Bench in England, the previous judgment was confirmed. In spite of this decision, however, the tithe continued to be a subject of litigation, and the landed proprietors even formed themselves into associations for the purpose of resisting the clergy's claim. In 1734 the House of Commons aggravated matters by passing resolutions against the claims, many of which were then the subject of legal actions, and prevented decisions being come to while it had the matter under its consideration. From the pamphlets written at the time it may easily be seen that this interference on the part of the lower House was both unseemly and unjust. Its conduct so roused Swift that his indignation found expression in one of his bitterest and most terrible poetical satires—" The Legion Club "—a satire so bitter and so scathing that reading it now, after the lapse of more than a century and a half, one shudders at its invective—" a blasting flood of filth and vitriol, out of some hellish fountain," Mr. Churton Collins calls it. We are told that its composition brought on a violent attack of vertigo, and it remained unfinished.

The text here given is that of the first edition collated with those given by Faulkner, Hawkesworth, and Scott.

[T. S.]

# SOME
# REASONS
### AGAINST THE
Bill for settling the Tyth of *Hemp*, *Flax*, &c. by a *Modus*.

---

---

DUBLIN:
Printed by GEORGE FAULKNER in *Essex-Street*, opposite to the Bridge.  M DCC XXIV.

# SOME REASONS AGAINST THE BILL FOR SETTLING THE TITHE OF HEMP, FLAX, &c., BY A MODUS.

THE Clergy did little expect to have any cause of complaint against the present House of Commons; who in the last sessions, were pleased to throw out a Bill[1] sent them from the Lords, which that reverend body apprehended would be very injurious to them, if it passed into a law; and who, in the present sessions, defeated the arts and endeavours of schismatics to repeal the Sacramental Test.

For, although it hath been allowed on all hands, that the former of those Bills might, by its necessary consequences, be very displeasing to the lay gentlemen of the kingdom, for many reasons purely secular; and, that this last attempt for repealing the Test, did much more affect, at present, the temporal interest than the spiritual; yet the whole body of the lower Clergy have, upon both these occasions, expressed equal gratitude to that honourable House, for their justice and steadiness, as if the clergy alone were to receive the benefit.

It must needs be, therefore, a great addition to the Clergy's grief, that such an assembly as the present House of Commons; should now, with an expedition more than usual, agree to a bill for encouraging the linen manufacture; with a clause, whereby the Church is to lose two parts in three, of the legal tithe in flax and hemp.

Some reasons, why the Clergy think such a law will be a great hardship upon them, are, I conceive, those that follow.

[1] For the bishops to divide livings. See the two preceding Tracts. [T. S.]

I shall venture to enumerate them with all deference due to that honourable assembly.

*First;* the Clergy suppose that they have not, by any fault or demerit, incurred the displeasure of the nation's representatives : neither can the declared loyalty of the present set, from the highest prelate to the lowest vicar, be in the least disputed : because, there are hardly ten clergymen, through the whole kingdom, for more than nineteen years past, who have not been either preferred entirely upon account of their declared affection to the Hanover line ; or higher promoted as the due reward of the same merit.

There is not a landlord in the whole kingdom, residing some part of the year at his country-seat, who is not, in his own conscience, fully convinced, that the tithes of his minister have gradually sunk, for some years past, one-third, or at least one-fourth of their former value, exclusive of all non-solvencies.

The payment of tithes in this kingdom, is subject to so many frauds, brangles, and other difficulties, not only from Papists and Dissenters, but even from those who profess themselves Protestants ; that by the expense, the trouble, and vexation of collecting, or bargaining for them, they are, of all other rents, the most precarious, uncertain, and ill paid.

The landlords in most parishes expect, as a compliment, that they shall pay little more than half, the value of their tithes for the lands they hold in their own hands ; which often consist of large domains : And it is the minister's interest to make them easy upon that article, when he considers what influence those gentlemen have upon their tenants.

The Clergy cannot but think it extremely severe, that in a bill for encouraging the linen manufacture, they alone must be the sufferers, who can least afford it : If, as I am told, there be a tax of three thousand pounds a year, paid by the public, for a further encouragement to the said manufacture ; are not the Clergy equal sharers in the charge with the rest of their fellow subjects? What satisfactory reason can be therefore given, why they alone should bear the whole additional weight, unless it will be alleged that their property is not upon an equal foot with the properties of other men? They acquire their own small pittance, by at least as honest means, as their neighbours, the landlords, possess their estates; and have been always supposed, except in rebellious or fanatical times, to have as good a title: For, no families now in being can shew a more ancient. Indeed, if it be true, that some persons (I hope they were not many) were seen to laugh when the rights of the Clergy were mentioned; in this case, an opinion may possibly be soon advanced, that they have no rights at all. And this is likely enough to gain ground, in proportion as the contempt of all religion shall increase; which is already in a very forward way.

It is said, there will be also added to this Bill a clause for diminishing the tithe of hops, in order to cultivate that useful plant among us: And here likewise the load is to lie entirely on the shoulders of the Clergy, while the landlords reap all the benefit. It will not be easy to foresee where such proceedings are like to stop: Or whether by the same authority, in civil times, a parliament may not as justly challenge the same power in reducing all things titheable, not below the tenth part of the product, (which is and ever will be the Clergy's equitable right) but from a tenth-part to a sixtieth or eightieth, and from thence to nothing.

I have heard it granted by skilful persons, that the practice of taxing the Clergy by parliament, without their own consent, is a new thing, not much above the date of seventy years: before which period, in times of peace, they always taxed themselves. But things are extremely altered at present: It is not now sufficient to tax them in common with their fellow subjects, without imposing an additional tax upon them, from which, or from anything equivalent, all their fellow-subjects are exempt; and this in a country professing Christianity.

The greatest part of the Clergy throughout this kingdom, have been stripped of their glebes by the confusion of times, by violence, fraud, oppression, and other unlawful means: All which glebes are now in the hands of the laity. So that they now are generally forced to lie at the mercy of landlords, for a small piece of ground in their parishes, at a most exorbitant rent, and usually for a short term of years; whereon to build a house, and enable them to reside. Yet, in spite of these disadvantages, I am a witness that they are generally more constant residents than their brethren in England; where the meanest vicar hath a convenient dwelling, with a barn, a garden, and a field or two for his cattle; besides the certainty of his little income from honest farmers, able and willing, not only to pay him his dues, but likewise to make him presents, according to their ability, for his better support. In all which circumstances, the Clergy of Ireland meet with a treatment directly contrary.

It is hoped, the honourable House will consider that it is impossible for the most ill-minded, avaricious, or cunning clergyman, to do the least injustice to the meanest cottager in his parish, in any bargain for tithes, or other ecclesiastical dues. He can, at the utmost, only demand to have his tithe fairly laid out; and does not once in a hundred times obtain his demand. But every tenant, from the poorest cottager to the most substantial farmer, can, and generally doth impose upon the minister, by fraud, by theft, by lies, by perjuries, by insolence, and sometimes by force; notwithstanding the utmost vigilance and skill of himself and his proctor. Insomuch, that it is allowed, that the Clergy in general receive little more than one-half of their legal dues; not including the charges they are at in collecting or bargaining for them.

The land rents of Ireland are computed to about two millions, whereof one-tenth amounts to two hundred thousand pounds. The beneficed clergymen, excluding those of this city, are not reckoned to be above five hundred; by which computation, they should each of them possess two hundred pounds a year, if those tithes were equally divided, although in well cultivated corn countries it ought to be more; whereas they hardly receive one half of that sum; with great defalcations, and in very bad payments. There are indeed, a few glebes in the north pretty considerable, but if these and all the rest were in like manner equally divided, they would not add five pounds a year to every clergyman. Therefore, whether the condition of the Clergy in general among us be justly liable to envy, or able to bear a heavy burden, which neither the nobility, nor gentry, nor tradesmen, nor farmers, will touch with one of their fingers; this, I say, is submitted to the honourable House.

One terrible circumstance in this Bill, is, that of turning the tithe of flax and hemp into what the lawyers call a *Modus*, or a certain sum in lieu of a tenth part of the product. And by this practice of claiming a *Modus* in many parishes by ancient custom, the Clergy in both kingdoms have been almost incredible sufferers. Thus, in the present case, the tithe of a tolerable acre of flax, which by a medium is worth twelve shillings, is by the present Bill reduced to four shillings. Neither is this the worst part in a *Modus;* every determinate sum must in process of time sink from a fourth to a four-and-twentieth part, or a great deal lower, by that necessary fall attending the value of money, which is now at least nine tenths lower all over Europe than it was four hundred years ago, by a gradual decline ; and even a third part at least within our own memories, in purchasing almost everything required for the necessities or conveniencies of life ; as any gentleman can attest, who hath kept house for twenty years past. And this will equally affect poor countries as well as rich. For, although, I look upon it as an impossibility that this kingdom should ever thrive under its present disadvantages, which without a miracle must still increase ; yet, when the whole cash of the nation shall sink to fifty thousand pounds ; we must in all our traffic abroad, either of import or export, go by the general rate at which money is valued in those countries that enjoy the common privileges of human kind. For this reason, no corporation, (if the Clergy may presume to call themselves one) should by any means grant away their properties in perpetuity upon any consideration whatsoever ; Which is a rock that many corporations have split upon, to their great impoverishment, and sometimes to their utter undoing. Because they are supposed to subsist for ever ; and because no determination of money is of any certain perpetual intrinsic value. This is known enough in England, where estates let for ever, some hundred years ago, by several ancient noble families, do not at this present pay their posterity a twentieth part of what they are now worth at an easy rate.

A tax affecting one part of a nation, which already bears its full share in all parliamentary impositions, cannot possibly be just, except it be inflicted as a punishment upon that body of men which is taxed, for some great demerit or danger to the public apprehended from those upon whom it is laid: Thus the Papists and Nonjurors have been doubly taxed for refusing to give proper securities to the government; which cannot be objected against the Clergy. And therefore, if this Bill should pass; I think it ought to be with a preface, shewing wherein they have offended, and for what disaffection or other crime they are punished.

If an additional excise upon ale, or a duty upon flesh and bread, were to be enacted, neither the victualler, butcher, or baker would bear any more of the charge than for what themselves consumed; but it would be an equal general tax through the whole kingdom: Whereas, by this Bill, the Clergy alone are avowedly condemned to be deprived of their ancient, inherent, undisputed rights, in order to encourage a manufacture by which all the rest of the kingdom are supposed to be gainers.

This Bill is directly against *Magna Charta*, whereof the first clause is for confirming the inviolable rights of Holy Church; as well as contrary to the oath taken by all our kings at their coronation, where they swear to defend and protect the Church in all its rights.

A tax laid upon employments is a very different thing. The possessors of civil and military employments are no corporation; neither are they any part of our constitution: Their salaries, pay, and perquisites are all changeable at the pleasure of the prince who bestows them, although the army be paid from funds raised and appropriated by the legislature. But the Clergy as they have little reason to expect, so they desire no more than their ancient legal dues; only indeed with the removal of many grievous impediments in the collection of them; which it is to be feared they must wait for until more favourable times. It is well known, that they have already of their own accord shewn great indulgence to their people upon this very article of flax, seldom taking above a fourth part of their tithe for small parcels, and oftentimes nothing at all from new beginners; waiting with patience until the farmers were able, and until greater quantities of land were employed in that part of husbandry; never suspecting that their good intentions should be perverted in so singular a manner to their detriment, by that very assembly, which, during the time that convocations (which are an original part of our constitution ever since Christianity became national among us) are thought fit to be suspended, God knows for what reason, or from what provocations; I say, from that very assembly, who, during the intervals of convocations, should rather be supposed to be guardians of the rights and properties of the Clergy, than to make the least attempt upon either.

I have not heard upon inquiry, that any of those gentlemen, who, among us without doors, are called the Court Party, discover the least zeal in this affair. If they had thoughts to interpose, it might be conceived they would shew their displeasure against this Bill, which must very much lessen the value of the King's patronage upon promotion to vacant sees; in the disposal of deaneries, and other considerable preferments in the Church, which are in the donation of the Crown; whereby the viceroys will have fewer good preferments to bestow on their dependants, as well as upon the kindred of members, who may have a sufficient stock of that sort of merit, whatever it may be, which may in future times most prevail.

The Dissenters, by not succeeding in their endeavours to procure a repeal of the Test, have lost nothing, but continue in full enjoyment of their toleration; while the Clergy without giving the least offence, are by this Bill deprived of a considerable branch of their ancient legal rights, whereby the schismatical party will have the pleasure of gratifying their revenge. *Hoc Graii voluere.*

The farmer will find no relief by this *Modus,* because, when his present lease shall expire, his landlord will infallibly raise the rent in an equal proportion, upon every part of land where flax is sown, and have so much a better security for payment at the expense of the Clergy.

If we judge by things past, it little avails that this Bill is to be limited to a certain time of ten, twenty, or thirty years. For no landlord will ever consent that a law shall expire, by which he finds himself a gainer; and of this there are many examples, as well in England, as in this kingdom.

The great end of this Bill is, by proper encouragement to extend the linen manufacture into those counties where it hath hitherto been little cultivated: But this encouragement *of lessening the tithe of flax and hemp* is one of such a kind as, it is to be feared, will have a directly contrary effect. Because, if I am rightly informed, no set of men hath for their number and fortunes been more industrious and successful than the Clergy, in introducing that manufacture into places which were unacquainted with it; by persuading their people to sow flax and hemp, by procuring seed for them and by having them instructed in the management thereof; and this they did not without reasonable hopes of increasing the value of their parishes after some time, as well as of promoting the benefit of the public. But if this *Modus* should take place, the Clergy will be so far from gaining that they will become losers by any extraordinary care, by having their best arable lands turned to flax and hemp, which are reckoned great impoverishers of land: They cannot therefore be blamed, if they should shew as much zeal to prevent its being introduced or improved in their parishes as they hitherto have shewed in the introducing and improving of it. This, I am told, some of them have already declared at least so far as to resolve not to give themselves any more trouble than other men about promoting a manufacture by the success of which, they only of all men are to be sufferers. Perhaps the giving them even a further encouragement than the law doth, as it now stands, to a set of men who might on many accounts be so useful to this purpose, would be no bad method of having the great end of the Bill more effectually answered: But this is what they are far from desiring; all they petition for is no more than to continue on the same footing with the rest of their fellow-subjects.

If this *Modus* of paying by the acre be to pass into a law, it were to be wished that the same law would appoint one or more sworn surveyors in each parish to measure the lands on which flax and hemp are sown, as also would settle the price of surveying, and determine whether the incumbent or farmer is to pay for each annual survey. Without something of this kind, there must constantly be disputes between them, and the neighbouring justices of peace must be teazed as often as those disputes happen.

I had written thus far, when a paper was sent to me with

several reasons against the Bill, some whereof although they have been already touched, are put in a better light, and the rest did not occur to me. I shall deliver them in the author's own words.

N.B. Some Alterations have been made in the Bill about the *Modus*, since the above paper was writ; but they are of little moment.

SOME
# FURTHER REASONS

AGAINST

## THE BILL FOR SETTLING THE TITHE

OF

## HEMP, FLAX, &C.

I. That tithes are the patrimony of the Church: And if not of Divine original, yet at least of great antiquity.

II. That all purchases and leases of titheable lands, for many centuries past, have been made and taken, subject to the demand of tithes, and those lands sold and taken just so much the cheaper on that account.

III. That if any lands are exempted from tithes; or the legal demands of such tithes lessened by act of parliament, so much value is taken from the proprietor of the tithes, and vested in the proprietor of the lands, or his head tenants.

IV. That no innocent unoffending person can be so deprived of his property without the greatest violation of common justice.

V. That to do this upon a prospect of encouraging the linen, or any other manufacture, is acting upon a very mistaken and unjust supposition, inasmuch as the price of the lands so occupied will be no way lessened to the farmer by such a law.

VI. That the Clergy are content cheerfully to bear (as they now do) any burden in common with their fellow-subjects, either for the support of his Majesty's government, or the encouragement of the trade of the nation but think it very hard, that they should be singled out to pay heavier taxes than others, at a time when by the decrease of the value of their parishes they are less able to bear them.

VII. That the legislature hath heretofore distinguished the Clergy by exemptions, and not by additional loads, and the present Clergy of the kingdom hope they have not deserved worse of the legislature than their predecessors.

VIII. That by the original constitution of these kingdoms, the Clergy had the sole right of taxing themselves, and were in possession of that right as low as the Restoration: And if that right be now devolved upon the Commons by the cession of the Clergy, the Commons can be considered in this case in no other light than as the guardians of the Clergy.

IX. That besides those tithes always in the possession of the Clergy; there are some portion of tithes lately come into their possession by purchase; that if this clause should take place, they would not be allowed the benefit of these purchases, upon an equal footing of advantage with the rest of their fellow-subjects. And that some tithes in the hands of impropriators, are under settlements and mortgages.

X. That the gentlemen of this House should consider, that loading the Clergy is loading their own younger brothers and children; with this additional grievance, that it is taking from the younger and poorer, to give to the elder and richer. And,

*Lastly*, That, if it were at any time just and proper to do this, it would however be too severe to do it now, when all the tithes of the kingdom are known for some years past to have sunk above one-third part in their value.

Any income in the hands of the Clergy, is at least as useful to the public, as the same income in the hands of the laity.

It were more reasonable to grant the clergy in three parts of the nation an additional support, than to diminish their present subsistence.

Great employments are and will be in the hands of Englishmen; nothing left for the younger sons of Irishmen but vicarages, tide-waiters' places, &c.; therefore no reason to make them worse.

The *Modus* upon the flax in England, affects only lands reclaimed since the year 1690, and is at the rate of five shillings the English acre, which is equivalent to eight shillings and eightpence Irish, and that to be paid before the farmer removed it from the field. Flax is a manufacture of little consequence in England, but is the staple in Ireland, and if it increases (as it probably will) must in many places jostle out corn, because it is more gainful.

The Clergy of the Established Church, have no interest like those of the Church of Rome, distinct from the true interest of their country; and therefore ought to suffer under no distinct impositions or taxes of any kind.

The Bill for settling the *Modus* of flax in England, was brought in, in the first year of the reign of King George I., when the Clergy lay very unjustly under the imputation of some disaffection. And to encourage the bringing in of some fens in Lincolnshire, which were not to be continued under flax: But it left all lands where flax had been sown before that time, under the same condition of tithing, in which they were before the passing of that Bill: Whereas this bill takes away what the Clergy are actually possessed of.

That the woollen manufacture is the staple of England, as the linen is that of Ireland, yet no attempt was ever made in England to reduce the tithe of wool, for the encouragement of that manufacture.

This manufacture hath already been remarkably favoured by the Clergy, who have hitherto been generally content with less than half—some with sixpence a garden—and some have taken nothing.

Employments they say have been taxed, the reasons for which taxation will not hold with regard to property, at least till employments become inheritances.

The Commons always have had so tender a regard to property; that they never would suffer any law to pass, whereby any particular persons might be aggrieved without their own consent.

# AN ESSAY
### ON THE
# FATES OF CLERGYMEN.

**III.**                              **U**

## NOTE.

THIS essay was first printed in Nos. v. and vii. of "The Intelligencer" (Dublin, 1728). In that periodical it bore the title: "A Description of what the World calls Discretion;" and had the following lines from Ben Jonson as a text:

> "Described it's thus: Defined would you it have?
> Then the World's honest Man's an errant knave."

The text here printed is based on the original issue, and collated with the "Miscellanies," vol. iii. of 1732, and the "Miscellanies," vol. ii., 1747. [T. S.]

# AN ESSAY ON THE FATES OF CLERGYMEN.

THERE is no talent so useful towards rising in the world, or which puts men more out of the reach of fortune, than that quality generally possessed by the dullest sort of people, and is in common speech called discretion; a species of lower prudence, by the assistance of which, people of the meanest intellectuals, without any other qualification, pass through the world in great tranquillity, and with universal good treatment, neither giving nor taking offence. Courts are seldom unprovided of persons under this character, on whom, if they happen to be of great quality, most employments, even the greatest, naturally fall, when competitors will not agree; and in such promotions, nobody rejoices or grieves. The truth of this I could prove by several instances within my own memory; for I say nothing of present times.

And, indeed, as regularity and forms are of great use in carrying on the business of the world, so it is very convenient, that persons endued with this kind of discretion, should have that share which is proper to their talents, in the conduct of affairs, but by no means meddle in matters which require genius, learning, strong comprehension, quickness of conception, magnanimity, generosity, sagacity, or any other superior gift of human minds. Because this sort of discretion is usually attended with a strong desire of money, and few scruples about the way of obtaining it; with servile flattery and submission; with a want of all public spirit or principle; with a perpetual wrong judgment, when the owners come into power and high place, how to dispose of favour and preferment; having no measures for merit and virtue in others, but those very steps by which themselves ascended; nor the least intention of doing good or hurt to the public, farther than either one or t'other is likely to be subservient to their own security or interest. Thus, being void of all friendship and enmity, they never complain or find fault with the times, and indeed never have reason to do so.

Men of eminent parts and abilities, as well as virtues, do sometimes rise in the court, sometimes in the law, and sometimes even in the Church. Such were the Lord Bacon, the Earl of Strafford, Archbishop Laud, in the reign of King Charles I., and others in our own times, whom I shall not name; but these, and many more, under different princes, and in different kingdoms, were disgraced or banished, or suffered death, merely in envy to their virtues and superior genius, which emboldened them in great exigencies and distresses of state, (wanting a reasonable infusion of this aldermanly discretion,) to attempt the service of their prince and country, out of the common forms.

This evil fortune, which generally attends extraordinary men in the management of great affairs, has been imputed to divers causes that need not be here set down, when so obvious a one occurs, if what a certain writer observes be true, that when a great genius appears in the world, the dunces are all in confederacy against him. And if this be his fate when he employs his talents[1] wholly in his closet, without interfering with any man's ambition or avarice, what must he expect, when he ventures out to seek for preferment in a court, but universal opposition when he is mounting the ladder, and every hand ready to turn him off when he is at the top? And in this point, fortune generally acts directly contrary to nature; for in nature we find, that bodies full of life and spirits mount easily, and are hard to fall, whereas heavy bodies are hard to rise, and come down with greater velocity, in proportion to their weight; but we find fortune every day acting just the reverse of this.

This talent of discretion, as I have described it in its

---

[1] "And thus although he employs his talents." This is the reading of "The Intelligencer." [T. S.]

several adjuncts and circumstances, is nowhere so serviceable as to the clergy, to whose preferment nothing is so fatal as the character of wit, politeness in reading or manners, or that kind of behaviour which we contract by having too much conversation with persons of high station and eminency: these qualifications being reckoned, by the vulgar of all ranks, to be marks of levity, which is the last crime the world will pardon in a clergyman; to this I may add a free manner of speaking in mixed company, and too frequent an appearance in places of much resort, which are equally noxious to spiritual promotion.

I have known, indeed, a few exceptions to some parts of these observations.[1] I have seen some of the dullest men alive aiming at wit, and others, with as little pretensions, affecting politeness in manners and discourse: But never being able to persuade the world of their guilt, they grew into considerable stations, upon the firm assurance which all people had of their discretion, because they were of a size too low to deceive the world to their own disadvantage. But this, I confess, is a trial too dangerous often to engage in.

There is a known story of a clergyman, who was recommended for a preferment by some great men at court, to an archbishop.[2] His grace said, "he had heard that the clergyman used to play at whist and swobbers;[3] that as to playing now and then a sober game at whist for pastime, it might be pardoned, but he could not digest those wicked swobbers;" and it was with some pains that my Lord Somers could undeceive him. I ask, by what talents we may suppose that great prelate ascended so high, or what sort of qualifications he would expect in those whom he took into his patronage, or would probably recommend to court for the government of distant churches?

---

[1] This word is "regulations" in "The Intelligencer." [T. S.]

[2] Archbishop Tenison, who, by all contemporary accounts, was a very dull man. There was a bitter sarcasm upon him usually ascribed to Swift, "That he was as hot and heavy as a tailor's goose." [S.]

In "The Intelligencer" the word "archbishop" is replaced by the letters A. B. C. T. [T. S.]

[3] "Swobbers" were four privileged cards used, at one time, for betting purposes, in the game of whist. [T. S.]

Two clergymen, in my memory, stood candidates for a small free school in Yorkshire, where a gentleman of quality and interest in the country, who happened to have a better understanding than his neighbours, procured the place for him who was the better scholar, and more gentlemanly person, of the two, very much to the regret of all the parish: The other, being disappointed, came up to London, where he became the greatest pattern of this lower discretion that I have known, and possessed it with as heavy intellectuals; which, together with the coldness of his temper, and gravity of his deportment, carried him safe through many difficulties, and he lived and died in a great station; while his competitor is too obscure for fame to tell us what became of him.

This species of discretion, which I so much celebrate, and do most heartily recommend, hath one advantage not yet mentioned, that it will carry a man safe through all the malice and variety of parties, so far, that whatever faction happens to be uppermost, his claim is usually allowed for a share of what is going. And the thing seems to me highly reasonable: For in all great changes, the prevailing side is usually so tempestuous, that it wants the ballast of those whom the world calls moderate men, and I call men of discretion; whom people in power may, with little ceremony, load as heavy as they please, drive them through the hardest and deepest roads without danger of foundering, or breaking their backs, and will be sure to find them neither rusty nor vicious.

I[1] will here give the reader a short history of two clergymen in England, the characters of each, and the progress of their fortunes in the world; by which the force of worldly discretion, and the bad consequences from the want of that virtue, will strongly appear.

Corusodes, an Oxford student, and a farmer's son, was never absent from prayers or lecture, nor once out of his

---

[1] In "The Intelligencer," No. v., this paragraph reads as follows: "In some following Paper I will give the reader a short history of two Clergymen in England, the characters of each, and the progress of their fortunes in the world. By which the force of worldly discretion, and the bad consequences from the want of that virtue, will strongly appear." In No. vii. the subject is continued as in the next paragraph. [T. S.]

college, after Tom had tolled. He spent every day ten hours in his closet, in reading his courses, dozing, clipping papers, or darning his stockings; which last he performed to admiration. He could be soberly drunk at the expense of others, with college ale, and at those seasons was always most devout. He wore the same gown five years without draggling or tearing. He never once looked into a play-book or a poem. He read Virgil and Ramus in the same cadence, but with a very different taste. He never understood a jest, or had the least conception of wit.

For one saying he stands in renown to this day. Being with some other students over a pot of ale, one of the company said so many pleasant things, that the rest were much diverted, only Corusodes was silent and unmoved. When they parted, he called this merry companion aside, and said, "Sir, I perceive by your often speaking, and your friends laughing, that you spoke many jests; and you could not but observe my silence: But sir, this is my humour, I never make a jest myself, nor ever laugh at another man's."

Corusodes, thus endowed, got into holy orders; having, by the most extreme parsimony, saved thirty-four pounds out of a very beggarly fellowship, he went up to London, where his sister was waitingwoman to a lady, and so good a solicitor, that by her means he was admitted to read prayers in the family twice a-day, at fourteen[1] shillings a month. He had now acquired a low, obsequious, awkward bow, and a talent of gross flattery both in and out of season; he would shake the butler by the hand; he taught the page his catechism, and was sometimes admitted to dine at the steward's table. In short, he got the good word of the whole family, and was recommended by my lady for chaplain to some other noble houses, by which his revenue (besides vales) amounted to about thirty pounds a-year: His sister procured him a scarf from my lord, who had a small design of gallantry upon her; and by his lordship's solicitation he got a lectureship in town of sixty pounds a-year; where he preached constantly in person, in a grave manner, with an audible voice, a style ecclesiastic, and the matter (such as it was) well suited to the intellectuals of his hearers. Some time after, a country living

---

[1] Scott has "ten shillings." [T. S.]

fell in my lord's disposal; and his lordship, who had now some encouragement given him of success in his amour, bestowed the living on Corusodes, who still kept his lectureship and residence in town; where he was a constant attendant at all meetings relating to charity, without ever contributing further than his frequent pious exhortations. If any woman of better fashion in the parish happened to be absent from church, they were sure of a visit from him in a day or two, to chide and to dine with them.

He had a select number of poor constantly attending at the street door of his lodgings, for whom he was a common solicitor to his former patroness, dropping in his own half-crown among the collection, and taking it out when he disposed of the money. At a person of quality's house, he would never sit down till he was thrice bid, and then upon the corner of the most distant chair. His whole demeanour was formal and starch, which adhered so close, that he could never shake it off in his highest promotion.

His lord was now in high employment at court, and attended by him with the most abject assiduity; and his sister being gone off with child to a private lodging, my lord continued his graces to Corusodes, got him to be a chaplain in ordinary, and in due time a parish in town, and a dignity in the Church.

He paid his curates punctually, at the lowest salary, and partly out of the communion money; but gave them good advice in abundance. He married a citizen's widow, who taught him to put out small sums at ten per cent., and brought him acquainted with jobbers in Change-alley. By her dexterity he sold the clerkship of his parish, when it became vacant.

He kept a miserable house, but the blame was laid wholly upon madam; for the good doctor was always at his books, or visiting the sick, or doing other offices of charity and piety in his parish.

He treated all his inferiors of the clergy with a most sanctified pride; was rigorously and universally censorious upon all his brethren of the gown, on their first appearance in the world, or while they continued meanly preferred; but gave large allowance to the laity of high rank, or great riches, using neither eyes nor ears for their faults: He was never sensible of the least corruption in courts, parliaments, or ministries, but made the most favourable constructions of all public proceedings; and power, in whatever hands, or whatever party, was always secure of his most charitable opinion. He had many wholesome maxims ready to excuse all miscarriages of state: Men are but men; *Erunt vitia donec homines;* and, *Quod supra nos, nil ad nos;* with several others of equal weight.

It would lengthen my paper beyond measure to trace out the whole system of his conduct; his dreadful apprehensions of Popery; his great moderation toward dissenters of all denominations; with hearty wishes, that, by yielding somewhat on both sides, there might be a general union among Protestants; his short, inoffensive sermons in his turns at court, and the matter exactly suited to the present juncture of prevailing opinions; the arts he used to obtain a mitre, by writing against Episcopacy; and the proofs he gave of his loyalty, by palliating or defending the murder of a martyred prince.

Endowed with all these accomplishments, we leave him in the full career of success, mounting fast toward the top of the Ladder Ecclesiastical, which he hath a fair probability to reach; without the merit of one single virtue, moderately stocked with the least valuable parts of erudition, utterly devoid of all taste, judgment, or genius; and, in his grandeur, naturally choosing to haul up others after him, whose accomplishments most resemble his own, except his beloved sons, nephews, or other kindred, be in competition; or, lastly, except his inclinations be diverted by those who have power to mortify, or further advance him.

Eugenio set out from the same university, and about the same time with Corusodes; he had the reputation of an arch lad at school, and was unfortunately possessed with a talent for poetry; on which account he received many chiding letters from his father, and grave advice from his tutor. He did not neglect his college learning, but his chief study was the authors of antiquity, with a perfect knowledge in the Greek and Roman tongues. He could never procure himself to be chosen fellow: For it was objected against him, that he had written verses, and particularly some wherein he glanced at a certain reverend doctor famous for dulness:

That he been seen bowing to ladies, as he met them in the streets; and it was proved, that once he had been found dancing in a private family, with half a dozen of both sexes.

He was the younger son to a gentleman of good birth, but small estate; and his father dying, he was driven to London to seek his fortune: He got into orders, and became reader in a parish church at twenty pounds a-year; was carried by an Oxford friend to Will's coffee-house, frequented in those days by men of wit, where in some time he had the bad luck to be distinguished. His scanty salary compelled him to run deep in debt for a new gown and cassock, and now and then forced him to write some paper of wit or humour, or preach a sermon for ten shillings, to supply his necessities. He was a thousand times recommended by his poetical friends to great persons, as a young man of excellent parts who deserved encouragement, and received a thousand promises; but his modesty, and a generous spirit, which disdained the slavery of continual application and attendance, always disappointed him, making room for vigilant dunces, who were sure to be never out of sight.

He had an excellent faculty in preaching, if he were not sometimes a little too refined, and apt to trust too much to his own way of thinking and reasoning.

When, upon the vacancy of a preferment, he was hardly drawn to attend upon some promising lord, he received the usual answer, "That he came too late, for it had been given to another the very day before." And he had only this comfort left, that everybody said, "It was a thousand pities something could not be done for poor Mr. Eugenio."

The remainder of his story will be dispatched in a few words: Wearied with weak hopes, and weaker pursuits, he accepted a curacy in Derbyshire, of thirty pounds a-year, and when he was five-and-forty, had the great felicity to be preferred by a friend of his father's to a vicarage worth annually sixty pounds, in the most desert parts of Lincolnshire; where, his spirit quite sunk with those reflections that solitude and disappointments bring, he married a farmer's widow, and is still alive, utterly undistinguished and forgotten; only some of the neighbours have accidentally heard, that he had been a notable man in his youth.

CONCERNING THAT
# UNIVERSAL HATRED,
**WHICH PREVAILS**
## AGAINST THE CLERGY.

# CONCERNING THAT UNIVERSAL HATRED, WHICH PREVAILS AGAINST THE CLERGY.

*May 24, 1736.*

I HAVE been long considering and conjecturing, what could be the causes of that great disgust, of late, against the clergy of both kingdoms, beyond what was ever known till that monster and tyrant, Henry VIII. who took away from them, against law, reason, and justice, at least two-thirds of their legal possessions; and whose successors (except Queen Mary) went on with their rapine, till the accession of King James I. That detestable tyrant Henry VIII. although he abolished the Pope's power in England, as universal bishop, yet what he did in that article, however just it were in itself, was the mere effect of his irregular appetite, to divorce himself from a wife he was weary of, for a younger and more beautiful woman, whom he afterwards beheaded. But, at the same time, he was an entire defender of all the Popish doctrines, even those which were the most absurd. And, while he put people to death for denying him to be head of the Church, he burned every offender against the doctrines of the Roman faith; and cut off the head of Sir Thomas More, a person of the greatest virtue this kingdom ever produced, for not directly owning him to be head of the Church. Among all the princes who ever reigned in the world there was never so infernal a beast as Henry VIII. in every vice of the most odious kind, without any one appearance of virtue: But cruelty, lust, rapine, and atheism, were his peculiar talents. He rejected the power of the Pope for no other reason, than to give his full swing to commit sacrilege, in which no tyrant, since Christianity became national, did ever equal him by many degrees. The abbeys, endowed with lands by the mistaken notions of well-disposed men, were indeed too numerous, and hurtful to the kingdom; and, therefore, the legislature might, after the Reformation, have justly applied them to some pious or public uses.

In a very few centuries after Christianity became national in most parts of Europe, although the church of Rome had already introduced many corruptions in religion; yet the piety of early Christians, as well as new converts, was so great, and particularly of princes, as well as noblemen and other wealthy persons, that they built many religious houses, for those who were inclined to live in a recluse or solitary manner, endowing those monasteries with land. It is true, we read of monks some ages before, who dwelt in caves and cells, in desert places. But, when public edifices were erected and endowed, they began gradually to degenerate into idleness, ignorance, avarice, ambition, and luxury, after the usual fate of all human institutions. The Popes, who had already aggrandized themselves, laid hold of the opportunity to subject all religious houses with their priors and abbots, to their peculiar authority; whereby these religious orders became of an interest directly different from the rest of mankind, and wholly at the Pope's devotion. I need say no more on this article, so generally known and so frequently treated, or of the frequent endeavours of some other princes, as well as our own, to check the growth, and wealth, and power of the regulars.

In later times, this mistaken piety, of erecting and endowing abbeys, began to decrease. And therefore, when some new-invented sect of monks and friars began to start up, not being able to procure grants of land, they got leave from the Pope to appropriate the tithes and glebes of certain parishes, as contiguous or near as they could find, obliging themselves to send out some of their body to take care of the people's souls: And, if some of those parishes were at too great a distance from the abbey, the monks appointed to attend them were paid, for the cure, either a small stipend of a determined sum, or sometimes a third part, or what are now called the vicarial tithes.

As to the church-lands, it hath been the opinion of many writers, that, in England, they amounted to a third part of the whole kingdom. And therefore, if that wicked prince above-mentioned, when he had cast off the Pope's power, had introduced some reformation in religion, he could not have been blamed for taking away the abbey-lands by authority of parliament. But, when he continued the most cruel persecutor of all those who differed in the least article of the Popish religion, which was then the national and established faith, his seizing on those lands, and applying them to profane uses, was absolute sacrilege, in the strongest sense of the word; having been bequeathed by princes and pious men to sacred uses.

In the reign of this prince, the church and court of Rome had arrived to such a height of corruption, in doctrine and discipline, as gave great offence to many wise, learned, and pious men, through most parts of Europe; and several countries agreed to make some reformation in religion. But, although a proper and just reformation were allowed to be necessary, even to preserve Christianity itself, yet the passions and vices of men had mingled themselves so far, as to pervert and confound all the good endeavours of those who intended well: And thus the reformation, in every country where it was attempted, was carried on in the most impious and scandalous manner that can possibly be conceived. To which unhappy proceedings we owe all the just reproachings that Roman Catholics have cast upon us ever since. For, when the northern kingdoms and states grew weary of the Pope's tyranny, and when their preachers, beginning with the scandalous abuses of indulgencies, and proceeding farther to examine several points of faith, had credit enough with their princes, who were in some fear lest such a change might affect the peace of their countries, because their bishops had great influence on the people by their wealth and power; these politic teachers had a ready answer to this purpose. "Sir, your Majesty need not be in any pain or apprehension: Take away the lands, and sink the authority of the bishops: Bestow those lands on your courtiers, on your nobles, and your great officers in your army; and then you will be secure of the people." This advice was exactly followed. And, in the Protestant monarchies abroad, little more than the shadow of Episcopacy is left; but, in the republics, is wholly extinct.

In England, the Reformation was brought in after a somewhat different manner, but upon the same principle of robbing the Church. However, Henry VIII. with great dexterity, discovered an invention to gratify his insatiable thirst for blood, on both religions, * * * * *

## THOUGHTS ON RELIGION.

III.                    X

## NOTE.

IN the "Gent. Mag.," vol. xxxv., p. 372 (August, 1765), is a reprint of these "Thoughts," and "Further Thoughts" from Deane Swift's edition of his relative's works, just then published. The note introducing the reprint is signed "T. B."; but neither the note nor T. B.'s remarks are of much importance. The present text is that of Scott, and collated with the quarto edition of Swift's Works, vol. viii. 1765.

[T. S.]

# THOUGHTS ON RELIGION.

I AM in all opinions to believe according to my own impartial reason; which I am bound to inform and improve, as far as my capacity and opportunities will permit.

It may be prudent in me to act sometimes by other men's reason, but I can think only by my own.

If another man's reason fully convinceth me, it becomes my own reason.

To say a man is bound to believe, is neither truth nor sense.

You may force men, by interest or punishment, to say or swear they believe, and to act as if they believed: You can go no further.

Every man, as a member of the commonwealth, ought to be content with the possession of his own opinion in private, without perplexing his neighbour or disturbing the public.

Violent zeal for truth hath an hundred to one odds to be either petulancy, ambition, or pride.

There is a degree of corruption wherein some nations, as bad as the world is, will proceed to an amendment; till which time particular men should be quiet.

To remove opinions fundamental in religion is impossible, and the attempt wicked, whether those opinions be true or false; unless your avowed design be to abolish that religion altogether. So, for instance, in the famous doctrine of Christ's divinity, which hath been universally received by all bodies of Christians, since the condemnation of Arianism under Constantine and his successors: Wherefore the proceedings of the Socinians are both vain and unwarrantable; because they will be never able to advance their own opinion, or meet any other success than breeding doubts and disturbances in the world. *Qui ratione suâ disturbant mænia mundi.*

The want of belief is a defect that ought to be concealed when it cannot be overcome.

The Christian religion, in the most early times, was proposed to the Jews and heathens without the article of Christ's divinity; which, I remember, Erasmus accounts for, by its being too strong a meat for babes. Perhaps, if it were now softened by the Chinese missionaries, the conversion of those infidels would be less difficult: And we find by the Alcoran, it is the great stumbling-block of the Mahometans. But, in a country already Christian, to bring so fundamental a point of faith into debate, can have no consequences that are not pernicious to morals and public peace.

I have been often offended to find St. Paul's allegories, and other figures of Grecian eloquence, converted by divines into articles of faith.

God's mercy is over all His works, but divines of all sorts lessen that mercy too much.

I look upon myself, in the capacity of a clergyman, to be one appointed by Providence for defending a post assigned me, and for gaining over as many enemies as I can. Although I think my cause is just, yet one great motive is my submitting to the pleasure of Providence, and to the laws of my country.

I am not answerable to God for the doubts that arise in my own breast, since they are the consequence of that reason which He hath planted in me; if I take care to conceal those doubts from others, if I use my best endeavours to subdue them, and if they have no influence on the conduct of my life.

I believe that thousands of men would be orthodox enough in certain points, if divines had not been too curious, or too narrow, in reducing orthodoxy within the compass of subtleties, niceties, and distinctions, with little warrant from Scripture and less from reason or good policy.

I never saw, heard, nor read, that the clergy were beloved in any nation where Christianity was the religion of the country. Nothing can render them popular but some degree of persecution.

Those fine gentlemen who affect the humour of railing at

the clergy, are, I think, bound in honour to turn parsons themselves, and shew us better examples.

Miserable mortals! Can we contribute to the honour and glory of God? I wish that expression were struck out of our Prayer-books.

Liberty of conscience, properly speaking, is no more than the liberty of possessing our own thoughts and opinions, which every man enjoys without fear of the magistrate: But how far he shall publicly act in pursuance of those opinions, is to be regulated by the laws of the country. Perhaps, in my own thoughts, I prefer a well-instituted commonwealth before a monarchy; and I know several others of the same opinion. Now, if, upon this pretence, I should insist upon liberty of conscience, form conventicles of republicans, and print books preferring that government and condemning what is established, the magistrate would, with great justice, hang me and my disciples. It is the same case in religion, although not so avowed, where liberty of conscience, under the present acceptation, equally produces revolutions, or at least convulsions and disturbances in a state; which politicians would see well enough, if their eyes were not blinded by faction, and of which these kingdoms, as well as France, Sweden, and other countries, are flaming instances. Cromwell's notion upon this article was natural and right; when, upon the surrender of a town in Ireland, the Popish governor insisted upon an article for liberty of conscience, Cromwell said, he meddled with no man's conscience; but, if by liberty of conscience, the governor meant the liberty of the mass, he had express orders from the Parliament of England against admitting any such liberty at all.

It is impossible that anything so natural, so necessary, and so universal as death, should ever have been designed by Providence as an evil to mankind.

Although reason were intended by Providence to govern our passions, yet it seems that, in two points of the greatest moment to the being and continuance of the world, God hath intended our passions to prevail over reason. The first is, the propagation of our species, since no wise man ever married from the dictates of reason. The other is, the love of life, which, from the dictates of reason, every man would despise, and wish it at an end, or that it never had a beginning.

# FURTHER THOUGHTS ON RELIGION.

THE Scripture system of man's creation is what Christians are bound to believe, and seems most agreeable of all others to probability and reason. Adam was formed from a piece of clay, and Eve from one of his ribs. The text mentioneth nothing of his Maker's intending him for, except to rule over the beasts of the field and birds of the air. As to Eve, it doth not appear that her husband was her monarch, only she was to be his help meet, and placed in some degree of subjection. However, before his fall, the beasts were his most obedient subjects, whom he governed by absolute power. After his eating the forbidden fruit, the course of nature was changed, the animals began to reject his government; some were able to escape by flight, and others were too fierce to be attacked. The Scripture mentioneth no particular acts of royalty in Adam over his posterity, who were cotemporary with him, or of any monarch until after the flood; whereof the first was Nimrod, the mighty hunter, who, as Milton expresseth it, made men, and not beasts, his prey. For men were easier caught by promises, and subdued by the folly or treachery of their own species. Whereas the brutes prevailed only by their courage or strength, which, among them, are peculiar to certain kinds. Lions, bears, elephants, and some other animals are strong or valiant, and their species never degenerates in their native soil, except they happen to be enslaved or destroyed by human fraud: But men degenerate every day, merely by the folly, the perverseness, the avarice, the tyranny, the pride, the treachery, or inhumanity of their own kind.

# THREE PRAYERS

USED BY THE DEAN FOR MRS JOHNSON,

IN HER LAST SICKNESS, 1727.[1]

### I.

#### A Prayer for Stella.

ALMIGHTY and most gracious Lord God, extend, we beseech Thee, Thy pity and compassion towards this Thy languishing servant: Teach her to place her hope and confidence entirely in Thee; give her a true sense of the emptiness and vanity of all earthly things; make her truly sensible of all the infirmities of her life past, and grant to her such a true sincere repentance as is not to be repented of. Preserve her, O Lord, in a sound mind and understanding, during this Thy visitation: Keep her from both the sad extremes of presumption and despair. If Thou shalt please to restore her to her former health, give her grace to be ever mindful of that mercy, and to keep those good resolutions she now makes in her sickness, so that no length of time, nor prosperity, may entice her to forget them. Let no thought of her misfortunes distract her mind, and prevent the means towards her recovery, or disturb her in her preparations for a better life. We beseech Thee also, O Lord, of Thy infinite goodness to remember the good actions of this Thy servant; that the naked she hath clothed, the hungry

---

[1] "Dr. Swift, after his return to Ireland in the beginning of October [1727], having visited her [Stella] frequently during her sickness, not only as a friend, but a clergyman; he used the following prayers on that occasion; which are here printed from his own handwriting." [Note in volume viii. of Swift's Works, Dublin, 1746.]

she hath fed, the sick and the fatherless whom she hath relieved, may be reckoned according to Thy gracious promise, as if they had been done unto Thee. Hearken, O Lord, to the prayers offered up by the friends of this Thy servant in her behalf, and especially those now made by us unto Thee. Give Thy blessing to those endeavours used for her recovery; but take from her all violent desire, either of life or death, further than with resignation to Thy holy will. And now, O Lord, we implore Thy gracious favour towards us here met together; grant that the sense of this Thy servant's weakness may add strength to our faith, that we, considering the infirmities of our nature, and the uncertainty of life, may, by this example, be drawn to repentance before it shall please Thee to visit us in the like manner. Accept these prayers, we beseech Thee, for the sake of Thy dear Son Jesus Christ, our Lord; who, with Thee and the Holy Ghost, liveth and reigneth ever one God world without end. Amen.

## II.

### A Prayer used by the Dean for Mrs Johnson in her last Sickness, written Oct. 17, 1727.

Most merciful Father, accept our humblest prayers in behalf of this Thy languishing servant: Forgive the sins, the frailties, and infirmities of her life past. Accept the good deeds she hath done, in such a manner, that at whatever time Thou shalt please to call her, she may be received into everlasting habitations. Give her grace to continue sincerely thankful to Thee for the many favours Thou hast bestowed upon her; The ability and inclination and practice to do good, and those virtues, which have procured the esteem and love of her friends, and a most unspotted name in the world. O God, Thou dispensest Thy blessings and Thy punishments, as it becometh infinite justice and mercy; and since it was Thy pleasure to afflict her with a long, constant, weakly state of health, make her truly sensible, that it was for very wise ends, and was largely made up to her in other blessings, more valuable and less common. Continue to her, O Lord, that firmness and constancy of mind, wherewith Thou hast most graciously endowed her, together with that contempt of worldly things and vanities, that she hath shewn in the whole conduct of her life. O all-powerful Being, the least motion of Whose will can create or destroy a world; pity us the mournful friends of Thy distressed servant, who sink under the weight of her present condition, and the fear of losing the most valuable of our friends: Restore her to us, O Lord, if it be Thy gracious will, or inspire us with constancy and resignation, to support ourselves under so heavy an affliction. Restore her, O Lord, for the sake of those poor, who by losing her will be desolate, and those sick, who will not only want her bounty, but her care and tending: Or else, in Thy mercy, raise up some other in her place with equal disposition and better abilities. Lessen, O Lord, we beseech Thee, her bodily pains, or give her a double strength of mind to support them. And if Thou wilt soon take her to Thyself, turn our thoughts rather upon that felicity, which we hope she shall enjoy, than upon that unspeakable loss we shall endure. Let her memory be ever dear unto us; and the example of her many virtues, as far as human infirmity will admit, our constant imitation. Accept, O Lord, these prayers poured from the very bottom of our hearts, in Thy mercy, and for the merits of our blessed Saviour. Amen.

### III.

#### WRITTEN NOV. 6, 1727.

O Merciful Father, Who never afflictest Thy children, but for their own good, and with justice, over which Thy mercy always prevaileth, either to turn them to repentance, or to punish them in the present life, in order to reward them in a better; take pity, we beseech Thee, upon this Thy poor afflicted servant, languishing so long and so grievously under the weight of Thy hand. Give her strength, O Lord, to support her weakness; and patience to endure her pains, without repining at Thy correction. Forgive every rash and inconsiderate expression, which her anguish may at any time force from her tongue, while her heart continueth in an entire submission to Thy will. Suppress in her, O Lord, all eager desires of life, and lessen her fears of death, by inspiring into her an humble, yet assured, hope of Thy mercy. Give her a sincere repentance for all her transgressions and omissions, and a firm resolution to pass the remainder of her life in endeavouring to her utmost to observe all Thy precepts. We beseech Thee likewise to compose her thoughts; and preserve to her the use of her memory and reason during the course of her sickness. Give her a true conception of the vanity, folly, and insignificancy of all human things; and strengthen her so as to beget in her a sincere love of Thee in the midst of her sufferings. Accept and impute all her good deeds, and forgive her all those offences against Thee, which she hath sincerely repented of, or through the frailty of memory hath forgot. And now, O Lord, we turn to Thee in behalf of ourselves, and the rest of her sorrowful friends. Let not our grief afflict her mind, and thereby have an ill effect on her present distempers. Forgive the sorrow and weakness of those among us, who sink under the grief and terror of losing so dear and useful a friend. Accept and pardon our most earnest prayers and wishes for her longer continuance in this evil world, to do what Thou art pleased to call Thy service, and is only her bounden duty; that she may be still a comfort to us, and to all others who will want the benefit of her conversation, her advice, her good offices, or her charity. And since Thou hast promised, that where two or three are gathered together in Thy name, Thou wilt be in the midst of them, to grant their request; O gracious Lord, grant to us who are here met in Thy name, that those requests, which in the utmost sincerity and earnestness of our hearts we have now made in behalf of this Thy distressed servant, and of ourselves, may effectually be answered; through the merits of Jesus Christ our Lord. Amen.

# AN EVENING PRAYER,

### FROM THE ORIGINAL MANUSCRIPT FOUND AMONGST DR LYON'S PAPERS.

OH! Almighty God, the searcher of all hearts, and from whom no secrets are hid, who hast declared that all such as shall draw nigh to thee with their lips, when their hearts are far from thee, are an abomination unto thee; cleanse, we beseech thee, the thoughts of our hearts, by the inspiration of thy Holy Spirit, that no wandering, vain, nor idle thoughts may put out of our minds that reverence and godly fear, that becomes all those who come in thy presence.

We know, O Lord, that while we are in these bodies, we are absent from the Lord, for no man can see thy face and live. The only way that we can draw near unto thee in this life, is by prayer; but, O Lord, we know not how to pray, nor what to ask for as we ought. We cannot pretend by our supplications or prayers to turn or change thee, for thou art the same yesterday, to-day, and for ever; but the coming into thy presence, the drawing near unto thee, is the only means to be changed ourselves, to become like thee in holiness and purity, to be followers of thee as thy dear children. O, therefore, turn not away thy face from us, but let us see so much of the excellencies of thy divine nature, of thy goodness, and justice, and mercy, and forbearance, and holiness, and purity, as may make us hate everything in ourselves that is unlike to thee, that so we may abhor and repent of and forsake those sins that we so often fall into when we forget thee. Lord! We acknowledge and confess we have lived in a course of sin, and folly, and vanity, from our youth up, forgetting our latter end, and our great account that we must one day make, and turning a deaf ear to thy many calls to us, either by thy holy word, by our teachers, or by our own consciences; and even thy more severe messages by afflictions, sicknesses, crosses, and disappointments, have not been of force enough to turn us from the vanity and folly of our own ways. What then can we expect in justice, when thou shalt enter into judgment with us, but to have our portion with the hypocrites and unbelievers? to depart for ever from the presence of the Lord; to be turned into hell with those that forget God! But, O God, most holy! O God, most mighty! O holy and most merciful Saviour, deliver us not into the bitter pains of eternal death, but have mercy upon us, most merciful Father, and forgive us our sins for thy name's sake; for thou hast declared thyself to be a God slow to anger, full of goodness, forbearance, and long-suffering, and forgiving iniquity, transgression, and sin. O Lord, therefore, shew thy mercy upon us. O let it be in pardoning our sins past, and in changing our natures, in giving us a new heart, and a new spirit, that we may lead a new life, and walk before thee in newness of life, that so sin may not have dominion over us for the time to come. O let thy good Spirit, without which we can do nothing, O let that work in us both to will and do such things as may be well pleasing to thee. O let it change our thoughts and minds, and take them off the vain pleasures of this world, and place them there where only the true joys are to be found. O fill our minds every day more and more with the happiness of that blessed state of living for ever with thee, that we may make it our great work and business to work out our salvation,—to improve in the knowledge of thee, whom to know is life eternal. But, Lord, since we cannot know thee but by often drawing near unto thee, and coming into thy presence, which in this life, we can do only by prayer, O make us, therefore, ever sensible of these great benefits of prayer, that we may rejoice at all opportunities of coming into thy presence, and may ever find ourselves the better and more heavenly minded by it, and may never wilfully neglect any opportunity of thy worship and service. Awaken thoroughly in us a serious sense of these things, that so to-day, while it is called to-day, we may see and know the things that belong to our peace, before they be hid from our eyes, before that long night cometh when no man can work. O that every night may so effectually put us in mind of our last, that we may every day take care so to live, as we shall then wish we had lived when we come to die; that so when that night shall come, we may as willingly put off these bodies, as we now put off our clothes, and may rejoice to rest from our labours, and that our war with the world, the devil, and our own corrupt nature, is at an end. In the meanwhile, we beseech thee to take us, and ours, and all that belongs to us, into thy fatherly care this night. Let thy holy angels be our guard, while we are not in a condition to defend ourselves, that we may not be under the power of devils or wicked men; and preserve us also, O Lord, from every evil accident, that, after a comfortable and refreshing sleep, we may find ourselves, and all that belongs to us, in peace and safety. And now, O Lord, being ourselves still in the body, and compassed about with infirmities, we can neither be ignorant nor unmindful of the sufferings of our fellow-creatures. O Lord, we must acknowledge, that they are all but the effects of sin; and, therefore, we beseech thee so to sanctify their several chastisements to them, that at length they may bring forth the peaceable fruits of righteousness, and then be thou graciously pleased to remove thy heavy and afflicting hand from them. And O that the rest of mankind, who are not under such trials, may, by thy goodness, be led to repentance, that the consciences of hard-hearted sinners may be awakened, and the understandings of poor ignorant creatures enlightened, and that all that love and fear thee may ever find the joy and comfort of a good conscience, beyond all the satisfactions that this world can afford. And now, blessed Lord, from whom every good gift comes, it is meet, right, and our bounden duty, that we should offer up unto thee our thanks and praise for all thy goodness towards us, for preserving peace in our land, the light of thy Gospel, and the true religion in our churches; for giving us the fruits of the earth in due season, and preserving us from the plague and sickness that rages in other lands. We bless thee for that support and maintenance, which thou art pleased to afford us, and that thou givest us a heart to be sensible of this thy goodness, and to return our thanks at this time for the same; and as to our persons, for that measure of health that any of us do enjoy, which is more than any of us do deserve. We bless thee, more particularly, for thy protection over us the day past; that thy good spirit has kept us from falling into even the greatest sins, which, by our wicked and corrupt nature, we should greedily have been hurried into; and that, by the guard of thy holy angels, we have been kept safe from any of those evils that might have befallen us, and which many are now groaning under, who rose up in the morning in safety and peace as well as we. But above all, for that great mercy of contriving and effecting our redemption, by the death of our Saviour Jesus Christ, whom, of thy great love to mankind, thou didst send into this world, to take upon him our flesh, to teach us thy will, and to bear the guilt of our transgressions, to die for our sins, and to rise again for our justification; and for enabling us to lay hold of that salvation, by the gracious assistances of thy Holy Spirit. Lord, grant that the sense of this wonderful love of thine to us, may effectually encourage us to walk in thy fear, and live to thy glory, that so when we shall put off this mortal state, we may be made partakers of that glory that shall then be revealed, which we beg of thee, for the sake of thy Son Jesus Christ, who died to procure it for us, and in whose name and words we do offer up the desires of our souls unto thee, saying,

"Our Father," &c.

# OBSERVATIONS

ON

## HEYLIN'S HISTORY OF THE PRESBYTERIANS.[1]

THIS book, by some errors and neglects in the style, seems not to have received the author's[2] last correction. It is written with some vehemence, very pardonable in one who had been an observer and a sufferer, in England, under that diabolical fanatic sect which then destroyed Church and State. But, by comparing in my memory what I have read in other histories, he neither aggravates nor falsifies any facts. His partiality appears chiefly in setting the actions of the Calvinists in the strongest light, without equally dwelling on those of the other side; which, however, to say the truth, was not his proper business. And yet he might have spent some more words on the inhuman massacre of Paris and other parts of France, which no provocation (and yet the King had the greatest possible) could excuse, or much extenuate. The author, according to the current opinion of the age he lived in, had too high notions of regal power; led

---

[1] Written by the Dean in the beginning of the book, on one of the blank leaves. [Note in vol. ix. 1775 edition of Swift's Works.]

[2] Peter Heylin, D.D. (1600-1662) was born at Burford, Oxfordshire. Educated at Magdalen College, Oxford, and became in succession, chaplain to Charles I., rector of Hemmingford, rector of Islip, and a prebendary of Westminster. He wrote the weekly paper, "Mercurius Aulicus," and lost his estates during the Civil War. He was reinstated at the Restoration into all his preferments. His works are voluminous, consisting of a "Cosmography," "A Help to English History," a "Life of Charles I.," a "History of the Reformation," a "History of Presbyterians," a "Life of Archbishop Laud," and a few theological works. The work on the Presbyterians, here referred to by Swift, was published in 1670. [T. S.]

by the common mistake of the term Supreme Magistrate, and not rightly distinguishing between the legislature and administration: into which mistake the clergy fell, or continued, in the reign of Charles II., as I have shewn and explained in a treatise, &c.

J. SWIFT.

March 6, 1727-8.

# AN ALPHABETICAL LIST

OF BOOKS CONTAINED IN

# BOHN'S LIBRARIES.

*Detailed Catalogue, arranged according to the various Libraries, will be sent on application.*

---

**ADDISON'S Works.** With the Notes of Bishop Hurd, Portrait, and 8 Plates of Medals and Coins. Edited by H. G. Bohn. 6 vols. 3s. 6d. each.

**ÆSCHYLUS, The Dramas of.** Translated into English Verse by Anna Swanwick. 4th Edition, revised. 5s.

—— **The Tragedies of.** Translated into Prose by T. A. Buckley, B.A. 3s. 6d.

**AGASSIZ and GOULD'S Outline of Comparative Physiology.** Enlarged by Dr. Wright. With 390 Woodcuts. 5s.

**ALFIERI'S Tragedies.** Translated into English Verse by Edgar A. Bowring, C.B. 2 vols. 3s. 6d. each.

**ALLEN'S (Joseph, R. N.) Battles of the British Navy.** Revised Edition, with 57 Steel Engravings. 2 vols. 5s. each.

**AMMIANUS MARCELLINUS. History of Rome** during the Reigns of Constantius, Julian, Jovianus, Valentinian, and Valens. Translated by Prof. C. D. Yonge, M.A. 7s. 6d.

**ANDERSEN'S Danish Legends and Fairy Tales.** Translated by Caroline Peachey. With 120 Wood Engravings. 5s.

**ANTONINUS (M. Aurelius). The Thoughts of.** Trans. literally, with Notes and Introduction by George Long, M.A. 3s. 6d.

**APOLLONIUS RHODIUS.** 'The Argonautica.' Translated by E. P. Coleridge, B.A.

**APPIAN'S Roman History.** Translated by Horace White, M.A., LL.D. With Maps and Illustrations. 2 vols. 6s. each.

**APULEIUS, The Works of.** Comprising the Golden Ass, God of Socrates, Florida, and Discourse of Magic. 5s.

**ARIOSTO'S Orlando Furioso.** Translated into English Verse by W. S. Rose. With Portrait, and 24 Steel Engravings. 2 vols. 5s. each

**ARISTOPHANES' Comedies.** Translated by W. J. Hickie. 2 vols. 5s. each.

**ARISTOTLE'S Nicomachean Ethics.** Translated, with Introduction and Notes, by the Venerable Archdeacon Browne. 5s.

—— **Politics and Economics.** Translated by E. Walford, M A., with Introduction by Dr. Gillies. 5s.

—— **Metaphysics.** Translated by the Rev. John H. M'Mahon, M.A. 5s.

—— **History of Animals.** Trans. by Richard Cresswell, M A. 5s.

—— **Organon;** or, Logical Treatises, and the Introduction of Porphyry. Translated by the Rev. O F. Owen, M.A. 2 vols. 3s. 6d. each.

—— **Rhetoric and Poetics.** Trans. by T. Buckley, B.A. 5s.

**ARRIAN'S Anabasis of Alexander,** together with the Indica. Translated by E. J. Chinnock, M.A., LL.D. With Maps and Plans. 5s.

**ATHENÆUS. The Deipnosophists;** or, the Banquet of the Learned. Trans. by Prof. C. D. Yonge, M.A. 3 vols. 5s. each.

**BACON'S Moral and Historical Works,** including the Essays, Apophthegms, Wisdom of the Ancients, New Atlantis, Henry VII., Henry VIII., Elizabeth, Henry Prince of Wales, History of Great Britain, Julius Cæsar, and Augustus Cæsar. Edited by J. Devey, M.A. 3s. 6d.

—— **Novum Organum and Advancement of Learning.** Edited by J. Devey, M.A. 5s.

**BASS'S Lexicon to the Greek Testament.** 2s.

**BAX'S Manual of the History of Philosophy,** for the use of Students. By E. Belfort Bax. 5s.

**BEAUMONT and FLETCHER,** their finest Scenes, Lyrics, and other Beauties, selected from the whole of their works, and edited by Leigh Hunt. 3s. 6d.

**BECHSTEIN'S Cage and Chamber Birds,** their Natural History, Habits, Food, Diseases, and Modes of Capture. Translated, with considerable additions on Structure, Migration, and Economy, by H. G. Adams. Together with SWEET BRITISH WARBLERS. With 43 coloured Plates and Woodcut Illustrations. 5s.

**BEDE'S (Venerable) Ecclesiastical History of England.** Together with the ANGLO-SAXON CHRONICLE. Edited by J. A. Giles, D.C.L. With Map. 5s.

**BELL (Sir Charles). The Anatomy and Philosophy of Expression,** as connected with the Fine Arts. By Sir Charles Bell, K.H. 7th edition, revised. 5s.

**BERKELEY (George), B·shop of Cloyne, The Works of.** Edited by George Sampson. With Biographical Introduction by the Right Hon. A. J. Balfour, M.P. 3 vols. 5s. each.

**BION.** See THEOCRITUS.

**BJÖRNSON'S Arne and the Fisher Lassie.** Translated by W. H. Low, M.A. 3s. 6d.

**BLAIR'S Chronological Tables** Revised and Enlarged. Comprehending the Chronology and History of the World, from the Earliest Times to the Russian Treaty of Peace, April 1856. By J. Willoughby Rosse. Double vol. 10s.

**BLAIR'S Index of Dates.** Comprehending the principal Facts in the Chronology and History of the World, alphabetically arranged; being a complete Index to Blair's Chronological Tables. By J. W. Rosse. 2 vols. 5s. each.

**BLEEK, Introduction to the Old Testament.** By Friedrich Bleek. Edited by Johann Bleek and Adolf Kamphausen. Translated by G. H. Venables, under the supervision of the Rev. Canon Venables. 2 vols. 5s. each.

**BOETHIUS'S Consolation of Philosophy.** King Alfred's Anglo-Saxon Version of. With a literal English Translation on opposite pages, Notes, Introduction, and Glossary, by Rev. S. Fox, M.A. 5s.

**BOHN'S Dictionary of Poetical Quotations.** 4th edition. 6s.

—— **Handbooks of Athletic Sports.** In 8 vols., each containing numerous Illustrations. 3s. 6d. each.
    I.—Cricket, Lawn Tennis, Tennis, Rackets, Fives, Golf.
    II.—Rowing and Sculling, Sailing, Swimming.
    III.—Boxing, Broadsword, Single Stick, &c., Wrestling, Fencing.
    IV.—Rugby Football, Association Football, Baseball, Rounders, Fieldball, Quoits, Skittles, Bowls, Curling.
    V.—Cycling, Athletics, Skating.
    VI.—Practical Horsemanship, including Riding for Ladies.
    VII.—Camping Out, Canoeing.
    VIII.—Gymnastics, Indian Clubs.

**BOHN'S Handbooks of Games.** New edition. In 2 vols., with numerous Illustrations. 3s. 6d. each.
    Vol. I.—TABLE GAMES:—Billiards, Chess, Draughts, Backgammon, Dominoes, Solitaire, Reversi, Go-Bang, Rouge et Noir, Roulette, E.O., Hazard, Faro.
    Vol. II.—CARD GAMES:—Whist, Solo Whist, Poker, Piquet, Ecarté, Euchre, Bézique, Cribbage, Loo, Vingt-et-un, Napoleon, Newmarket, Pope Joan, Speculation, &c., &c.

**BOND'S A Handy Book of Rules and Tables** for verifying Dates with the Christian Era, &c. Giving an account of the Chief Eras and Systems used by various Nations; with the easy Methods for determining the Corresponding Dates. By J. J. Bond. 5s.

**BONOMI'S Nineveh and its Palaces.** 7 Plates and 294 Woodcut Illustrations. 5s.

**BOSWELL'S Life of Johnson,** with the TOUR IN THE HEBRIDES and JOHNSONIANA. Edited by the Rev. A. Napier, M.A. With Frontispiece to each vol. 6 vols. 3s. 6d. each.

**BRAND'S Popular Antiquities of England, Scotland, and Ireland.** Arranged, revised, and greatly enlarged, by Sir Henry Ellis, K.H., F.R.S., &c., &c. 3 vols. 5s. each.

**BREMER'S (Frederika) Works.** Translated by Mary Howitt. 4 vols. 3s. 6d. each.

**BRIDGWATER TREATISES.**
Bell (Sir Charles) on the Hand. With numerous Woodcuts. 5s.

Kirby on the History, Habits, and Instincts of Animals. Edited by T. Rymer Jones. With upwards of 100 Woodcuts. 2 vols. 5s. each.

## An Alphabetical List of Books

BRIDGWATER TREATISES *continued.*

Kidd on the Adaptation of External Nature to the Physical Condition of Man. 3s. 6d.

Chalmers on the Adaptation of External Nature to the Moral and Intellectual Constitution of Man. 5s.

BRINK (B. ten) Early English Literature. By Bernhard ten Brink. Vol. I. To Wyclif. Translated by Horace M. Kennedy. 3s. 6d.

Vol. II. Wyclif, Chaucer, Earliest Drama Renaissance. Translated by W. Clarke Robinson, Ph.D. 3s. 6d.

Vol. III. From the Fourteenth Century to the Death of Surrey. Edited by Dr. Alois Brandl. Trans. by L. Dora Schmitz. 3s. 6d.

—— Five Lectures on Shakespeare. Trans. by Julia Franklin. 3s. 6d.

BROWNE'S (Sir Thomas) Works Edited by Simon Wilkin. 3 vols. 3s. 6d. each.

BURKE'S Works. 8 vols. 3s. 6d. each.

I.—Vindication of Natural Society—Essay on the Sublime and Beautiful, and various Political Miscellanies.

II.—Reflections on the French Revolution — Letters relating to the Bristol Election — Speech on Fox's East India Bill, &c.

III.—Appeal from the New to the Old Whigs—On the Nabob of Arcot's Debts—The Catholic Claims, &c.

BURKE'S WORKS *continued.*

IV.—Report on the Affairs of India, and Articles of Charge against Warren Hastings.

V.—Conclusion of the Articles of Charge against Warren Hastings—Political Letters on the American War, on a Regicide Peace, to the Empress of Russia.

VI.—Miscellaneous Speeches — Letters and Fragments—Abridgments of English History, &c. With a General Index.

VII. & VIII.—Speeches on the Impeachment of Warren Hastings; and Letters. With Index. 2 vols. 3s. 6d. each.

—— Life By Sir J. Prior. 3s. 6d.

BURNEY'S Evelina. By Frances Burney (Mme. D'Arblay). With an Introduction and Notes by A. R. Ellis. 3s. 6d.

—— Cecilia. With an Introduction and Notes by A. R. Ellis. 2 vols. 3s. 6d. each.

BURN (R.) Ancient Rome and its Neighbourhood. An Illustrated Handbook to the Ruins in the City and the Campagna, for the use of Travellers. By Robert Burn, M.A. With numerous Illustrations, Maps, and Plans. 7s. 6d.

BURNS (Robert). Life of. By J. G. Lockhart, D.C.L. A new and enlarged Edition. Revised by William Scott Douglas. 3s. 6d.

BURTON'S (Robert) Anatomy of Melancholy. Edited by the Rev. A. R. Shilleto, M.A. With Introduction by A. H. Bullen, and full Index. 3 vols. 3s. 6d. each.

BURTON (Sir R. F.) Personal Narrative of a Pilgrimage to Al-Madinah and Mecoah. By Captain Sir Richard F. Burton, K.C.M.G. With an Introduction by Stanley Lane-Poole, and all the original Illustrations  2 vols. 3s. 6d. each.

\*\*\* This is the copyright edition, containing the author's latest notes.

BUTLER'S (Bishop) Analogy of Religion, Natural and Revealed, to the Constitution and Course of Nature; together with two Dissertations on Personal Identity and on the Nature of Virtue, and Fifteen Sermons. 3s. 6d.

BUTLER'S (Samuel) Hudibras. With Variorum Notes, a Biography, Portrait, and 28 Illustrations. 5s.

—— or, further Illustrated with 60 Outline Portraits. 2 vols. 5s. each.

CÆSAR. Commentaries on the Gallic and Civil Wars. Translated by W. A. McDevitte, B.A. 5s.

CAMOENS' Lusiad; or, the Discovery of India. An Epic Poem. Translated by W. J. Mickle. 5th Edition, revised by E. R. Hodges, M.C.P. 3s. 6d.

CARAFAS (The) of Maddaloni. Naples under Spanish Dominion. Translated from the German of Alfred de Reumont. 3s. 6d.

CARLYLE'S French Revolution. Edited by J. Holland Rose, Litt.D. Illus. 3 vols. 5s. each.

—— Sartor Resartus. With 75 Illustrations by Edmund J. Sullivan. 5s.

CARPENTER'S (Dr. W. B.) Zoology. Revised Edition, by W. S. Dallas, F.L.S. With very numerous Woodcuts. Vol. I. 6s.
— [Vol. II. out of print.

CARPENTER'S Mechanical Philosophy, Astronomy, and Horology. 181 Woodcuts. 5s.

—— Vegetable Physiology and Systematic Botany. Revised Edition, by E. Lankester, M.D., &c. With very numerous Wood cuts. 6s.

—— Animal Physiology. Revised Edition. With upwards of 300 Woodcuts. 6s.

CASTLE (E.) Schools and Masters of Fence, from the Middle Ages to the End of the Eighteenth Century. By Egerton Castle, M.A., F.S.A. With a Complete Bibliography. Illustrated with 140 Reproductions of Old Engravings and 6 Plates of Swords, showing 114 Examples. 6s.

CATTERMOLE'S Evenings at Haddon Hall. With 24 Engravings on Steel from designs by Cattermole, the Letterpress by the Baroness de Carabella. 5s.

CATULLUS, Tibullus, and the Vigil of Venus. A Literal Prose Translation. 5s.

CELLINI (Benvenuto). Memoirs of, written by Himself. Translated by Thomas Roscoe. 3s. 6d.

CERVANTES' Don Quixote de la Mancha. Motteaux's Translation revised. 2 vols. 3s. 6d. each.

—— Galatea. A Pastoral Romance. Translated by G. W. J. Gyll. 3s. 6d.

—— Exemplary Novels. Translated by Walter K. Kelly. 3s. 6d.

CHAUCER'S Poetical Works. Edited by Robert Bell. Revised Edition, with a Preliminary Essay by Prof. W. W. Skeat, M.A. 4 vols. 3s. 6d. each.

**CHESS CONGRESS of 1862.** A Collection of the Games played. Edited by J. Lowenthal. 5s.

**CHEVREUL on Colour.** Translated from the French by Charles Martel. Third Edition, with Plates, 5s.; or with an additional series of 16 Plates in Colours, 7s. 6d.

**CHILLINGWORTH'S Religion of Protestants.** A Safe Way to Salvation. 3s. 6d.

**CHINA, Pictorial, Descriptive, and Historical.** With Map and nearly 100 Illustrations. 5s.

**CHRONICLES OF THE CRUSADES.** Contemporary Narratives of the Crusade of Richard Cœur de Lion, by Richard of Devizes and Geoffrey de Vinsauf; and of the Crusade at St. Louis, by Lord John de Joinville. 5s.

**CICERO'S Orations.** Translated by Prof. C. D. Yonge, M.A. 4 vols. 5s. each.

—— **Letters.** Translated by Evelyn S. Shuckburgh. 4 vols. 5s. each.

—— **On Oratory and Orators.** With Letters to Quintus and Brutus. Translated by the Rev. J. S. Watson, M.A. 5s.

—— **On the Nature of the Gods, Divination, Fate, Laws, a Republic, Consulship.** Translated by Prof. C. D. Yonge, M.A., and Francis Barham. 5s.

—— **Academics, De Finibus, and Tusculan Questions.** By Prof. C. D. Yonge, M.A. 5s.

**CICERO'S Offices; or, Moral Duties.** Cato Major, an Essay on Old Age; Lælius, an Essay on Friendship; Scipio's Dream; Paradoxes; Letter to Quintus on Magistrates. Translated by C. R. Edmonds. 3s. 6d.

**CORNELIUS NEPOS.**—See JUSTIN.

**CLARK'S (Hugh) Introduction to Heraldry.** 18th Edition, Revised and Enlarged by J. R. Planché, Rouge Croix. With nearly 1000 Illustrations. 5s. Or with the Illustrations Coloured, 15s.

**CLASSIC TALES.** containing Rasselas, Vicar of Wakefield, Gulliver's Travels, and The Sentimental Journey. 3s. 6d.

**COLERIDGE'S (S. T.) Friend** A Series of Essays on Morals, Politics, and Religion. 3s. 6d.

—— **Aids to Reflection, and the CONFESSIONS OF AN INQUIRING SPIRIT,** to which are added the ESSAYS ON FAITH and the BOOK OF COMMON PRAYER. 3s. 6d.

—— **Lectures and Notes on Shakespeare and other English Poets.** Edited by T. Ashe 3s. 6d.

—— **Biographia Literaria;** together with Two Lay Sermons. 3s. 6d.

—— **Table-Talk and Omniana.** Edited by T. Ashe, B.A. 3s. 6d.

—— **Miscellanies, Æsthetic and Literary;** to which is added, THE THEORY OF LIFE. Collected and arranged by T. Ashe, B.A. 3s. 6d.

**COMTE'S Positive Philosophy.** Translated and condensed by Harriet Martineau. With Introduction by Frederic Harrison. 3 vols. 5s. each.

**COMTE'S Philosophy of the Sciences,** being an Exposition of the Principles of the *Cours de Philosophie Positive*. By G. H. Lewes. 5s.

**CONDÉ'S History of the Dominion of the Arabs in Spain.** Translated by Mrs. Foster. 3 vols. 3s. 6d. each.

**COOPER'S** Biographical Dictionary. Containing Concise Notices (upwards of 15,000) of Eminent Persons of all Ages and Countries. By Thompson Cooper, F.S.A. With a Supplement, bringing the work down to 1883. 2 vols. 5s. each.

**COXE'S** Memoirs of the Duke of Marlborough. With his original Correspondence. By W. Coxe, M.A., F.R.S. Revised edition by John Wade. 3 vols. 3s. 6d. each.

\*\*\* An Atlas of the plans of Marlborough's campaigns, 4to. 10s. 6d.

—— History of the House of Austria (1218-1792). With a Continuation from the Accession of Francis I. to the Revolution of 1848. 4 vols. 3s. 6d. each.

**CRAIK'S (G. L.)** Pursuit of Knowledge under Difficulties. Illustrated by Anecdotes and Memoirs. Revised edition, with numerous Woodcut Portraits and Plates. 5s.

**CRUIKSHANK'S** Punch and Judy. The Dialogue of the Puppet Show; an Account of its Origin, &c. With 24 Illustrations, and Coloured Plates, designed and engraved by G. Cruikshank. 5s.

**CUNNINGHAM'S** Lives of the Most Eminent British Painters. A New Edition, with Notes and Sixteen fresh Lives. By Mrs. Heaton. 3 vols. 3s. 6d. each.

**DANTE**. Divine Comedy. Translated by the Rev. H. F. Cary, M.A. 3s. 6d.

—— Translated into English Verse by I. C. Wright, M.A. 3rd Edition, revised. With Portrait, and 34 Illustrations on Steel, after Flaxman.

**DANTE**. The Inferno. A Literal Prose Translation, with the Text of the Original printed on the same page. By John A. Carlyle, M.D. 5s.

—— The Purgatorio. A Literal Prose Translation, with the Text printed on the same page. By W. S. Dugdale. 5s.

**DE COMMINES (Philip)**, Memoirs of. Containing the Histories of Louis XI. and Charles VIII., Kings of France, and Charles the Bold, Duke of Burgundy. Together with the Scandalous Chronicle, or Secret History of Louis XI., by Jean de Troyes. Translated by Andrew R. Scoble. With Portraits. 2 vols. 3s. 6d. each.

**DEFOE'S** Novels and Miscellaneous Works. With Prefaces and Notes, including those attributed to Sir W. Scott. 7 vols. 3s. 6d. each.

    I.—Captain Singleton, and Colonel Jack.

    II.—Memoirs of a Cavalier, Captain Carleton, Dickory Cronke, &c.

    III.—Moll Flanders, and the History of the Devil.

    IV.—Roxana, and Life of Mrs. Christian Davies.

    V.—History of the Great Plague of London, 1665; The Storm (1703); and the True-born Englishman.

    VI.—Duncan Campbell, New Voyage round the World, and Political Tracts.

    VII.—Robinson Crusoe.

**DE LOLME** on the Constitution of England. Edited by John Macgregor. 3s. 6d.

**DEMMIN'S History of Arms and Armour** from the Earliest Period. By Auguste Demmin. Translated by C. C. Black, M.A. With nearly 2000 Illustrations. 7s. 6d.

**DEMOSTHENES Orations.** Translated by C. Rann Kennedy. 5 vols. Vol. I., 3s. 6d.; Vols. II.-V., 5s. each.

**DE STAËL'S Corinne or Italy.** By Madame de Stael. Translated by Emily Baldwin and Paulina Driver. 3s. 6d.

**DEVEY'S Logic,** or the Science of Inference. A Popular Manual. By J. Devey. 5s.

**DICTIONARY of Latin and Greek Quotations**; including Proverbs, Maxims, Mottoes, Law Terms and Phrases. With all the Quantities marked, and English Translations. With Index Verborum (622 pages). 5s.

**DICTIONARY of Obsolete and Provincial English.** Compiled by Thomas Wright, M.A., F.S.A., &c. 2 vols. 5s. each.

**DIDRON'S Christian Iconography**: a History of Christian Art in the Middle Ages. Translated by E. J Millington and completed by Margaret Stokes. With 240 Illustrations. 2 vols. 5s. each.

**DIOGENES LAERTIUS. Lives and Opinions of the Ancient Philosophers** Translated by Prof. C. D. Yonge, M A. 5s.

**DOBREE'S Adversaria.** Edited by the late Prof. Wagner. 2 vols. 5s. each.

**DODD'S Epigrammatists.** A Selection from the Epigrammatic Literature of Ancient, Mediæval, and Modern Times. By the Rev. Henry Philip Dodd, M.A. Oxford. 2nd Edition, revised and enlarged. 6s.

**DONALDSON'S The Theatre of the Greeks.** A Treatise on the History and Exhibition of the Greek Drama. With numerous Illustrations and 3 Plans. By John William Donaldson, D.D. 5s.

**DRAPER'S History of the Intellectual Development of Europe.** By John William Draper, M.D., LL.D. 2 vols. 5s. each.

**DUNLOP'S History of Fiction.** A new Edition. Revised by Henry Wilson. 2 vols. 5s. each.

**DYER (Dr T. H.). Pompeii;** its Buildings and Antiquities. By T. H. Dyer, LL.D. With nearly 300 Wood Engravings, a large Map, and a Plan of the Forum. 7s. 6d.

—— **The City of Rome**: its History and Monuments. With Illustrations. 5s.

**DYER (T. F. T.) British Popular Customs, Present and Past.** An Account of the various Games and Customs associated with Different Days of the Year in the British Isles, arranged according to the Calendar. By the Rev. T. F. Thiselton Dyer, M.A. 5s.

**EBERS' Egyptian Princess.** An Historical Novel. By George Ebers. Translated by E. S. Buchheim. 3s. 6d.

**EDGEWORTH'S Stories for Children.** With 8 Illustrations by L. Speed. 3s. 6d.

**ELZE'S William Shakespeare.** —See SHAKESPEARE.

**EMERSON'S Works.** 3 vols 3s. 6d. each.
I.—Essays, Lectures and Poems.
II.—English Traits, Nature, and Conduct of Life.

EMERSON'S WORKS *continued.*
III.—Society and Solitude—Letters and Social aims — Miscellaneous Papers (hitherto uncollected) — May Day, and other Poems.

ELLIS (G.) Specimens of Early English Metrical Romances. With an Historical Introduction on the Rise and Progress of Romantic Composition in France and England. Revised Edition. By J. O. Halliwell, F.R.S. 5*s.*

ENNEMOSER'S History of Magic. Translated by William Howitt. 2 vols. 5*s.* each.

EPICTETUS, The Discourses of. With the ENCHEIRIDION and Fragments. Translated by George Long, M.A. 5*s.*

EURIPIDES. A New Literal Translation in Prose. By E P. Coleridge, M.A. 2 vols. 5*s.* each.

EUTROPIUS.—*See* JUSTIN.

EUSEBIUS PAMPHILUS, Ecclesiastical History of. Translated by Rev. C. F. Cruse, M.A. 5*s.*

EVELYN'S Diary and Correspondence. Edited from the Original MSS. By W. Bray, F.A.S. With 45 engravings. 4 vols. 5*s.* each.

FAIRHOLT'S Costume in England. A History of Dress to the end of the Eighteenth Century. 3rd Edition, revised, by Viscount Dillon, V.P.S.A. Illustrated with above 700 Engravings. 2 vols. 5*s.* each.

FIELDING'S Adventures of Joseph Andrews and his Friend Mr. Abraham Adams. With Cruikshank's Illustrations. 3*s.* 6*d.*

—— History of Tom Jones, a Foundling. With Cruikshank's Illustrations. 2 vols. 3*s.* 6*d.* each.

—— Amelia. With Cruikshank's Illustrations. 5*s.*

FLAXMAN'S Lectures on Sculpture. By John Flaxman, R.A. With Portrait and 53 Plates. 6*s.*

FLORENCE of WORCESTER'S Chronicle, with the Two Continuations: comprising Annals of English History, from the Departure of the Romans to the Reign of Edward I. Translated by Thomas Forester, M.A. 5*s.*

FOSTER'S (John) Life and Correspondence. Edited by J. E. Ryland. 2 vols. 3*s.* 6*d.* each.

—— Critical Essays. Edited by J. E. Ryland. 2 vols. 3*s.* 6*d.* each.

—— Essays: on Decision of Character; on a Man's writing Memoirs of Himself; on the epithet Romantic; on the aversion of Men of Taste to Evangelical Religion. 3*s.* 6*d.*

—— Essays on the Evils of Popular Ignorance; to which is added, a Discourse on the Propagation of Christianity in India. 3*s.* 6*d.*

—— Essays on the Improvement of Time. With NOTES OF SERMONS and other Pieces. 3*s.* 6*d.*

GASPARY'S History of Italian Literature. Translated by Herman Oelsner, M.A., Ph.D. Vol. I. 3*s.* 6*d.*

GEOFFREY OF MONMOUTH, Chronicle of.—*See Old English Chronicles.*

GESTA ROMANORUM, or Entertaining Moral Stories invented by the Monks. Translated by the Rev. Charles Swan Revised Edition, by Wynnard Hooper, B.A. 5*s.*

GILDAS, Chronicles of.—*See Old English Chronicles.*

**IBBON'S Decline and Fall of the Roman Empire.** Complete and Unabridged, with Variorum Notes. Edited by an English Churchman. With 2 Maps and Portrait. 7 vols. 3s. 6d. each.

**GILBART'S History, Principles, and Practice of Banking.** By the late J. W. Gilbart, F.R.S. New Edition, revised by A. S. Michie. 2 vols. 10s.

**GIL BLAS, The Adventures of.** Translated from the French of Lesage by Smollett. With 24 Engravings on Steel, after Smirke, and 10 Etchings by George Cruikshank. 6s.

**GIRALDUS CAMBRENSIS' Historical Works.** Translated by Th. Forester, M.A., and Sir R. Colt Hoare. Revised Edition, Edited by Thomas Wright, M.A., F.S.A. 5s.

**GOETHE'S Faust.** Part I. German Text with Hayward's Prose Translation and Notes. Revised by C. A. Buchheim, Ph.D. 5s.

**GOETHE'S Works.** Translated into English by various hands. 14 vols. 3s. 6d. each.
   I. and II.—Autobiography and Annals.
   III.—Faust. Two Parts, complete. (Swanwick.)
   IV.—Novels and Tales.
   V.—Wilhelm Meister's Apprenticeship.
   VI.—Conversations with Eckermann and Soret.
   VIII.—Dramatic Works.
   IX.—Wilhelm Meister's Travels.
   X.—Tour in Italy, and Second Residence in Rome.
   XI.—Miscellaneous Travels.
   XII.—Early and Miscellaneous Letters.
   XIII.—Correspondence with Zelter.
   XIV.—Reineke Fox, West-Eastern Divan and Achilleid.

**GOLDSMITH'S Works.** A new Edition, by J. W. M. Gibbs. 5 vols. 3s. 6d. each.

**GRAMMONT'S Memoirs of the Court of Charles II** Edited by Sir Walter Scott. Together with the BOSCOBEL TRACTS, including two not before published, &c. New Edition. 5s.

**GRAY'S Letters.** Including the Correspondence of Gray and Mason. Edited by the Rev. D. C. Tovey, M.A. Vols. I. and II. 3s. 6d. each.

**GREEK ANTHOLOGY.** Translated by George Burges, M.A. 5s.

**GREEK ROMANCES of Heliodorus, Longus, and Achilles Tatius**—viz., The Adventures of Theagenes & Chariclea; Amours of Daphnis and Chloe; and Loves of Clitopho and Leucippe. Translated by Rev. R. Smith, M.A. 5s.

**GREGORY'S Letters on the Evidences, Doctrines, & Duties of the Christian Religion.** By Dr. Olinthus Gregory. 3s. 6d.

**GREENE, MARLOWE, and BEN JONSON.** Poems of. Edited by Robert Bell. 3s. 6d.

**GRIMM'S TALES.** With the Notes of the Original. Translated by Mrs. A. Hunt. With Introduction by Andrew Lang, M.A. 2 vols. 3s. 6d. each.

—— **Gammer Grethel; or, German Fairy Tales and Popular Stories.** Containing 42 Fairy Tales. Trans. by Edgar Taylor. With numerous Woodcuts after George Cruikshank and Ludwig Grimm. 3s. 6d.

**GROSSI'S Marco Visconti.** Translated by A. F. D. The Ballads rendered into English Verse by C. M. P. 3s. 6d.

GUIZOT'S History of the English Revolution of 1640. From the Accession of Charles I. to his Death. Translated by William Hazlitt. 3s. 6d.

—— History of Civilisation, from the Fall of the Roman Empire to the French Revolution. Translated by William Hazlitt. 3 vols. 3s. 6d. each.

HALL'S (Rev. Robert) Miscellaneous Works and Remains. 3s. 6d.

HAMPTON COURT: A Short History of the Manor and Palace. By Ernest Law, B.A. With numerous Illustrations. 5s.

HARDWICK'S History of the Articles of Religion. By the late C. Hardwick. Revised by the Rev. Francis Procter, M.A. 5s.

HAUFF'S Tales. The Caravan— The Sheik of Alexandria—The Inn in the Spessart. Trans. from the German by S. Mendel. 3s. 6d.

HAWTHORNE'S Tales. 4 vols. 3s. 6d. each.
   I.—Twice-told Tales, and the Snow Image.
   II.—Scarlet Letter, and the House with the Seven Gables.
   III.—Transformation [The Marble Faun], and Blithedale Romance.
   IV.—Mosses from an Old Manse.

HAZLITT'S Table-talk. Essays on Men and Manners. By W. Hazlitt. 3s. 6d.

—— Lectures on the Literature of the Age of Elizabeth and on Characters of Shakespeare's Plays. 3s. 6d.

—— Lectures on the English Poets, and on the English Comic Writers. 3s. 6d.

—— The Plain Speaker. Opinions on Books, Men, and Things. 3s. 6d.

—— Round Table. 3s. 6d.

HAZLITT'S Sketches and Essays. 3s. 6d.

—— The Spirit of the Age; or, Contemporary Portraits. Edited by W. Carew Hazlitt. 3s. 6d.

—— View of the English Stage. Edited by W. Spencer Jackson. 3s. 6d.

HEATON'S Concise History of Painting. New Edition, revised by Cosmo Monkhouse. 5s.

HEGEL'S Lectures on the Philosophy of History. Translated by J. Sibree, M.A.

HEINE'S Poems, Complete. Translated by Edgar A. Bowring, C.B. 3s. 6d.

—— Travel-Pictures, including the Tour in the Harz, Norderney, and Book of Ideas, together with the Romantic School. Translated by Francis Storr. A New Edition, revised throughout. With Appendices and Maps. 3s. 6d.

HELP'S Life of Christopher Columbus, the Discoverer of America. By Sir Arthur Helps, K.C.B. 3s. 6d.

—— Life of Hernando Cortes, and the Conquest of Mexico. 2 vols. 3s. 6d. each.

—— Life of Pizarro. 3s. 6d.

—— Life of Las Casas the Apostle of the Indies. 3s. 6d.

HENDERSON (E.) Select Historical Documents of the Middle Ages, including the most famous Charters relating to England, the Empire, the Church, &c., from the 6th to the 14th Centuries. Translated from the Latin and edited by Ernest F. Henderson, A.B., A.M., Ph.D. 5s.

HENFREY'S Guide to English Coins, from the Conquest to the present time. New and revised Edition by C. F. Keary, M.A., F.S.A. 6s.

HENRY OF HUNTINGDON'S History of the English. Translated by T. Forester, M.A. 5s.

**HENRY'S (Matthew) Exposition of the Book of the Psalms.** 5s.

**HELIODORUS. Theagenes and Charicles.** — *See* GREEK ROMANCES.

**HERODOTUS** Translated by the Rev. Henry Cary, M.A. 3s. 6d

—— **Notes on.** Original and Selected from the best Commentators. By D. W. Turner, M.A. With Coloured Map. 5s.

—— **Analysis and Summary of** By J. T. Wheeler. 5s.

**HESIOD, CALLIMACHUS, and THEOGNIS.** Translated by the Rev. J. Banks, M.A. 5s.

**HOFFMANN'S (E. T. W.) The Serapion Brethren.** Translated from the German by Lt.-Col. Alex. Ewing. 2 vols. 3s. 6d. each.

**HOLBEIN'S Dance of Death and Bible Cuts** Upwards of 150 Subjects, engraved in facsimile, with Introduction and Descriptions by Francis Douce and Dr. Thomas Frognall Dibden. 5s.

**HOMER'S Iliad.** Translated into English Prose by T. A. Buckley, B.A. 5s.

—— **Odyssey.** Hymns, Epigrams, and Battle of the Frogs and Mice. Translated into English Prose by T. A. Buckley, B.A. 5s.

—— *See also* POPE.

**HOOPER'S (G.) Waterloo The Downfall of the First Napoleon:** a History of the Campaign of 1815. By George Hooper. With Maps and Plans. 3s. 6d.

—— **The Campaign of Sedan:** The Downfall of the Second Empire, August - September, 1870. With General Map and Six Plans of Battle. 3s. 6d.

**HORACE.** A new literal Prose translation, by A. Hamilton Bryce, LL.D. 3s. 6d.

**HUGO'S (Victor) Dramatic Works. Hernani**—Ruy Blas—The King's Diversion. Translated by Mrs. Newton Crosland and F. L. Slous. 3s. 6d.

—— **Poems, chiefly Lyrical.** Translated by various Writers, now first collected by J. H. L. Williams. 3s. 6d.

**HUMBOLDT'S Cosmos.** Translated by E. C. Otté, B. H. Paul, and W. S. Dallas, F.L.S. 5 vols. 3s. 6d. each, excepting Vol. V. 5s.

—— **Personal Narrative** of his Travels to the Equinoctial Regions of America during the years 1799-1804. Translated by T. Ross. 3 vols. 5s. each.

—— **Views of Nature.** Translated by E. C. Otté and H. G. Bohn. 5s.

**HUMPHREYS' Coin Collector's Manual.** By H. N. Humphreys. with upwards of 140 Illustrations on Wood and Steel. 2 vols. 5s. each.

**HUNGARY:** its History and Revolution, together with a copious Memoir of Kossuth. 3s. 6d.

**HUTCHINSON (Colonel). Memoirs of the Life of.** By his Widow, Lucy: together with her Autobiography, and an Account of the Siege of Lathom House. 3s. 6d.

**HUNT'S Poetry of Science.** By Richard Hunt. 3rd Edition, revised and enlarged. 5s.

**INDIA BEFORE THE SEPOY MUTINY.** A Pictorial, Descriptive, and Historical Account, from the Earliest Times to the Annexation of the Punjab. with upwards of 100 Engravings on Wood, and a Map. 5s.

**INGULPH'S Chronicles of the Abbey of Croyland,** with the CONTINUATION by Peter of Blois and other Writers. Translated by H. T. Riley, M.A. 5s.

IRVING'S (Washington) Complete Works. 15 vols. With Portraits, &c. 3s. 6d. each.
  I.—Salmagundi, Knickerbocker's History of New York.
  II.—The Sketch-Book, and the Life of Oliver Goldsmith.
  III.—Bracebridge Hall, Abbotsford and Newstead Abbey.
  IV.—The Alhambra, Tales of a Traveller.
  V.—Chronicle of the Conquest of Granada, Legends of the Conquest of Spain.
  VI. & VII.—Life and Voyages of Columbus, together with the Voyages of his Companions.
  VIII.—Astoria, A Tour on the Prairies.
  XI.—Life of Mahomet, Lives of the Successors of Mahomet.
  X.—Adventures of Captain Bonneville, U.S.A., Wolfert's Roost.
  XI.—Biographies and Miscellaneous Papers.
  XII.-XV.—Life of George Washington. 4 vols.

—— Life and Letters. By his Nephew, Pierre E. Irving. 2 vols. 3s. 6d. each.

ISOCRATES, The Orations of Translated by J. H. Freese, M.A. Vol. I. 5s.

JAMES'S (G. P. R.) Life of Richard Cœur de Lion. 2 vols. 3s. 6d. each.

—— The Life and Times of Louis XIV. 2 vols. 3s. 6d. each.

JAMESON'S (Mrs.) Shakespeare's Heroines. Characteristics of Women: Moral, Poetical, and Historical. By Mrs. Jameson. 3s. 6d.

JESSE'S (E.) Anecdotes of Dogs. With 40 Woodcuts and 34 Steel Engravings. 5s.

JESSE'S (J. H.) Memoirs of the Court of England during the Reign of the Stuarts, including the Protectorate. 3 vols. With 42 Portraits. 5s. each.

—— Memoirs of the Pretenders and their Adherents. With 6 Portraits. 5s.

JOHNSON'S Lives of the Poets. Edited by Mrs. Alexander Napier, with Introduction by Professor Hales. 3 vols. 3s. 6d. each.

JOSEPHUS (Flavius), The Works of. Whiston's Translation, revised by Rev. A. R. Shilleto, M.A. With Topographical and Geographical Notes by Colonel Sir C. W. Wilson, K.C.B. 5 vols. 3s. 6d. each.

JOYCE'S Scientific Dialogues. With numerous Woodcuts. 5s.

JUKES-BROWNE (A. J.), The Building of the British Isles: a Study in Geographical Evolution. Illustrated by numerous Maps and Woodcuts. 2nd Edition, revised, 7s. 6d.

—— Student's Handbook of Physical Geology. With numerous Diagrams and Illustrations. 2nd Edition, much enlarged, 7s. 6d.

JULIAN, the Emperor. Containing Gregory Nazianzen's Two Invectives and Libanus' Monody, with Julian's extant Theosophical Works. Translated by C. W. King, M.A. 5s.

JUSTIN CORNELIUS NEPOS, and EUTROPIUS. Translated by the Rev. J. S. Watson, M.A. 5s.

JUVENAL, PERSIUS. SULPICIA and LUCILIUS. Translated by L. Evans, M.A. 5s.

JUNIUS'S Letters. With all the Notes of Woodfall's Edition, and important Additions. 2 vols. 3s. 6d. each.

KANT'S Critique of Pure Reason. Translated by J. M. D. Meiklejohn. 5s.
—— Prolegomena and Metaphysical Foundations of Natural Science. Translated by E. Belfort Bax. 5s.

KEIGHTLEY'S (Thomas) Mythology of Ancient Greece and Italy. 4th Edition, revised by Leonard Schmitz, Ph.D., LL.D. With 12 Plates from the Antique. 5s.
—— Fairy Mythology, illustrative of the Romance and Superstition of Various Countries. Revised Edition, with Frontispiece by Cruikshank. 5s.

LA FONTAINE'S Fables. Translated into English Verse by Elizur Wright. New Edition, with Notes by J. W. M. Gibbs. 3s. 6d.

LAMARTINE'S History of the Girondists. Translated by H. T. Ryde. 3 vols. 3s. 6d. each.
—— History of the Restoration of Monarchy in France (a Sequel to the History of the Girondists). 4 vols. 3s. 6d. each.
—— History of the French Revolution of 1848. 3s. 6d.

LAMB'S (Charles) Essays of Elia and Eliana. Complete Edition. 3s. 6d.
—— Specimens of English Dramatic Poets of the Time of Elizabeth. 3s. 6d.
—— Memorials and Letters of Charles Lamb. By Serjeant Talfourd. New Edition, revised, by W. Carew Hazlitt. 2 vols. 3s. 6d. each.
—— Tales from Shakespeare With Illustrations by Byam Shaw. 3s. 6d.

LANZI'S History of Painting in Italy, from the Period of the Revival of the Fine Arts to the End of the Eighteenth Century. Translated by Thomas Roscoe. 3 vols. 3s. 6d. each.

LAPPENBERG'S History of England under the Anglo-Saxon Kings. Translated by B. Thorpe, F.S.A. New edition, revised by E. C. Otté. 2 vols. 3s. 6d. each.

LECTURES ON PAINTING, by Barry, Opie, Fuseli. Edited by R. Wornum. 5s.

LEONARDO DA VINCI'S Treatise on Painting. Translated by J. F. Rigaud, R.A., With a Life of Leonardo by John William Brown. With numerous Plates. 5s.

LEPSIUS'S Letters from Egypt, Ethiopia, and the Peninsula of Sinai Translated by L. and J. B. Horner. With Maps. 5s.

LESSING'S Dramatic Works, Complete. Edited by Ernest Bell, M.A. With Memoir of Lessing by Helen Zimmern. 2 vols. 3s. 6d. each.
—— Laokoon, Dramatic Notes, and the Representation of Death by the Ancients. Translated by E. C. Beasley and Helen Zimmern. Edited by Edward Bell, M.A. With a Frontispiece of the Laokoon group. 3s. 6d.

LILLY'S Introduction to Astrology. With a GRAMMAR OF ASTROLOGY and Tables for Calculating Nativities, by Zadkiel. 5s.

LIVY'S History of Rome. Translated by Dr. Spillan, C. Edmonds, and others. 4 vols. 5s. each.

LOCKE'S Philosophical Works. Edited by J. A. St. John. 2 vols. 3s. 6d each.
—— Life and Letters: By Lord King. 3s. 6d.

LOCKHART (J. G.)—*See* BURNS.

**LODGE'S Portraits of Illustrious Personages of Great Britain,** with Biographical and Historical Memoirs. 240 Portraits engraved on Steel, with the respective Biographies unabridged. 8 vols. 5s. each.

**LONGFELLOW'S Prose Works.** With 16 full-page Wood Engravings. 5s.

**LOUDON'S (Mrs.) Natural History.** Revised edition, by W. S. Dallas, F.L.S. With numerous Woodcut Illus. 5s.

**LOWNDES' Bibliographer's Manual of English Literature.** Enlarged Edition. By H. G. Bohn. 6 vols. cloth, 5s. each. Or 4 vols. half morocco, 2l. 2s.

**LONGUS.** Daphnis and Chloe. —See GREEK ROMANCES.

**LUCAN'S Pharsalia.** Translated by H. T. Riley, M.A. 5s.

**LUCIAN'S Dialogues of the Gods, of the Sea Gods, and of the Dead.** Translated by Howard Williams, M.A. 5s.

**LUCRETIUS.** Translated by the Rev. J. S. Watson, M.A. 5s.

**LUTHER'S Table-Talk.** Translated and Edited by William Hazlitt. 3s. 6d.

—— **Autobiography.** — See MICHELET.

**MACHIAVELLI'S History of Florence,** together with the Prince, Savonarola, various Historical Tracts, and a Memoir of Machiavelli. 3s. 6d.

**MALLET'S Northern Antiquities,** or an Historical Account of the Manners, Customs, Religions and Laws, Maritime Expeditions and Discoveries, Language and Literature, of the Ancient Scandinavians. Translated by Bishop Percy. Revised and Enlarged Edition, with a Translation of the PROSE EDDA, by J. A. Blackwell. 5s.

**MANTELL'S (Dr.) Petrifactions and their Teachings.** With numerous illustrative Woodcuts. 6s.

—— **Wonders of Geology.** 8th Edition, revised by T. Rupert Jones, F G.S. With a coloured Geological Map of England, Plates, and upwards of 200 Woodcuts. 2 vols. 7s. 6d. each.

**MANZONI.** The Betrothed: being a Translation of 'I Promessi Sposi.' By Alessandro Manzoni. With numerous Woodcuts. 5s.

**MARCO POLO'S Travels;** the Translation of Marsden revised by T. Wright, M.A., F.S.A. 5s.

**MARRYAT'S (Capt. R.N.) Masterman Ready.** With 93 Woodcuts. 3s. 6d.

—— **Mission;** or, Scenes in Africa. Illustrated by Gilbert and Dalziel. 3s. 6d.

—— **Pirate and Three Cutters.** With 8 Steel Engravings, from Drawings by Clarkson Stanfield, R.A. 3s. 6d.

—— **Privateersman.** 8 Engravings on Steel. 3s. 6d.

—— **Settlers in Canada.** 10 Engravings by Gilbert and Dalziel. 3s. 6d.

—— **Poor Jack.** With 16 Illustrations after Clarkson Stansfield, R.A. 3s. 6d.

—— **Peter Simple.** With 8 full-page Illustrations. 3s. 6d.

—— **Midshipman Easy.** With 8 full-page Illustrations. 3s. 6d.

**MARTIAL'S Epigrams,** complete. Translated into Prose, each accompanied by one or more Verse Translations selected from the Works of English Poets, and other sources. 7s. 6d.

**MARTINEAU'S (Harriet)** History of England, from 1800-1815. 3s. 6d.

—— History of the Thirty Years' Peace, A.D. 1815-46. 4 vols. 3s. 6d. each.

—— *See Comte's Positive Philosophy.*

**MATTHEW PARIS'S** English History, from the Year 1235 to 1273. Translated by Rev. J. A. Giles, D.C.L. 3 vols. 5s. each.

**MATTHEW OF WESTMINSTER'S** Flowers of History, from the beginning of the World to A.D. 1307. Translated by C. D. Yonge, M.A. 2 vols. 5s. each.

**MAXWELL'S** Victories of Wellington and the British Armies. Frontispiece and 5 Portraits. 5s.

**MENZEL'S** History of Germany, from the Earliest Period to 1842. 3 vols. 3s. 6d. each.

**MICHAEL ANGELO AND RAPHAEL**, their Lives and Works. By Duppa and Quatremere de Quincy. With Portraits, and Engravings on Steel. 5s.

**MICHELET'S** Luther's Autobiography. Trans. by William Hazlitt. With an Appendix (110 pages) of Notes. 3s. 6d.

—— History of the French Revolution from its earliest indications to the flight of the King in 1791. 3s. 6d.

**MIGNET'S** History of the French Revolution, from 1789 to 1814. 3s. 6d.

**MILL (J. S.)** Early Essays by John Stuart Mill. Collected from various sources by J. W. M. Gibbs. 3s. 6d.

**MILLER (Professor).** History Philosophically Illustrated, from the Fall of the Roman Empire to the French Revolution. 4 vols. 3s. 6d. each.

**MILTON'S Prose Works.** Edited by J. A. St. John. 5 vols. 3s. 6d. each.

—— Poetical Works, with a Memoir and Critical Remarks by James Montgomery, an Index to Paradise Lost, Todd's Verbal Index to all the Poems, and a Selection of Explanatory Notes by Henry G. Bohn. Illustrated with 120 Wood Engravings from Drawings by W. Harvey. 2 vols. 3s. 6d. each.

**MITFORD'S (Miss) Our Village** Sketches of Rural Character and Scenery. With 2 Engravings on Steel. 2 vols. 3s. 6d. each.

**MOLIERE'S Dramatic Works.** A new Translation in English Prose, by C. H. Wall. 3 vols. 3s. 6d. each.

**MONTAGU.** The Letters and Works of Lady Mary Wortley Montagu. Edited by her great-grandson, Lord Wharncliffe's Edition, and revised by W. Moy Thomas. New Edition, revised, with 5 Portraits. 2 vols. 5s. each.

**MONTAIGNE'S Essays.** Cotton's Translation, revised by W. C. Hazlitt. New Edition. 3 vols. 3s. 6d. each.

**MONTESQUIEU'S Spirit of Laws.** New Edition, revised and corrected. By J. V. Pritchard, A.M. 2 vols. 3s. 6d. each.

**MOTLEY (J. L.).** The Rise of the Dutch Republic. A History. By John Lothrop Motley. New Edition, with Biographical Introduction by Moncure D. Conway. 3 vols. 3s. 6d. each.

**MORPHY'S Games of Chess.** Being the Matches and best Games played by the American Champion, with Explanatory and Analytical Notes by J. Lowenthal. 5s.

**MUDIE'S British Birds**; or, History of the Feathered Tribes of the British Islands. Revised by W. C. L. Martin. With 52 Figures of Birds and 7 Coloured Plates of Eggs. 2 vols.

**NEANDER (Dr. A.). History of the Christian Religion and Church.** Trans. from the German by J. Torrey. 10 vols. 3s. 6d. each.

—— **Life of Jesus Christ.** Translated by J. McClintock and C. Blumenthal. 3s. 6d.

—— **History of the Planting and Training of the Christian Church by the Apostles.** Translated by J. E. Ryland. 2 vols. 3s. 6d. each.

—— **Memorials of Christian Life in the Early and Middle Ages**; including Light in Dark Places. Trans. by J. E. Ryland. 3s. 6d.

**NIBELUNGEN LIED.** The Lay of the Nibelungs, metrically translated from the old German text by Alice Horton, and edited by Edward Bell, M.A. To which is prefixed the Essay on the Nibelungen Lied by Thomas Carlyle. 5s.

**NEW TESTAMENT (The) in Greek.** Griesbach's Text, with various Readings at the foot of the page, and Parallel References in the margin; also a Critical Introduction and Chronological Tables. By an eminent Scholar, with a Greek and English Lexicon. 3rd Edition, revised and corrected. Two Facsimiles of Greek Manuscripts. 900 pages. 5s.
The Lexicon may be had separately, price 2s.

**NICOLINI'S History of the Jesuits**: their Origin, Progress, Doctrines, and Designs. With 8 Portraits. 5s.

**NORTH (R.) Lives of the Right Hon. Francis North, Baron Guildford, the Hon. Sir Dudley North, and the Hon. and Rev. Dr. John North.** By the Hon. Roger North. Together with the Autobiography of the Author. Edited by Augustus Jessopp, D.D. 3 vols. 3s. 6d. each.

**NUGENT'S (Lord) Memorials of Hampden, his Party and Times.** With a Memoir of the Author, an Autograph Letter, and Portrait. 5s.

**OCKLEY (S.) History of the Saracens and their Conquests in Syria, Persia, and Egypt.** By Simon Ockley, B.D., Professor of Arabic in the University of Cambridge. 3s. 6d.

**OLD ENGLISH CHRONICLES,** including Ethelwerd's Chronicle, Asser's Life of Alfred, Geoffrey of Monmouth's British History, Gildas, Nennius, and the spurious chronicle of Richard of Cirencester. Edited by J. A. Giles, D.C.L. 5s.

**OMAN (J. C.) The Great Indian Epics**: the Stories of the RAMAYANA and the MAHABHARATA. By John Campbell Oman, Principal of Khalsa College, Amritsar. With Notes, Appendices, and Illustrations. 3s. 6d.

**ORDERICUS VITALIS' Ecclesiastical History of England and Normandy.** Translated by T. Forester, M.A. To which is added the CHRONICLE OF ST. EVROULT. 4 vols. 5s. each.

**OVID'S Works,** complete. Literally translated into Prose. 3 vols. 5s. each.

**PASCAL'S Thoughts.** Translated from the Text of M. Auguste Molinier by C. Kegan Paul. 3rd Edition. 3s. 6d.

**PAULI'S (Dr. R.) Life of Alfred the Great.** Translated from the German. To which is appended Alfred's ANGLO-SAXON VERSION OF OROSIUS. With a literal Translation interpaged, Notes, and an ANGLO-SAXON GRAMMAR and GLOSSARY, by B. Thorpe. 5*s.*

**PAUSANIAS' Description of Greece.** Newly translated by A. R. Shilleto, M.A. 2 vols. 5*s.* each.

**PEARSON'S Exposition of the Creed.** Edited by E. Walford, M.A. 5*s.*

**PEPYS' Diary and Correspondence.** Deciphered by the Rev. J. Smith, M.A., from the original Shorthand MS. in the Pepysian Library. Edited by Lord Braybrooke. 4 vols. With 31 Engravings. 5*s.* each.

**PERCY'S Reliques of Ancient English Poetry.** With an Essay on Ancient Minstrels and a Glossary. Edited by J. V. Pritchard, A.M. 2 vols. 3*s.* 6*d.* each.

**PERSIUS.**—*See* JUVENAL.

**PETRARCH'S Sonnets, Triumphs and other Poems.** Translated into English Verse by various Hands. With a Life of the Poet by Thomas Campbell. With Portrait and 15 Steel Engravings. 5*s.*

**PHILO-JUDÆUS, Works of.** Translated by Prof. C. D. Yonge, M.A. 4 vols. 5*s.* each.

**PICKERING'S History of the Races of Man,** and their Geographical Distribution. With AN ANALYTICAL SYNOPSIS OF THE NATURAL HISTORY OF MAN by Dr. Hall. With a Map of the World and 12 coloured Plates. 5*s.*

**PINDAR.** Translated into Prose by Dawson W. Turner. To which is added the Metrical Version by Abraham Moore. 5*s.*

**PLANCHE. History of British Costume,** from the Earliest Time to the Close of the Eighteenth Century. By J. R. Planché, Somerset Herald. With upwards of 400 Illustrations. 5*s.*

**PLATO'S Works.** Literally translated, with Introduction and Notes. 6 vols. 5*s.* each.

I.—The Apology of Socrates, Crito, Phædo, Gorgias, Protagoras, Phædrus, Theætetus, Euthyphron, Lysis. Translated by the Rev. H. Carey.

II.—The Republic, Timæus, and Critias. Translated by Henry Davis.

III.—Meno, Euthydemus, The Sophist, Statesman, Cratylus, Parmenides, and the Banquet. Translated by G. Burges.

IV.—Philebus, Charmides, Laches, Menexenus, Hippias, Ion, The Two Alcibiades, Theages, Rivals, Hipparchus, Minos, Clitopho, Epistles. Translated by G. Burges.

V.—The Laws. Translated by G. Burges.

VI.—The Doubtful Works. Translated by G. Burges.

—— **Summary and Analysis of the Dialogues.** With Analytical Index. By A. Day, LL.D. 5*s.*

**PLAUTUS'S Comedies.** Translated by H. T. Riley, M.A. 2 vols. 5*s.* each.

**PLINY'S Natural History.** Translated by the late John Bostock, M.D., F.R.S., and H T. Riley, M.A. 6 vols. 5*s.* each.

**PLINY. The Letters of Pliny the Younger.** Melmoth's translation, revised by the Rev. F. C. T. Bosanquet, M.A. 5*s.*

**PLOTINUS, Select Works of.** Translated by Thomas Taylor. With an Introduction containing the substance of Porphyry's Plotinus. Edited by G. R. S. Mead, B.A., M.R.A.S. 5*s.*

PLUTARCH'S Lives. Translated by A. Stewart, M.A., and George Long, M.A. 4 vols. 3s. 6d. each.

—— Morals. Theosophical Essays. Translated by C. W. King, M.A. 5s.

—— Morals Ethical Essays. Translated by the Rev. A. R. Shilleto, M.A. 5s.

POETRY OF AMERICA. Selections from One Hundred American Poets, from 1776 to 1876. By W. J. Linton. 3s. 6d.

POLITICAL CYCLOPÆDIA. A Dictionary of Political, Constitutional, Statistical, and Forensic Knowledge; forming a Work of Reference on subjects of Civil Administration, Political Economy, Finance, Commerce, Laws, and Social Relations. 4 vols. 3s. 6d. each.

POPE'S Poetical Works. Edited, with copious Notes, by Robert Carruthers. With numerous Illustrations. 2 vols. 5s. each.

—— Homer's Iliad. Edited by the Rev. J. S. Watson, M.A. Illustrated by the entire Series of Flaxman's Designs. 5s.

—— Homer's Odyssey, with the Battle of Frogs and Mice, Hymns, &c., by other translators. Edited by the Rev. J. S. Watson, M.A. With the entire Series of Flaxman's Designs. 5s.

—— Life, including many of his Letters. By Robert Carruthers. With numerous Illustrations. 5s.

POUSHKIN'S Prose Tales: The Captain's Daughter—Doubrovsky—The Queen of Spades—An Amateur Peasant Girl—The Shot—The Snow Storm—The Postmaster—The Coffin Maker—Kirdjali—The Egyptian Nights—Peter the Great's Negro. Translated by T. Keane. 3s. 6d.

PRESCOTT'S Conquest of Mexico. Copyright edition, with the notes by John Foster Kirk, and an introduction by G. P. Winship. 3 vols. 3s. 6d. each.

—— Conquest of Peru. Copyright edition, with the notes of John Foster Kirk. 2 vols. 3s. 6d. each.

—— Reign of Ferdinand and Isabella. Copyright edition, with the notes of John Foster Kirk. 3 vols. 3s. 6d. each.

PROPERTIUS. Translated by Rev. P. J. F. Gantillon, M.A., and accompanied by Poetical Versions, from various sources. 3s. 6d.

PROVERBS, Handbook of. Containing an entire Republication of Ray's Collection of English Proverbs, with his additions from Foreign Languages and a complete Alphabetical Index; in which are introduced large additions as well of Proverbs as of Sayings, Sentences, Maxims, and Phrases, collected by H. G. Bohn. 5s.

PROVERBS, A Polyglot of Foreign. Comprising French, Italian, German, Dutch, Spanish, Portuguese, and Danish. With English Translations & a General Index by H. G Bohn. 5s.

POTTERY AND PORCELAIN, and other Objects of Vertu. Comprising an Illustrated Catalogue of the Bernal Collection of Works of Art, with the prices at which they were sold by auction, and names of the possessors. To which are added, an Introductory Lecture on Pottery and Porcelain, and an Engraved List of all the known Marks and Monograms. By Henry G. Bohn. With numerous Wood Engravings, 5s.; or with Coloured Illustrations, 10s. 6d.

PROUT'S (Father) Reliques. Collected and arranged by Rev. F. Mahony. New issue, with 21 Etchings by D. Maclise, R.A. Nearly 600 pages. 5s.

QUINTILIAN'S Institutes of Oratory, or Education of an Orator. Translated by the Rev. J. S. Watson, M.A. 2 vols. 5s. each.

RACINE'S (Jean) Dramatic Works. A metrical English version. By R. Bruce Boswell, M.A. Oxon. 2 vols. 3s. 6d. each.

RANKE'S History of the Popes, their Church and State, and especially of their Conflicts with Protestantism in the 16th and 17th centuries. Translated by E. Foster. 3 vols. 3s. 6d. each.

—— History of Servia and the Servian Revolution. With an Account of the Insurrection in Bosnia. Translated by Mrs. Kerr. 3s. 6d.

RECREATIONS in SHOOTING. By 'Craven.' With 62 Engravings on Wood after Harvey, and 9 Engravings on Steel, chiefly after A. Cooper, R.A. 5s.

RENNIE'S Insect Architecture. Revised and enlarged by Rev. J. G. Wood, M.A. With 186 Woodcut Illustrations. 5s.

REYNOLD'S (Sir J.) Literary Works. Edited by H. W. Beechy. 2 vols. 3s. 6d. each.

RICARDO on the Principles of Political Economy and Taxation. Edited by E. C. K. Gonner, M.A. 5s.

RICHTER (Jean Paul Friedrich). Levana, a Treatise on Education: together with the Autobiography (a Fragment), and a short Prefatory Memoir. 3s. 6d.

—— Flower, Fruit, and Thorn Pieces, or the Wedded Life, Death, and Marriage of Firmian Stanislaus Siebenkaes, Parish Advocate in the Parish of Kuhschnappcel. Newly translated by Lt.-Col. Alex. Ewing. 3s. 6d.

ROGER DE HOVEDEN'S Annals of English History, comprising the History of England and of other Countries of Europe from A.D. 732 to A.D. 1201. Translated by H. T. Riley, M.A. 2 vols. 5s. each.

ROGER OF WENDOVER'S Flowers of History, comprising the History of England from the Descent of the Saxons to A.D. 1235, formerly ascribed to Matthew Paris. Translated by J. A. Giles, D.C.L. 2 vols. 5s. each.

ROME in the NINETEENTH CENTURY. Containing a complete Account of the Ruins of the Ancient City, the Remains of the Middle Ages, and the Monuments of Modern Times. By C. A. Eaton. With 34 Steel Engravings. 2 vols. 5s. each.

—— See BURN and DYER.

ROSCOE'S (W.) Life and Pontificate of Leo X. Final edition, revised by Thomas Roscoe. 2 vols. 3s. 6d. each.

—— Life of Lorenzo de' Medici, called 'the Magnificent.' With his poems, letters, &c. 10th Edition, revised, with Memoir of Roscoe by his Son. 3s. 6d.

RUSSIA. History of, from the earliest Period, compiled from the most authentic sources by Walter K. Kelly. With Portraits. 2 vols. 3s. 6d. each.

SALLUST, FLORUS, and VELLEIUS PATERCULUS. Translated by J. S. Watson, M.A. 5s.

SCHILLER'S Works. Translated by various hands. 7 vols. 3s. 6d. each:—

I.—History of the Thirty Years' War.

SCHILLER'S WORKS *continued.*

II.—History of the Revolt in the Netherlands, the Trials of Counts Egmont and Horn, the Siege of Antwerp, and the Disturbances in France preceding the Reign of Henry IV.

III.—Don Carlos, Mary Stuart, Maid of Orleans, Bride of Messina, together with the Use of the Chorus in Tragedy (a short Essay). These Dramas are all translated in metre.

IV.—Robbers (with Schiller's original Preface), Fiesco, Love and Intrigue, Demetrius, Ghost Seer, Sport of Divinity. The Dramas in this volume are translated into Prose.

V.—Poems.

VI.—Essays, Æsthetical and Philosophical.

VII.—Wallenstein's Camp, Piccolomini and Death of Wallenstein, William Tell.

SCHILLER and GOETHE. Correspondence between, from A.D. 1794-1805. Translated by L. Dora Schmitz. 2 vols. 3*s*. 6*d*. each.

SCHLEGEL'S (F.) Lectures on the Philosophy of Life and the Philosophy of Language. Translated by the Rev. A. J. W. Morrison, M.A. 3*s*. 6*d*.

—— Lectures on the History of Literature, Ancient and Modern. Translated from the German. 3*s*.6*d*.

—— Lectures on the Philosophy of History. Translated by J. B. Robertson. 3*s*. 6*d*.

SCHLEGEL'S Lectures on Modern History, together with the Lectures entitled Cæsar and Alexander, and The Beginning of our History. Translated by L. Purcell and R. H. Whitelock. 3*s*. 6*d*.

—— Æsthetic and Miscellaneous Works. Translated by E. J. Millington. 3*s*. 6*d*.

SCHLEGEL (A. W.) Lectures on Dramatic Art and Literature. Translated by J. Black. Revised Edition, by the Rev. A. J. W. Morrison, M.A. 3*s*. 6*d*.

SCHOPENHAUER on the Fourfold Root of the Principle of Sufficient Reason, and On the Will in Nature. Translated by Madame Hillebrand. 5*s*.

—— Essays. Selected and Translated. With a Biographical Introduction and Sketch of his Philosophy, by E. Belfort Bax. 5*s*.

SCHOUW'S Earth, Plants, and Man. Translated by A. Henfrey. With coloured Map of the Geography of Plants. 5*s*.

SCHUMANN (Robert). His Life and Works, by August Reissmann. Translated by A. L. Alger. 3*s*. 6*d*.

—— Early Letters. Originally published by his Wife. Translated by May Herbert. With a Preface by Sir George Grove, D.C.L. 3*s*. 6*d*.

SENECA on Benefits. Newly translated by A. Stewart, M.A. 3*s*. 6*d*.

—— Minor Essays and On Clemency. Translated by A. Stewart, M.A. 5*s*.

SHAKESPEARE DOCUMENTS. Arranged by D. H. Lambert, B.A. 3*s*. 6*d*.

SHAKESPEARE'S Dramatic Art. The History and Character of Shakespeare's Plays. By Dr. Hermann Ulrici. Translated by L. Dora Schmitz. 2 vols. 3*s*. 6*d*. each.

**SHAKESPEARE (William).** A Literary Biography by Karl Elze, Ph.D., LL.D. Translated by L. Dora Schmitz. 5s.

**SHARPE (S.)** The History of Egypt, from the Earliest Times till the Conquest by the Arabs, A.D. 640. By Samuel Sharpe. 2 Maps and upwards of 400 Illustrative Woodcuts. 2 vols. 5s. each.

**SHERIDAN'S Dramatic Works,** Complete. With Life by G. G. S. 3s. 6d.

**SISMONDI'S History of the Literature of the South of Europe.** Translated by Thomas Roscoe. 2 vols. 3s. 6d. each.

**SMITH'S Synonyms and Antonyms, or Kindred Words and their Opposites.** Revised Edition. 5s.

——— Synonyms Discriminated. A Dictionary of Synonymous Words in the English Language, showing the Accurate signification of words of similar meaning. Edited by the Rev. H. Percy Smith, M.A. 6s.

**SMITH'S (Adam) The Wealth of Nations.** Edited by E. Belfort Bax. 2 vols. 3s. 6d. each.

——— Theory of Moral Sentiments. With a Memoir of the Author by Dugald Stewart. 3s. 6d.

**SMYTH'S (Professor) Lectures on Modern History.** 2 vols. 3s. 6d. each

**SMYTH'S (Professor) Lectures on the French Revolution.** 2 vols. 3s. 6d. each.

**SMITH'S (Pye) Geology and Scripture.** 2nd Edition. 5s.

**SMOLLETT'S Adventures of Roderick Random.** With short Memoir and Bibliography, and Cruikshank's Illustrations. 3s. 6d.

**SMOLLETT'S Adventures of Peregrine Pickle.** With Bibliography and Cruikshank's Illustrations. 2 vols. 3s. 6d. each.

——— The Expedition of Humphry Clinker. With Bibliography and Cruikshank's Illustrations. 3s. 6d.

**SOCRATES (surnamed 'Scholasticus').** The Ecclesiastical History of (A.D. 305-445). Translated from the Greek. 5s.

**SOPHOCLES, The Tragedies of.** A New Prose Translation, with Memoir, Notes, &c., by E. P. Coleridge, M.A. 5s.

**SOUTHEY'S Life of Nelson.** With Portraits, Plans, and upwards of 50 Engravings on Steel and Wood. 5s.

——— Life of Wesley, and the Rise and Progress of Methodism. 5s.

——— Robert Southey. The Story of his Life written in his Letters. Edited by John Dennis. 3s. 6d.

**SOZOMEN'S Ecclesiastical History.** Translated from the Greek. Together with the ECCLESIASTICAL HISTORY OF PHILOSTORGIUS, as epitomised by Photius. Translated by Rev. E. Walford, M.A. 5s.

**SPINOZA'S Chief Works.** Translated, with Introduction, by R.H.M. Elwes. 2 vols. 5s. each.

**STANLEY'S Classified Synopsis of the Principal Painters of the Dutch and Flemish Schools.** By George Stanley. 5s.

**STARLING'S (Miss) Noble Deeds of Women.** With 14 Steel Engravings. 5s.

**STAUNTON'S Chess-Player's Handbook.** 5s.

——— Chess Praxis. A Supplement to the Chess-player's Handbook. 5s.

STAUNTON'S Chess - player's Companion. Comprising a Treatise on Odds, Collection of Match Games, and a Selection of Original Problems. 5s.

—— Chess Tournament of 1851. With Introduction and Notes. 5s.

STOCKHARDT'S Experimental Chemistry. Edited by C. W. Heaton, F.C.S. 5s.

STRABO'S Geography. Translated by W. Falconer, M.A., and H. C. Hamilton. 3 vols. 5s. each.

STRICKLAND'S (Agnes) Lives of the Queens of England, from the Norman Conquest. Revised Edition. With 6 Portraits. 6 vols. 5s. each.

—— Life of Mary Queen of Scots. 2 vols. 5s. each.

—— Lives of the Tudor and Stuart Princesses. With Portraits. 5s.

STUART and REVETT'S Antiquities of Athens, and other Monuments of Greece. With 71 Plates engraved on Steel, and numerous Woodcut Capitals. 5s.

SUETONIUS' Lives of the Twelve Cæsars and Lives of the Grammarians. Thomson's translation, revised by T. Forester. 5s.

SWIFT'S Prose Works. Edited by Temple Scott. With a Biographical Introduction by the Right Hon. W. E. H. Lecky, M.P. With Portraits and Facsimiles. 12 vols. 3s. 6d. each.
[*Vols. I.-X. ready.*

I.—A Tale of a Tub, The Battle of the Books, and other early works. Edited by Temple Scott. With a Biographical Introduction by W. E. H. Lecky.

II.—The Journal to Stella. Edited by Frederick Ryland, M.A. With 2 Portraits and Facsimile.

SWIFT'S PROSE WORKS *continued.*

III. & IV.—Writings on Religion and the Church.

V.—Historical and Political Tracts (English).

VI.—The Drapier's Letters. With facsimiles of Wood's Coinage, &c.

VII.—Historical and Political Tracts (Irish).

VIII.—Gulliver's Travels. Edited by G. R. Dennis. With Portrait and Maps.

IX.—Contributions to Periodicals.

X.—Historical Writings.

XI.—Literary Essays.
[*In preparation.*

XII.—Index and Bibliography.
[*In preparation.*

STOWE (Mrs. H. B.) Uncle Tom's Cabin. Illustrated. 3s. 6d.

TACITUS. The Works of. Literally translated. 2 vols. 5s. each.

TALES OF THE GENII. Translated from the Persian by Sir Charles Morell. Numerous Woodcuts and 12 Steel Engravings. 5s.

TASSO'S Jerusalem Delivered. Translated into English Spenserian Verse by J. H. Wiffen. With 8 Engravings on Steel and 24 Woodcuts by Thurston. 5s.

TAYLOR'S (Bishop Jeremy) Holy Living and Dying. 3s. 6d.

TEN BRINK.—*See* BRINK.

TERENCE and PHÆDRUS. Literally translated by H. T. Riley, M.A. To which is added, Smart's Metrical Version of Phædrus. 5s.

THEOCRITUS, BION, MOSCHUS, and TYRTÆUS. Literally translated by the Rev. J. Banks, M.A. To which are appended the Metrical Versions of Chapman. 5s.

**THEODORET and EVAGRIUS.** Histories of the Church from A.D. 332 to A.D. 427; and from A.D. 431 to A.D. 544. Translated. 5*s.*

**THIERRY'S** History of the Conquest of England by the Normans Translated by William Hazlitt. 2 vols. 3*s.* 6*d.* each.

**THUCYDIDES.** The Peloponnesian War. Literally translated by the Rev. H. Dale. 2 vols 3*s.* 6*d.* each.

—— An Analysis and Summary of. By J. T. Wheeler. 5*s.*

**THUDICHUM (J. L. W.)** A Treatise on Wines. Illustrated. 5*s.*

**URE'S (Dr. A.)** Cotton Manufacture of Great Britain. Edited by P. L. Simmonds. 2 vols. 5*s.* each.

—— Philosophy of Manufactures. Edited by P. L. Simmonds. 7*s.* 6*d.*

**VASARI'S** Lives of the most Eminent Painters, Sculptors, and Architects. Translated by Mrs. J. Foster, with a Commentary by J. P. Richter, Ph.D. 6 vols. 3*s.* 6*d.* each.

**VIRGIL.** A Literal Prose Translation by A. Hamilton Bryce, LL.D. With Portrait. 3*s.* 6*d.*

**VOLTAIRE'S** Tales. Translated by R. B. Boswell. Containing Bebouc, Memnon, Candide, L'Ingénu, and other Tales. 3*s.* 6*d.*

**WALTON'S** Complete Angler. Edited by Edward Jesse. With Portrait and 203 Engravings on Wood and 26 Engravings on Steel. 5*s.*

—— Lives of Donne, Hooker, &c. New Edition revised by A. H. Bullen, with a Memoir of Izaak Walton by Wm. Dowling. With numerous Illustrations. 5*s.*

**WELLINGTON, Life of.** By 'An Old Soldier.' From the materials of Maxwell. With Index and 18 Steel Engravings. 5*s.*

**WELLINGTON, Victories of.** See MAXWELL.

**WERNER'S** Templars in Cyprus. Translated by E. A. M. Lewis. 3*s.* 6*d.*

**WESTROPP (H. M.)** A Handbook of Archæology, Egyptian, Greek, Etruscan, Roman. Illustrated. 5*s.*

**WHITE'S** Natural History of Selborne. With Notes by Sir William Jardine. Edited by Edward Jesse. With 40 Portraits and coloured Plates. 5*s.*

**WHEATLEY'S** A Rational Illustration of the Book of Common Prayer. 3*s.* 6*d.*

**WHEELER'S** Noted Names of Fiction, Dictionary of. 5*s*

**WIESELER'S** Chronological Synopsis of the Four Gospels. Translated by the Rev. Canon Venables. 3*s.* 6*d.*

**WILLIAM of MALMESBURY'S** Chronicle of the Kings of England. Translated by the Rev. J. Sharpe Edited by J. A. Giles, D.C.L. 5*s.*

**XENOPHON'S** Works. Translated by the Rev. J. S. Watson, M.A., and the Rev. H. Dale. In 3 vols. 5*s.* each.

**YOUNG (Arthur).** Travels in France during the years 1787, 1788, and 1789. Edited by M. Betham Edwards. 3*s.* 6*d.*

—— Tour in Ireland, with General Observations on the state of the country during the years 1776-79. Edited by A. W. Hutton. With Complete Bibliography by J. P. Anderson, and Map. 2 vols. 3*s.* 6*d.* each.

**YULE-TIDE STORIES.** A Collection of Scandinavian and North-German Popular Tales and Traditions. Edited by B. Thorpe. 5*s.*

www.ingramcontent.com/pod-product-compliance
Lightning Source LLC
Chambersburg PA
CBHW030745250426
43672CB00028B/616